Cooks of the
Green Door

Established 1911

The Green Door Cookbook has been underwritten by:

The Frey Foundation

The General Mills Foundation

Bernatello's Pizza

J. Peter and Mary Ritten

The Rosemarie S. Rosengren Trust

The Myser Family Foundation

The Scherer Family Fund

George and Gloria Allen

Mary Esther McKay

Host and guest sponsors at pre-publication events

This generous support for the League of Catholic Women
and its mission ensures that proceeds from the sale of the
Cooks of the Green Door cookbook will flow directly to the
social services the LCW initiates and sustains to enrich the
lives of women and families. We are grateful to these
foundations, companies and individuals and to all who
contribute to the work of the League by purchasing this book.

Cooks of the
Green Door

Recipes, table blessings and family
traditions to savor.
Enjoy the fullness of the feast.

The League of Catholic Women

207 South 9th Street
Minneapolis, MN 5402
www.mplsleagcatholicwomen.org

Celebrating 90 years
of supportive friendship
and creative community services
to women and families
in the Minneapolis/St. Paul metropolitan area.

Printed 2000
Japs-Olson Printing Company

Hospitality
in the heart of the city.

207 South Ninth Street
Minneapolis

A Message from the League of Catholic Women:

The League of Catholic Women is pleased to share with you some of its members' favorite recipes, family traditions and table blessings. We are happy that you are helping us commemorate our ninety-year history of community service and supportive friendship.

Throughout these pages you will be offered a sampling of the kinds of social services in which the LCW has been engaged since its founding in 1911.

The League's Downtown Center welcomes clients, members and anyone interested in attending our programs or learning more about out organization. Our door is painted a vibrant green - the color of hope, renewal and growth:

> **Hope** for a brighter future for the women and families our projects embrace.

> **Renewal** generated by awareness that our projects and programs must continually be evaluated and adjusted to answer the changing needs of the community.

> **Growth**, both outward toward responsive public service and inward toward deeper spiritual and personal development.

With this publication, the League of Catholic Women honors its past and looks forward to the future. We are confident that with the help of God and by working with others, we can continue to be a catalyst for positive change in the metropolitan community.

Our green door is open. Please pull up a chair and make yourself at home at the bountiful table ready and waiting inside for you.

Patricia S. Grier

President
League of Catholic Women

In every culture, food brings people together. Sharing a meal with family or friends nurtures the soul as well as the body. We gather around the table to talk, to listen, to laugh, to celebrate and to sustain one another in times of trouble.

We believe that the family meal has been, and can continue to be, a source of more than one kind of nourishment. That is why the **Cooks of the Green Door** includes a selection of table blessings to establish a mealtime mood of thoughtful thankfulness in young and old. It also features some of our members treasured traditions which, year by year, help knit together the generations and provide food for memories that last.

Please sample a recipe that intrigues. Try out a blessing that inspires. Establish a family tradition that seems to fit. And most of all, enjoy the fullness of the feast!

The Editors

The Advisory Committee of the **Cooks of the Green Door** has made every effort to check each recipe for accuracy of ingredients and preparation. If, however, you discover an error and would like clarification of terms, please contact the League's website: www.mplsleagcatholicwomen.org, and the editors will try to remedy the situation. Thank you.

Contents

An Irish Christmas Blessing

The light of the Christmas star to you...
The warmth of home and hearth to you...
The cheer and good will of friends to you...
The hope of a childlike heart to you...
The joy of a thousand angels to you...
The love of the Son and God's grace to you.

Polish Christmas Tradition

It is a Polish tradition in our family to serve Oplatek, a blessed but not sacred unleavened bread, at Christmas Eve or "Vigilia" dinner. The bread is broken and distributed by the head of the household to be shared as a sign of love and unity by all family members. Sometimes pieces of the bread are sent in advance to distant family members so they may share the family meal at least in spirit. Oplatek is available at Holy Cross Church and St. Charles Borromeo Church during Advent.

Irish Christmas Tradition

Both my husband and I are of Irish descent. It was the Christmas Eve custom in our home, just as it was in the Irish homes of our ancestors, to place a lighted candle in the front window for each child in the family. These tapers are meant to light the way for the Christ Child. Our older children always found great joy in lighting a candle for each new baby celebrating his or her first Christmas in our family. Last Christmas Eve as we walked up to our daughter's house, we were delighted to see four candles shining from her front window.

Appetizers

Beef-Tortilla Pinwheels

1	**(8-count) package 10-inch flour tortillas**
1	**(6-ounce) container soft cream cheese with herbs and garlic (i.e. Boursin)**
4	**tablespoons snipped fresh basil**
1	**pound thinly sliced Italian-style roast beef**
1	**(10-ounce) bag fresh spinach, trimmed**
1	**(7.5-ounce) jar roasted red bell peppers, drained**
1	**(6-ounce) jar marinated artichoke hearts, drained**

Separate tortillas and divide on flat surface. Divide herbed cream cheese evenly among tortillas, spreading to edge. Sprinkle with basil. Arrange single layer of beef on each tortilla, leaving 1/2-inch border around edge. Layer spinach leaves over basil. Cut peppers into thin strips. Arrange in single row across center of tortillas. Cut artichokes into strips and place beside peppers. Roll tortillas up tightly. Wrap with plastic wrap. Refrigerate 3 to 4 hours before slicing.

To serve, trim ends of tortillas. Cut each roll crosswise into 8 slices. Arrange on spinach lined platter.

Makes 24 appetizers.

Italian beef is available at most deli counters. It provides the zest for these appetizers.

Chicken Nips

4	**whole boneless skinless chicken breasts**
1/2	**cup (1 stick) butter, melted**
1	**cup crushed Champagne crackers or crackers of choice**
1/2	**cup grated Parmesan cheese**
1/4	**cup finely chopped walnuts**
1	**teaspoon dried thyme**
1	**teaspoon dried basil**
1/2	**teaspoon salt**
1/4	**teaspoon pepper**

Dip:

1/2	**cup Dijon mustard**
1/4	**cup sour cream**

Heat oven to 400°. Cut chicken into bite-size pieces. Dip each piece into melted butter.

In separate bowl combine crushed crackers, Parmesan cheese, walnuts, thyme, basil, salt and pepper. Roll chicken in coating mixture. Place pieces on foil on baking sheet. Refrigerate or bake immediately 10 to 15 minutes until lightly browned.

To prepare dip combine mustard and sour cream in a small bowl.

Serve chicken nips with sauce.

Makes about 30 appetizers.

Sesame Chicken Wings

1	**(5-pound) bag frozen chicken wings**
$1/3$	**cup vegetable oil**
$1/3$	**cup vermouth**
$1/3$	**cup soy sauce**
4	**tablespoons toasted sesame seed**

Thaw wings, snip off tips and excess skin. Combine oil, vermouth and soy sauce in small bowl. Place chicken wings and marinade in heavy sealed plastic bag. Refrigerate several hours, shaking bag occasionally.

Heat oven to 325°.

Place wings and marinade in 13x9-inch baking pan or larger one if needed. Sprinkle 2 tablespoons sesame seed over wings. Bake 45 minutes. Turn wings and sprinkle with remaining sesame seed. Bake another 45 minutes or until golden and sauce has thickened. Cooking time may vary depending on meatiness of chicken wings. Check to be sure they do not overcook.

Serves 8 generously.

An easy do-ahead treat for weekend company.

Sweet and Sour Meatballs

1	**pound lean hamburger**
$1/2$	**cup chopped mushrooms**
1	**small onion, chopped**
$1/2$	**green pepper, chopped**
1	**teaspoon salt**
1	**teaspoon pepper**
$1/2$	**teaspoon ground mustard**
2	**slices bread, dried and crumbled**
$1/2$	**cup all-purpose flour**
2	**tablespoons olive oil**

Sauce:

1	**(16-ounce) jar barbecue sauce**
1	**(16-ounce) jar grape jelly**

Combine 8 meatball ingredients in large bowl. Mix well. Using teaspoon shape meat mixture into small balls. Dip in flour and brown in batches in large skillet coated with olive oil.

In medium saucepan heat barbecue sauce and grape jelly until well blended. Place meatballs and sauce in Crock Pot or large saucepan. Simmer $1/2$ hour. After mixture cools it may be frozen and reheated before serving. Best served in chafing dish.

Makes about 30 meatballs.

White Castle Appetizers

1	pound lean ground beef
2	cups finely shredded Cheddar cheese
2	tablespoons mayonnaise
1	(1-ounce) Lipton onion soup mix
40	slices hamburger pickles
2	(20-count) packages Pepperidge Farm party rolls

Heat oven to 350°. Brown meat in large skillet. Stir in cheese while meat is hot. Add mayonnaise and soup mix. Slice rolls. Put small amount of meat mixture on bottom of each roll. Cover with pickle slice and top of roll. Return hamburgers to foil pans. Cover with aluminum foil. Bake 20 minutes or until warm.

Serves 40.

This is a terrific treat for teen parties and Super Bowl buffets. Guest sponsors at cookbook pre-publication parties loved them too!

Crabby Quesadillas

1/3	cup butter
1/4	cup safflower oil
1	clove garlic, minced
1/2	medium-sized onion
1	jalapeno pepper, seeded and finely chopped
1	pound crabmeat, fresh or canned (not frozen), rinsed and cartilage removed
1/4	cup mayonnaise
1/4	teaspoon salt
1	teaspoon minced cilantro
16	(10-inch) flour tortillas, plain or flavored
6	ounces Monterey Jack cheese, shredded
	Salsa of your choice

Heat butter and oil in medium saucepan until butter is melted. Pour all but 2 tablespoons into small cup and set aside. Add garlic and onion to remaining oil mixture and sauté over medium heat 2 minutes. Remove from heat. Add jalapenos, crabmeat, mayonnaise, salt and cilantro. Mix well and set aside.

Heat large nonstick skillet over medium-high heat for 3 minutes. Place 1 tortilla in skillet turning frequently until soft. If tortilla sticks to pan spray skillet with vegetable spray. Remove tortilla. Spread 1 spoonful crab mixture over half the tortilla. Top with cheese and fold over. Brush liberally with reserved oil mixture on both sides of tortilla. Repeat until all quesadillas are made. If desired refrigerate up to 24 hours.

Sauté quesadillas 3 to 4 minutes in skillet or warm on outdoor grill for 3 to 4 minutes. Cut each quesadilla into 3 triangles. Serve with salsa on the side if desired.

Makes 24 appetizers.

Crab Rolls

1/2	**pound Velveeta cheese**
1	**pound (4 sticks) butter, divided**
1	**(6-ounce) can crabmeat, rinsed and cartilage removed**
20	**slices white bread, crusts removed**
2	**cups toasted sesame seed**

Melt cheese and 2 sticks butter in medium saucepan. Cool slightly. Add crabmeat and stir until mixture is spreadable. Blend thoroughly butter and cheese tend to separate. Roll each slice of bread with rolling pin to flatten. Spread crab mixture to within 1/2 inch of bread edges. Roll up tightly. Melt remaining butter in small saucepan. Dip rolls into butter and sesame seeds. Place seam side down in shallow 13x9-inch baking pan. Cover and freeze. Transfer to heavy sealed plastic bag and store in freezer up to 1 month.

To serve thaw rolls slightly. Cut into 3 pieces. Heat broiler. Place rolls on baking sheet and broil until nicely browned, turning once. Watch carefully.

Makes 60 pieces.

Black Caviar Mousse

9	**ounces black caviar, unrinsed**
1/4	**cup chopped fresh parsley**
1 1/2	**tablespoons grated onion**
1	**teaspoon grated lemon rind**
2	**envelopes (4 teaspoons) unflavored gelatin**
1/2	**cup water**
2	**cups sour cream, divided**
1	**cup whipping cream, lightly whipped**
Pepper to taste	
50	**Melba toast rounds**

Lightly oil 6-cup mold. Set aside. Combine first 4 ingredients in small bowl. Set aside. In medium saucepan, sprinkle gelatin over 1/2 cup water. Let stand 1 minute. Cook over low heat until completely dissolved. Remove from heat. Add 1 cup sour cream stirring until well blended. Fold gelatin mixture and remaining sour cream into caviar. Fold in whipped cream and pepper. Pour into mold. Refrigerate at least 3 hours or until set. Unmold on platter and serve with Melba toast rounds or cucumber slices.

Serves 20.

Brought back by popular demand every New Year's Eve at this contributor's house.

Crabmeat Remick

1	pound crabmeat, fresh or canned (not frozen), rinsed and cartilage removed
6	strips bacon, crisply cooked
1	teaspoon ground mustard
$1/2$	teaspoon paprika
$1/2$	teaspoon celery salt
$1/2$	teaspoon Tabasco sauce
$1/2$	cup chili sauce
1	teaspoon tarragon vinegar
$1^1/_2$	cups mayonnaise

Heat oven to 350˚. Place equal amounts of crabmeat in 6 individual 1-cup ramekins. Bake about 5 minutes. Top with strips of crisp bacon. Blend mustard, paprika, celery salt and Tabasco sauce in small bowl. Add chili sauce and vinegar. Mix well. Blend in mayonnaise. Heat broiler. Spread warm crabmeat with sauce and glaze under broiler for 1 to 2 minutes.

Serves 6 as first course.

This recipe is a specialty of the Pontchatrain Hotel in New Orleans.

New Age Guacamole

1	ear fresh white corn or $3/4$ cup canned white corn
$3/4$	cup mashed avocado
$1/2$	cup chopped water chestnuts
2	tablespoons minced green onions
1	tablespoon minced fresh garlic
1	tablespoon lemon juice
1	teaspoon Chinese chili sauce
$1/4$	teaspoon salt
Taco chips or raw vegetables	

Stand corn ear on end and cut off all kernels. Add raw kernels to avocado in small bowl along with other ingredients. If preparing in advance sprinkle top with extra lemon juice and insert avocado pits to prevent discoloration. Cover and refrigerate up to 6 hours. When ready to serve, remove avocado pits and stir. Serve with taco chips or raw vegetables.

Makes 1 cup.

Phyllo Pizza

1	cup crumbled feta cheese
1	tablespoon chopped fresh oregano or 1 teaspoon dried
2	tablespoons extra virgin olive oil
$^1/_2$	teaspoon freshly ground pepper
8	sheets phyllo dough
$^1/_4$	cup ($^1/_2$ stick) butter
3	large plum tomatoes, sliced
$^1/_2$	cup thinly-sliced red onion

Heat oven to 375°. Lightly grease 15x10-inch jellyroll pan. Toss feta cheese with oregano, oil and pepper in small bowl until well combined. Arrange 1 sheet phyllo dough in prepared pan and brush lightly with a portion of melted butter. Keep remaining phyllo sheets covered with damp cloth. Layer with remaining phyllo sheets, buttering each layer. Arrange tomatoes on top. Sprinkle with feta cheese mixture and onion.

Bake 20 minutes. Cool. Cover loosely and store at room temperature up to 6 hours. Cut into 2-inch squares.

Makes 24 appetizers.

May substitute goat cheese for feta and sun-dried tomatoes for fresh. Kalamata olive slices also add a nice touch.

Quiche Cheese Puffs

1	(8-ounce) container cottage cheese
1	(4-ounce) package cream cheese
4	tablespoons plus 1 teaspoon sour cream
3	eggs
$^1/_2$	cup (1 stick) butter, melted
$^1/_2$	cup Bisquick
2	tablespoons chopped chives

Heat oven to 350°. Combine all ingredients in large bowl and mix well. Spray mini-muffin tins with vegetable spray. Fill almost to top. Bake 35 minutes. Remove from oven and let stand 1 minute. Run knife around each muffin. Remove muffins from pan and place on serving platter.

Makes 36 mini-muffins.

Cooked muffins may be placed in tightly sealed container and frozen until ready to serve. Reheat on baking sheet in 325° oven for about 10 minutes.

A rose window depicting the Assumption of the Virgin Mary was donated to the Basilica of Saint Mary by the League of Catholic Women in 1925. It was given in memory of Archbishop John Ireland who gave his last public address at a League gathering.

Creamy Shrimp Crostini

40	slices French bread, sliced $1/2$-inch thick
2	tablespoons olive oil
1	(8-ounce) package cream cheese, at room temperature
$1/2$	cup mayonnaise
2	tablespoons Dijon mustard
1	pound cooked shrimp, peeled, deveined and coarsely chopped
$1/2$	cup minced green onions
$1 1/2$	tablespoons chopped fresh dill weed or 1 teaspoon dried
1	teaspoon grated lemon rind

Salt and pepper to taste

$1/2$	cup chopped fresh parsley

Lightly brush one side of each bread slice with oil. Arrange on 2 baking sheets. Broil until lightly toasted, about 1 minute. May prepare 1 day in advance and store in airtight container.

Blend cream cheese, mayonnaise and mustard in large bowl. Mix in shrimp, green onions, dill weed and lemon rind. Season with salt and pepper. Cover and refrigerate up to 24 hours.

To serve spread 1 tablespoon shrimp mixture on each toast slice. Heat broiler. Arrange crostini on baking sheets. Broil about 2 minutes or until shrimp mixture begins to brown. Top each crostini with chopped parsley before serving.

Makes 40 crostini.

Crostini may also be served cold.

Curried Shrimp Spread

1	(8-ounce) package cream cheese
2	tablespoons mayonnaise
$1/4$	teaspoon curry powder
6	green onions, finely chopped
8	ounces cooked shrimp, chopped
2	hard boiled eggs, chopped

Salt and pepper to taste

12	lemon slices
$1/2$	cup chopped fresh parsley
1	pound loaf party rye bread

Blend cream cheese, mayonnaise and curry in medium bowl. Spread or mound on 12-inch serving plate. Sprinkle with green onions, shrimp and eggs. Season with salt and pepper. Garnish with lemon slices and parsley. Serve with party rye or crackers.

Serves 8.

Apple Slices with Gorgonzola Spread

2	(8-ounce) packages cream cheese, softened
8-12	ounces Gorgonzola cheese at room temperature
$\frac{1}{2}$	cup sour cream
3	tablespoons brandy
8	large Granny Smith apples, cored and thinly sliced

Combine cream cheese, Gorgonzola, sour cream and brandy. Mix well. Spread mixture on apple slices. Arrange on large serving platter.

Serves 12.

To prevent fruit from discoloring dip apple slices in 1 cup water mixed with 2 tablespoons lemon juice.

Asparagus Roll-Ups

1	(8-ounce) package cream cheese
2-4	ounces blue cheese
2	egg yolks
1	tablespoon mayonnaise
$\frac{1}{2}$	teaspoon Worcestershire sauce
20	slices white bread, crusts removed, Tastee preferred
1	(15-ounce) can green asparagus
1	cup (2 sticks) butter, melted

Mix first 5 ingredients in small bowl. Roll bread slices with rolling pin to flatten. Spread each slice with cheese mixture. Place one asparagus spear on each bread slice and roll up, pasting long ends together with cream cheese mixture. Dip in melted butter. Place on baking sheet and cover tightly. Freeze. May transfer to heavy sealed plastic bag and store in freezer up to 1 month.

When ready to bake, heat oven to 400°. Remove roll-ups from freezer. Thaw slightly. Cut each roll into 2 or 3 pieces. Place on baking sheet. Bake 15 to 20 minutes or until lightly browned.

Makes 60 appetizers.

Canned asparagus works better than fresh for this recipe.

Bruschetta Al Pomodora

3   ripe tomatoes, peeled and chopped

1½   teaspoon salt, divided

2   garlic cloves, chopped

1   cup chopped fresh basil leaves

½   cup chopped fresh parsley

Chili powder to taste

6   tablespoons extra virgin olive oil, divided

6   slices peasant bread, ½-inch thick

Sprinkle chopped tomatoes with 1 teaspoon or more salt to release juices. Drain in colander. Mix garlic, basil and parsley in small bowl. Stir in 4 tablespoons olive oil. Season to taste with remaining salt and chili powder.

Toast bread on grill or in toaster. Brush with remaining olive oil. Cover bread with tomato mixture and serve.

Serves 6.

Cheese Triangles

5   tablespoons butter, softened

6   ounces Gorgonzola cheese, broken into small pieces

2   tablespoons chopped fresh basil or parsley

2   tablespoons whole pine nuts

⅛   teaspoon pepper

10   slices thin-sliced Pepperidge Farm white bread

Heat oven to 400°. Combine first 5 ingredients in small bowl. Mix well. Spread on bread slices. Place prepared bread slices directly on middle oven rack. Bake until edges are brown. Carefully remove from oven rack. Cut each slice diagonally into 4 triangles. Bake 1 to 2 minutes more. Serve warm or at room temperature.

Triangles may be frozen. Bake until just slightly brown. Layer in aluminum foil, covering tightly. Place in freezer. Remove slices as needed and bake at 400° for 2 minutes.

Makes 10 to 20.

Crostini Al Formaggio Di Capra

16   slices French bread

2   tablespoons extra virgin olive oil

½   cup fresh goat cheese

6   walnuts, finely chopped

Coarsely ground pepper to taste

Heat oven to 350°. Place slices of bread on large baking sheet. Toast in oven about 5 minutes until golden brown. Cool. In medium bowl blend olive oil with cheese until creamy using a fork. Spread toasts with cheese mixture. Sprinkle with walnuts and pepper. Arrange on platter and serve.

Serves 6.

This contributor picked up this recipe while attending a cooking school in Florence, Italy.

Cucumber Canapes

1   (1.05-ounce) package Good
    Seasons Italian dressing mix

1   (8-ounce) package cream cheese

1   large cucumber, peeled or
    unpeeled, thinly sliced

1   pound loaf party rye bread

1   tablespoon dried dill weed

Combine salad dressing mix with cream cheese in
medium bowl. Cover and refrigerate several hours.
Spread small amount cream cheese mixture on each
bread slice. Top with cucumber slice. Sprinkle
generously with dill weed.

Makes 44 appetizers.

*Guests at the League's annual garden tour thought
these tasted great on a hot July day.*

*To make fluted cucumber or zucchini slices, stand whole
unpeeled vegetable on end and run dinner fork down
the sides before slicing.*

Fiesta Layered Dip

³/₄   cup sour cream

1   (3-ounce) package cream cheese,
     softened

³/₄   cup shredded Monterey Jack
     cheese

³/₄   cup canned refried beans

³/₄   cup thick and chunky salsa

1   (8-ounce) refrigerated guacamole

¹/₄   cup sliced ripe olives

Tortilla chips

Combine sour cream, cream cheese and Monterey Jack
in medium bowl. Mix well. Spread evenly on 10-inch
pie plate or serving dish. Refrigerate 10 minutes or until
set. Carefully spread refried beans over first layer.
Spread salsa over beans. Spoon guacamole onto salsa
leaving 1-inch edge. Sprinkle with ripe olives.
Refrigerate up to 6 hours. Serve with tortilla chips.

Serves 8 to 10.

Great for an office party.

In 1912, to meet the needs of an increasing number of immigrants living in northeast
Minneapolis, the League of Catholic Women initiated services to prepare non-English speaking
children for kindergarten. Mothers also received help in learning English. This work was the
forerunner of the **Margaret Barry Settlement House** established by the League in 1913. A
community center for children and their families, this settlement house provided enrichment
programs both cultural and practical. Later the program included a gymnasium, nursery school
for working mothers, dental clinic, well-baby clinic and a day camp.

Herbed Pita Crisps

3   tablespoons olive oil

1   tablespoon chopped fresh basil
     or 1 teaspoon dried

1/2 teaspoon coarse salt

5   large whole wheat pita bread
     pockets, cut into eighths

Heat oven to 450°. Combine olive oil, basil and salt in large bowl. Add pita pieces and toss to coat well. Spread pita pieces in a single layer on 1 or 2 baking sheets. Bake 4 minutes. Using tongs, turn pita pieces over and continue baking 4 more minutes until crisp and golden. Store up to 2 days in airtight container.

Makes 40 appetizers.

These make a wonderful accompaniment to a salad lunch.

Sherried Stilton and Green Peppercorn Spread

3   cups (3/4 pound) Stilton cheese,
     crumbled and softened

2   (3-ounce) packages cream cheese,
     softened

2-3 tablespoons drained green
     peppercorns packed in brine

1/4 cup medium-dry sherry

Salt and pepper to taste

Crackers of choice

In food processor or bowl, combine all ingredients except crackers. Blend until smooth. Transfer spread to 1-cup ramekins or 1-quart casserole. Cover tightly and refrigerate up to 1 week.

To serve, place ramekin on platter and surround with crackers.

Makes 2 cups.

Olive Spread

1/4 cup (1/2 stick) butter, softened

2   (8-ounce) packages cream cheese,
     softened

1   cup shredded sharp Cheddar
     cheese

1   cup sliced ripe olives

1   cup sliced green olives

Triscuits, other crackers or French bread
     slices

Blend butter, cream cheese and Cheddar cheese in large bowl. Beat well with electric mixer. Add olives. Spoon into 1-quart casserole dish or several small ramekins. Cover tightly and refrigerate or freeze.

To serve bring spread to room temperature and place casserole or ramekin on platter surrounded by crackers or French bread slices.

Makes 3 cups.

This spread in an attractive container makes a nice hostess gift.

Layered Cheese Paté

1	(8-ounce) package cream cheese
2	tablespoons milk
$1/2$	cup (1 stick) unsalted butter, softened
6	tablespoons finely grated Parmesan cheese, fresh or packaged
$1/2$	cup chopped green onions
4	ounces prosciutto, chopped

Salt and pepper to taste

$1/2$	cup bottled or homemade basil pesto, drained
$3/4$	cup sun-dried tomatoes, chopped and drained

Line 9x5-inch loaf pan with plastic wrap. Blend cream cheese, milk and butter in medium bowl. Add Parmesan cheese, onions, prosciutto and salt and pepper to taste. Spread $1/2$ cheese mixture on bottom of pan. Mix $1/4$ remaining cheese mixture with pesto and sun-dried tomatoes. Spread over first layer. Top with remaining $1/4$ cheese mixture. Cover and refrigerate several hours.

To unmold invert paté on plate and carefully remove plastic wrap. Garnish top with fresh herbs, olives or pimiento if desired.

Serves 8 to 10.

Zucchini Appetizers

1	cup Bisquick
4	eggs
3	cups sliced zucchini
$1/2$	cup minced onion
$1/2$	cup freshly grated Parmesan cheese
2	tablespoons chopped fresh parsley
$1/2$	teaspoon salt
$1/2$	teaspoon seasoned salt
$1/2$	teaspoon dried oregano
$1/8$	teaspoon pepper
1	clove garlic, minced
$1/2$	cup vegetable oil

Heat oven to 350˚. Mix all ingredients in large bowl until well blended. Pour into lightly greased 13x9-inch baking pan. Bake 25 minutes or until tester comes out clean. Cut into squares and serve.

Makes about 20 appetizers.

Shrimp and Snow Peas

Vinaigrette:

1	tablespoon Dijon mustard
1/4	cup sherry wine vinegar
1/4	teaspoon salt

Freshly ground pepper to taste

1	cup olive oil
1	pound fresh shrimp, cooked, peeled and deveined
1/2	pound snow pea pods

Combine vinaigrette ingredients in tightly covered container. Shake well. Marinate shrimp in vinaigrette in refrigerator overnight.

Trim pea pods and remove "strings." Drop into boiling water in medium saucepan. Blanch 1 minute. Immediately plunge into bowl of ice water. Drain and pat dry. Remove shrimp one at a time from vinaigrette. Wrap one pea pod around each shrimp. Secure with cocktail toothpick. Arrange on platter and drizzle with about 1/4 cup vinaigrette before serving.

Serves 6 to 8.

Oriental Spread

12	ounces cream cheese, softened
1/2	cup chopped salted peanuts
1/4	cup chopped green onions
1	clove garlic, minced
1/4	teaspoon ground ginger
2/3	cup shredded carrots
1/4	cup chopped water chestnuts
1	tablespoon chopped fresh cilantro
2	tablespoons soy sauce
4	tablespoons bottled sweet and sour sauce

Crackers of choice

Spread cream cheese into 10-inch round serving plate or pie plate. Combine remaining ingredients except sweet and sour sauce. Spoon evenly over cream cheese to within 1/2-inch from edge. Drizzle with sauce. Serve with crackers of choice.

Serves 12.

Spinach Balls with Mustard Sauce

Spinach Balls:

2   **(10-ounce) packages frozen chopped spinach, thawed and drained well**

2   **cups herbed stuffing mix**

1   **cup grated Parmesan cheese, fresh or packaged**

$3/4$ **cup ($1^{1}/_{2}$ sticks) butter, melted**

8   **green onions, finely chopped**

4   **eggs, beaten**

$1/4$ **teaspoon nutmeg**

Salt and pepper to taste

Sauce :

$1/2$ **cup ground mustard**

$1/2$ **cup white vinegar**

$1/4$ **cup sugar**

1   **pasteurized egg yolk**

Combine all spinach ball ingredients in large bowl and mix well. Form into small balls. Place on baking sheet. Cover tightly and refrigerate until ready to bake or freeze for future use.

Heat oven to 350°. Bake spinach balls on ungreased baking sheet 10 to 15 minutes or until golden brown.

Combine mustard and vinegar in small bowl. Cover and let stand at room temperature 4 hours. In separate small bowl, mix sugar and egg yolk. Add mustard mixture and beat until thick. Cover and chill. Let mustard sauce come to room temperature before serving.

To serve, place small bowl of sauce in center of large platter. Arrange spinach balls around sauce with a pretzel stick in each to act as a cocktail pick, if desired.

Makes 48 spinach balls.

Mushroom and Cream Cheese Appetizers

$1/2$ **cup sautéed fresh chopped mushrooms or 1 (3-ounce) can mushrooms, drained and chopped**

1   **(8-ounce) package cream cheese, softened**

$1/4$ **teaspoon seasoned salt**

1   **(8-ounce) package Pillsbury crescent rolls**

1   **egg, beaten**

1   **tablespoon poppy seed**

Heat oven to 375°. Blend mushrooms with cream cheese in small bowl. Add seasoned salt. Separate crescent rolls into 4 squares. Pinch diagonal lines together. Divide filling among squares and spread to edges. Roll up starting with long side. Seal seam. Cut into 1-inch pieces. Using a pastry brush, brush each piece with small amount beaten egg and sprinkle with poppy seed. Bake 10 to 12 minutes or until lightly browned.

Makes 24 appetizers.

During Advent...

When our children were in elementary school, we started a tradition of giving each of them a small empty box the last week of Advent. We asked them to think about what gift of the heart they wished to give to Baby Jesus. They wrote it out on a slip of paper, put it into the box and laid it in the manger or under the Christmas tree. This gift was between them and the Christ Child. We never peeked!

Instead of a commercial Advent Calendar, we make our own using a large piece of green or red poster board and Christmas card cutouts saved from the previous year. We write the dates in rows across the poster board, leaving big square spaces under each date. In each space we write something we might do that day to make someone happy, to bring about peace, to care for the earth, etc. Then we paste the top part of the Christmas card over each suggestion so that we can flip them up, one day at a time, as Christmas approaches. In this way we feel we are preparing our hearts for the coming of Jesus.

The first Sunday in Advent we set out a simple bare manger and a container of straw. For each secret good deed our children perform during Advent, they place one straw in the manger when no one is looking. Nobody knows what kind acts were done or what small sacrifices made or who made them. Miraculously, by Christmas Eve the manger is filled with straw, making a soft bed for Baby Jesus, and the crib is surrounded by beaming little faces.

Our children love a new custom we've started for Advent. We go to the library and find books related to Christmas. Each night we take time to read one of the books together and talk about it a little. We make sure to include books that feature Jesus, Mary and Joseph as well as Santa. This helps us all prepare for the feast in a quiet, thoughtful and fun way.

Salads

Wild Rice-Shrimp Salad

6	**cups water**
1½	**pounds medium size fresh shrimp, unpeeled**
1	**(6-ounce) package long grain and wild rice mix**
1	**(7-ounce) jar marinated artichoke quarters**
4	**green onions with tops, sliced**
½	**cup chopped green bell pepper**
12	**ripe olives, sliced**
⅓	**cup mayonnaise**
¾	**teaspoon curry powder**
	Leaf lettuce

Bring 6 cups water to boiling. Add shrimp and cook 3 to 5 minutes or until shrimp turn pink. Drain and rinse with cold water. Peel 16 shrimp leaving tails on. Set aside. Peel, devein and chop remaining shrimp. Cook rice according to package. Drain artichokes, reserving 3 tablespoons liquid. Stir together rice, chopped shrimp, artichokes, green onions and next 3 ingredients. Stir together reserved artichoke liquid, mayonnaise and curry powder. Toss with rice mixture. Cover and chill 5 hours. Serve on lettuce lined plates. Top with whole shrimp. May substitute chicken for shrimp.

Serves 4.

Tomato Vinaigrette

6	**vine ripe tomatoes, peeled, seeded and chopped**
2	**cups olive oil**
¾	**cup lemon juice**
¼	**cup chopped shallots**
1	**tablespoon minced garlic**
¼	**cup mixed herbs including fresh basil, Italian parsley and oregano, coarsely chopped**
¼	**cup chopped sun-dried tomatoes**
½	**teaspoon kosher salt or to taste**
½	**teaspoon coarse ground white pepper or to taste**

Combine first 7 ingredients. Season with kosher salt and white pepper.

Makes 3 cups.

A zesty summer dressing to use as a salad dressing for mixed greens, a sauce for pasta or as marinade for veal or fish.

Mandarin Salad

1/4	cup sliced almonds
1	tablespoon plus 1 teaspoon sugar
1/4	head lettuce, torn into bite-size pieces
1/4	bunch romaine, torn into bite-size pieces
2	medium stalks celery, chopped (about 1 cup)
2	green onions with tops, thinly sliced (about 2 tablespoons)
2	oranges, peeled and sectioned or 1 (11-ounce) can mandarin orange segments, drained

Sweet & Sour Dressing:

1/4	cup vegetable oil
2	tablespoons sugar
2	tablespoons vinegar
1	tablespoon snipped parsley
1/2	teaspoon salt

Dash of hot pepper sauce (i.e. Tabasco)

Cook almonds and sugar over low heat stirring constantly until sugar is melted and almonds are coated. Cool and break apart. Store at room temperature. Place lettuce and romaine in plastic bag or bowl. Add celery and onions. Toss. Add orange segments. Shake all dressing ingredients vigorously in a tightly covered container. Refrigerate. Just before serving pour a portion of Sweet and Sour Dressing over salad greens and orange segments. Toss until well coated. Add almonds and toss again. Refrigerate remaining dressing for up to 3 weeks.

Serves 4 to 6.

Fresh pineapple pieces or 1 (13.5-ounce) can pineapple chunks, drained, may be substituted for the mandarin orange segments and fresh snipped mint leaves may be substituted for the parsley. Add cooked, sliced chicken breasts to make a full-meal salad.

At a reunion gathering of this contributor's eight sisters, each planned one meal. All eight sisters declared this recipe the "winner".

In 1917-18, the Junior and Senior divisions of the League of Catholic Women collected and shipped tons of clothing to convents in Belgium and France which housed refugees and wounded soldiers during World War I. Members also formed a Red Cross unit to knit and sew whatever articles were needed in the war zones. They welcomed U.S. servicemen into their homes for meals and hosted dances and parties for them at the League's rented clubrooms.

Marinated Tomatoes, Cucumbers and Feta Cheese

4	tomatoes, thickly sliced
1	red onion, thinly sliced and separated into rings
1	cucumber, sliced
$^1/_2$-1	cup pitted Greek olives to taste
$^1/_2$	cup crumbled feta cheese
2	tablespoons fresh parsley

Dressing:

$^1/_2$	cup vegetable oil
3	tablespoons red wine vinegar
1	clove garlic, minced
3-4	fresh basil leaves, chopped
1	teaspoon chopped fresh oregano
$^1/_4$	teaspoon ground mustard

Salt and pepper to taste

Combine all dressing ingredients in a bowl or shake in tightly covered container.

Arrange tomatoes, onion rings and cucumbers in rimmed platter or pie plate. Pour dressing evenly over top. Scatter with olives. Cover. Refrigerate for several hours. Just before serving, sprinkle with feta cheese and parsley.

Serves 6.

Marinated Carrot Salad

1	cup white vinegar
$1^1/_2$	cups sugar
$^1/_3$	cup vegetable oil
2	(32-ounce) packages baby carrots, cooked just until tender
16	green onions, chopped
1	cup chopped green pepper
$^1/_2$	cup chopped red pepper

In a small bowl or jar combine vinegar, sugar and oil. In separate bowl blend last 4 ingredients. Mix dressing and vegetables together. Marinate at least 12 hours and up to 48 hours.

Serves 10.

Mixed Leaf Salad with Smoky Parmesan Walnuts

Walnuts:

1	**tablespoon unsalted butter or margarine**
1/4	**teaspoon hickory flavored salt**
1	**cup walnut pieces**
2	**tablespoons grated Parmesan cheese**

Salad:

2	**large heads Boston lettuce, torn in pieces**
1	**large head radicchio, torn in pieces**
1	**large bunch watercress, large stems removed**
1	**cup Smoky Parmesan Walnuts, divided**

Vinaigrette:

1	**small clove garlic, crushed**
1/2	**teaspoon freshly ground black pepper**
1/4	**cup olive oil**
1/4	**cup balsamic vinegar**
1	**teaspoon Dijon mustard**
1/2	**teaspoon salt**
2	**teaspoons cold water**

Heat oven to 350°. Melt butter in shallow baking dish in oven. Stir in salt and walnuts. Bake 5 minutes. Stir in cheese. Bake until cheese is lightly browned, about 4 minutes. Cool. Makes 1 cup.

In large salad bowl combine greens and half the walnuts. Set aside. In a tightly covered container combine dressing ingredients. Shake to blend. Pour over salad. Toss to coat evenly. Sprinkle with remaining walnuts.

Serves 12.

For crisp mixed green salads, always add dressing and toss just before serving.

Flaming Spinach Salad

1	**(16-ounce) bag fresh spinach**
8	**strips bacon**
4	**tablespoons sugar**
4	**tablespoons white wine vinegar**
1	**tablespoons Worcestershire sauce**

Juice of one lemon

$^1/_3$ **cup brandy**

Remove stems from spinach leaves and tear into bite-size pieces. Cut bacon into $^1/_2$-inch pieces and fry until crisp. Remove bacon and set aside. Add sugar, vinegar and Worcestershire to bacon drippings. Heat to boiling. Pour over spinach and toss. Squeeze lemon over salad and toss again. Put bacon back in skillet. Add brandy. Ignite. Let flame a minute. Spoon flaming brandy and bacon onto salad, toss again and serve.

Serves 6 to 8.

Salada

$^1/_2$	**cup walnut pieces**
1	**tablespoon butter**
6-8	**cups mixed salad greens**
6	**strawberries, sliced**
$^1/_2$	**medium size pear, unpeeled and sliced into small pieces**
2	**tablespoons crumbled blue cheese**
$^1/_2$	**medium sized red onion, sliced thinly into rings**
$^1/_2$	**cup pomegranate seeds, optional when in season**

Dressing:

1$^1/_2$	**tablespoons Dijon mustard**
1	**tablespoon honey**
3	**tablespoons sherry wine vinegar**
$^1/_4$	**cup walnut oil**

Salt and freshly ground white pepper, to taste

In small saucepan, sauté walnut pieces in 1 tablespoon melted butter until lightly toasted. Set aside.

Shake all dressing ingredients together in tightly covered container. Toss together salad greens, strawberries, pears, blue cheese, onion, pomegranate seeds and walnuts in large bowl. Cover and refrigerate for up to 6 hours. Just before serving toss again with enough dressing to moisten all ingredients. Refrigerate remaining dressing up to 3 weeks.

Serves 6 to 8.

Moroccan Chicken Salad

4	chicken breast halves, about 1³/₄ pounds
1	red bell pepper, cored, seeded and thinly sliced
1	red onion, peeled and thinly sliced
1	tablespoon cumin seed, toasted and ground
¹/₂	teaspoon cayenne
1	teaspoon paprika
2	tablespoons finely minced garlic
¹/₄	cup fresh lemon juice
¹/₄	cup red wine vinegar
1	cup chicken stock or broth
2	tablespoons olive oil
¹/₂	cup finely minced fresh cilantro
¹/₂	cup minced fresh Italian parsley

Salt and freshly ground pepper to taste

¹/₄	cup Nicoise or Kalamata olives

Roast, broil or poach chicken and shred into bite-size pieces. In large bowl combine chicken, pepper and onion. Cover and refrigerate. In a separate bowl combine cumin, cayenne, paprika and garlic. Whisk in lemon juice, vinegar, chicken broth and olive oil. Stir in cilantro, parsley, salt and pepper to taste. Remove chicken from refrigerator. Pour vinaigrette over and toss well. Garnish with olives. Serve from bowl or arrange on individual plates.

Serves 6.

The League of Catholic Women's 50th Anniversary in 1961 was a year of great celebration and accomplishment. A large home and carriage house at 2201 Pillsbury Avenue was purchased as a replacement for St. Mary's Hall which closed in 1945. To finance the project, the League conducted its first major Building Fund Appeal. After extensive remodeling and decorating the residence, named the **Catholic League Girls Club**, opened in January 1962. The Girls Club accommodated 42 young working women or students new to Minneapolis. This beautiful home provided low-cost rooms, meals and social activities in a Christian atmosphere. By 1975, young women preferred independent living and the Girls Club was sold to the Jesuit Order.

Spectacular Overnight Slaw

1	medium head cabbage or 2 pounds shredded cabbage
1	medium red onion, thinly sliced
$1/2$	cup chopped green pepper
$1/2$	cup chopped sweet red pepper
$1/2$	cup sliced, stuffed green olives

Dressing:

$1/2$	cup white wine vinegar
$1/2$	cup vegetable oil
$1/2$	cup sugar
2	teaspoons Dijon mustard
1	teaspoon salt
1	teaspoon celery seed
1	teaspoon mustard seed

In large bowl combine cabbage, onion, peppers and olives.

In saucepan combine vinegar, oil, sugar, mustard, salt, celery seed and mustard seed. Bring to a boil, cook and stir for 1 minute. Pour over vegetables in bowl. Stir gently until well mixed. Cover and refrigerate overnight. Mix well before serving.

Serves 12 to 16.

Thousand Island Dressing

1	cup sour cream
2	cups mayonnaise
2	eggs, hard-boiled and diced $1/4$-inch
$3/4$	cup chili sauce
$1/4$	cup ketchup
$1/2$	cup diced red peppers
$1 1/2$	tablespoons chopped parsley, leaves only
1	teaspoon fresh lemon juice
1	teaspoon Worcestershire sauce
$1/2$	teaspoon freshly ground black pepper
1	teaspoon salt

Combine all ingredients and mix together gently and thoroughly. Keep refrigerated in a covered container up to 30 days.

To make Russian dressing, add $1/2$ cup black caviar and fold in gently.

To make Sauce Remoulade, add 1 tablespoon capers and 10 anchovies finely minced.

This recipe comes from owner/chef John Schumacher of Schumacher's Historic European Hotel in New Prague. He serves it with his Fish Ruebens. It may also be served on wedges of iceberg lettuce and as a tasty addition to turkey sandwiches.

Honey Dressing

$1/3$	cup sugar
1	teaspoon salt
$1^1/2$	teaspoons dry mustard
1	teaspoon paprika
1	teaspoon celery seed
$1/3$	cup warm honey
5	tablespoon vinegar
1	tablespoon fresh lemon juice
1	cup vegetable oil

Blend first 8 ingredients in blender and slowly add oil.

Serve on a selection of either summer or winter fruits arranged on large lettuce leaves.

Makes 2 cups.

Festive Holiday Salad

1	(12 to 14-ounce) bag ready to use salad greens or the equivalent in mixed greens
$1/3$	cup chopped radicchio
$1/2$	cup dried cranberries
$1/2$	cup mandarin orange segments, drained
$1/4$	cup diced red onion
$1/2$	cup croutons
1	(4-ounce) package feta cheese

Dressing:

$1/4$	cup raspberry vinegar
2	tablespoons honey
$1/2$	teaspoons sugar
1	teaspoon fresh lemon juice
$1/4$	teaspoon salt
$1/4$	cup vegetable oil
$1/4$	cup olive oil
1	tablespoon poppy seed

Combine all ingredients for dressing in a tightly covered container. Shake well.

Combine all salad ingredients together in a large bowl. Lightly coat salad with dressing just before serving. To serve as entree, add 4 ounces cooked peeled shrimp or cubed chicken.

Serves 8.

If you are in a rush, use Brianna's Homestyle Blush Wine Vinaigrette Dressing.

Roquefort Dressing

4-8 **ounces Roquefort or blue cheese, softened**

¹/₄ **cup vinegar or fresh lemon juice**

³/₄ **cup olive, canola or grapeseed oil**

1 **cup regular or low fat mayonnaise, Hellmann's preferred**

1 **cup sour cream, regular or low fat**

1 **teaspoon salt**

1 **small onion, grated**

1 **teaspoon minced garlic**

With mixer or by hand, blend together all the ingredients. Refrigerate for up to 3 weeks.

Can be used on mixed salad greens, as a vegetable dip or as a topping for baked potatoes.

Fruited Turkey Bow-Tie Salad

¹/₂ **pound turkey or chicken, cooked and cut into ¹/₂-inch cubes**

2 **cups bow-tie pasta, cooked according to package directions and drained**

1 **medium red apple, chopped**

1 **(10¹/₂-ounce) can mandarin oranges, drained**

¹/₂ **cup chopped celery**

1 **cup seedless grapes, halved**

Dressing:

¹/₂ **cup low fat lemon yogurt**

2 **tablespoons frozen orange juice concentrate, defrosted**

¹/₄ **teaspoon ground ginger or to taste**

In large bowl combine turkey or chicken, pasta, apple, mandarin oranges, celery and grapes. In small bowl combine yogurt, juice and ginger. Fold dressing into turkey mixture and toss to coat. Cover and refrigerate up to 6 hours until ready to serve.

Serves 6.

Scallops Salad with Riesling

12	large sea scallops
1	bunch watercress
1/2	pound radicchio, torn
1	pound chicory
3	tablespoons peanut oil
1	tablespoon sherry vinegar

Salt and pepper to taste

2	tablespoons butter
2/3	cup Riesling wine

Wash and drain sea scallops. Set aside. Rinse watercress, radicchio and chicory. Pat dry. In small bowl, whisk together oil and vinegar, salt and pepper to taste to make vinaigrette. Set aside. Melt butter in large skillet over medium heat. Add scallops and sauté 3 to 4 minutes until just cooked. Remove from heat and cover.

Toss salad greens with vinaigrette. Divide evenly among four salad plates. Arrange scallops on top. Add Riesling to pan juices and bring to boiling. Cook about 2 minutes until liquid has reduced. Pour over scallops and serve immediately.

Serves 4.

Avocados and Mushrooms Continental

2	avocados, peeled and thinly sliced
1/2	pound fresh mushrooms, thinly sliced
1/3	cup olive oil

Juice of 1 lemon

1	tablespoon white wine vinegar
1	tablespoon chopped parsley
1	clove garlic, minced
1	teaspoon salt
1/2	teaspoon coarse ground pepper

In shallow bowl arrange layers of avocados and mushrooms. Combine remaining ingredients in small bowl or shake in covered container. Pour over avocados. Chill about an hour.

Serves 6 to 8.

Makes a beautiful salad served in a glass bowl.

Molded Gazpacho Salad with Avocado Dressing

2	envelopes unflavored gelatin
3	cups tomato juice
1/3	cup red wine vinegar
1	teaspoon salt
1/4	teaspoon Tabasco sauce
1	medium cucumber, peeled and diced
2	small tomatoes, peeled and diced
1/2	medium green bell pepper, chopped
1/4	cup chopped red onion
1	tablespoon chopped chives
1/4	cup chopped celery

Dressing:

1	(6-ounce) container avocado dip
1/4	cup regular or low-fat sour cream
1	clove garlic, minced
1/8	teaspoon sugar
1	teaspoon salt
1	tablespoon grated onion
1/4	teaspoon cayenne pepper

In large saucepan sprinkle gelatin over tomato juice and stir over low heat until dissolved. Remove from heat and stir in vinegar, salt and Tabasco sauce. Chill until partially set. Add vegetables and stir. Spray 1 1/2-quart mold or 8 (6-ounce) custard cups with vegetable spray. Pour mixture into mold and chill until firm. Serve with avocado dressing.

In a small bowl mix all dressing ingredients together well. Refrigerate for at least 1 hour and up to 2 days. Spoon over molded gazpacho salad.

Serves 6 to 8.

Asparagus, Tomato Pasta Salad

2   **cups diagonally sliced asparagus, cooked al dente**

2   **cups small seashell macaroni, cooked according to package directions**

1½   **cups cherry tomatoes, halved or quartered**

1   **cup yellow pepper, cut in small strips**

½   **cup thinly sliced fresh basil leaves**

⅓   **cup quartered Kalamata olives**

¼   **cup thinly sliced green onion**

2   **tablespoons capers**

5   **ounces feta cheese, crumbled**

⅔   **cup grated Parmesan cheese**

2   **tablespoons chopped fresh mint**

Dressing:

½   **cup light olive or vegetable oil**

3   **tablespoons red wine vinegar**

1   **teaspoon sugar**

½   **teaspoon salt or to taste**

¼   **teaspoon pepper**

Combine all salad ingredients in large bowl. Mix together dressing ingredients in a separate bowl or shake in tightly covered container. Toss salad ingredients lightly with dressing. Serve on individual plates or from large bowl.

Serves 6.

Real Tabbouleh

3/4   cup medium or #2 bulgur wheat

6-10   bunches fresh parsley or to taste

1/2   cup fresh mint leaves

3   medium tomatoes, finely chopped

16   green onions including tops, finely chopped

Dressing:

1   teaspoon salt or to taste

1/2   teaspoon black pepper

1/2   teaspoon ground cinnamon

1/2   cup fresh lemon juice

1/3   cup good quality olive oil

Cover bulgur with hot water and let soak for 1 hour or until all water is absorbed. While bulgur is soaking, snip parsley leaves from stems. Rinse parsley leaves several times in cold water. Drain and pat dry on clean towels, being sure to remove all excess moisture. Chop parsley and mint leaves by hand or using food processor being careful not to over process. Leaves should be chopped, not mashed. Drain off any excess water from bulgur. In a large bowl combine all salad ingredients. Mix all dressing ingredients in a small bowl or shake in a tightly covered container. Toss salad ingredients with dressing. Cover and chill for up to 12 hours.

Serves 8.

This contributor remembers her grandmother and her friends gathering in one another's kitchens to make huge bowls of this tabbouleh as they chatted - in Arabic of course!

Strawberry Tabbouleh

1 1/2 cups bulgur wheat

1-2   teaspoons salt

2   cups boiling water

1/4   cup extra virgin olive oil

1/4   cup freshly squeezed lemon juice

2   cups finely chopped fresh Italian parsley

3/4   cup finely chopped mint

4   cups chopped strawberries

1   cup pecan pieces, toasted

In large bowl combine bulgur and salt. Add boiling water, cover and let sit for 30 minutes. Remove cover and fluff with fork If any water remains, drain bulger completely. Stir in oil and lemon juice. Add parsley, mint and strawberries. Cover and refrigerate. When ready to serve add toasted pecans and toss to mix or sprinkle pecans on top.

Serves 8.

A slightly different flavor from traditional tabbouleh.

Apple Chicken and Wild Rice Salad

8   boneless skinless chicken breast halves

$1\frac{1}{2}$ cups apple juice

1   cup cooked wild rice, about $\frac{1}{3}$ cup raw rice

$1\frac{1}{2}$ cups green grapes, halved

$\frac{1}{2}$ cup chopped celery

$\frac{3}{4}$ cup slivered almonds, toasted

Dressing;

1   cup mayonnaise

$\frac{1}{2}$ teaspoon seasoned salt

$\frac{1}{4}$ teaspoon cinnamon

$\frac{1}{2}$-1 teaspoon salt to taste

Poach chicken breasts in apple juice 30 minutes. Cut up chicken and combine with other salad ingredients. Mix dressing ingredients until well blended and combine with salad ingredients. Chill before serving.

This salad is even better when refrigerated overnight.

Serves 6 to 8.

Spinach and Strawberry Salad

$\frac{1}{2}$ cup pecan or almond pieces

1   (10-ounce) package spinach, washed and torn

1   pint strawberries, halved

8   green onions with tops, thinly sliced

Dressing:

$\frac{1}{2}$ cup vegetable oil

$\frac{1}{2}$ cup vinegar

$\frac{1}{4}$ cup sugar

$\frac{1}{8}$ teaspoon pepper

$\frac{1}{2}$ teaspoon salt

$1\frac{1}{2}$ teaspoon Tabasco sauce or to taste

Heat oven to 300°. Spread nuts on a baking sheet and toast in oven 10 to 15 minutes or until lightly browned.

In large bowl combine spinach, berries and onion. In a small bowl or tightly covered container blend dressing ingredients. Just before serving, toss salad with just enough dressing to moisten spinach. Refrigerate left over sweet and sour dressing for up to 3 weeks.

Serves 4 to 6.

Grilled Escolar Salad

4 **Bosc pears, peeled and diced**

5 **tablespoons butter, divided**

Salt and pepper to taste, divided

2 **cups fresh blueberries**

3/4 **cup vegetable broth, divided**

1 **cup Riesling wine**

1 **seedless cucumber, thinly sliced**

1 **cup French green lentils, cooked**

1 **cup Napa cabbage, cut in julienne strips**

8 **(2-ounce) fresh escolar or sea bass medallions**

4 **baby bok choy, cleaned and blanched**

Heat oven to 350°. Toss pears with 1 tablespoon butter, salt and pepper. In baking dish roast pears in oven 5 to 8 minutes or until soft. Set aside half the pears for salad. Roast blueberries 3 to 5 minutes or until soft. In small saucepan bring 1/2 cup vegetable broth to boiling. Remove from heat. In blender puree blueberries and pears with hot broth. Strain pureed fruit through fine sieve. Transfer mixture to saucepan, add wine and simmer on low heat until reduced by half. Season with additional salt and pepper. Remove from heat and keep warm.

To prepare salad heat about 2 tablespoons butter in small skillet. Add remaining pears, cucumbers and lentils. Sauté until heated through and cucumbers are slightly wilted. Season with salt and pepper. Add cabbage and remaining 1/4 cup vegetable broth. Cook until cabbage is wilted.

Heat grill or skillet. Brush escolar medallions with remaining 2 tablespoons melted butter and season with salt and pepper. Grill approximately 1 1/2 minutes per side turning 1/4 turn after 45 seconds. If using skillet, sear and cook 30 to 40 seconds per side.

Place an equal amount of hot salad on each of four plates. Top with two escolar medallions and one lightly steamed seasoned baby bok choy per plate. Pour about 1 ounce sauce over each serving.

Serves 4.

Antonio Burrell, executive chef at The Vintage Restaurant in St. Paul, submitted this chic, unusual recipe.

In 1966, the League of Catholic Women contracted with Hennepin County to open a **Girls Group Home.** Hennepin County Social Services paid per diem for each resident. Catholic Charities provided professional staff and supervision. The League purchased, renovated, furnished and maintained the building. They also provided trained League members who worked with the young women in developing social and enrichment activities. These volunteers became "big sisters" and mentors to the group home residents.

Rustic Main Course Salad

1	pound small unpeeled new potatoes
4	tablespoons dry white wine
3	tablespoons white wine vinegar
3	tablespoons minced green onions
2	tablespoons Dijon mustard
3/4	teaspoon salt
1/4	teaspoon freshly ground pepper
1/2	cup plus 1 tablespoon olive oil
1/3	cup chopped parsley
3/4	pound ham, cut in julienne strips
1/2	pound Swiss cheese, cut in julienne strips
	Lettuce for garnish
2	beefsteak tomatoes, sliced
1	small red onion, thinly sliced

In large saucepan boil potatoes in lightly salted water until just tender. Drain and cut into thinly sliced rounds leaving skins intact whenever possible. In container with tight fitting lid combine wine, vinegar, green onions, mustard, salt and pepper. Cover and shake well. Add oil and parsley. Shake again. Pour half the dressing over warm potatoes and toss lightly. Cover. Cool to room temperature. Add ham, cheese and remaining dressing. Blend well. Line serving platter with lettuce. Mound salad on top and surround with tomato slices. Garnish with onion rings.

Serves 6.

Lebanese Salad Dressing

1-2	cloves garlic, minced
1/2	cup fresh lemon juice
1	cup extra virgin olive oil
3	tablespoons finely chopped mint
1	teaspoon salt
1/4	teaspoon black pepper

Shake all dressing ingredients in tightly covered container. Serve over a salad of mixed greens, cucumbers and tomatoes.

David George, who owned the Cedars Restaurant, gave lessons in Lebanese cooking to several local families. This is one of his recipes. Every family or village in Lebanon seems to have his or her own version of this salad dressing.

Cranberry Ginger Salad

½	cup orange or pineapple juice or ⅓ cup cherry liqueur
1	orange, peeled, seeded and sectioned
1	red apple, cored and cubed
1	green apple, cored and cubed
1	grapefruit, peeled, seeded and sectioned
1	cup pineapple tidbits, drained
½	pound red grapes, halved

Sauce:

½	cup water
6	tablespoons sugar
½-1	teaspoon cinnamon or to taste
1	teaspoon finely chopped or grated fresh ginger or to taste
1	cup fresh cranberries

Pour juice over cut-up fruit and fold gently to mix. Cover and refrigerate. Bring water, sugar, cinnamon and ginger to boil. Add cranberries and boil 2 to 4 minutes until berries pop. Fold cranberry sauce into mixed fruit. Refrigerate for 2 to 12 hours. Gently stir fruit and sauce again before serving. Drain and serve on individual lettuce leaves or serve with juice as buffet side dish. Provide a large slotted spoon for buffet guests to serve themselves.

Serves 8.

This is an appetizing light fruit salad especially appropriate for the holidays. It would be an excellent accompaniment for the Swiss Fondue in the Breads and Breakfast section.

Unused fresh ginger may be stored in the freezer for months.

Spinach Salad with Warm Dressing

3	tablespoons brown sugar
1	tablespoon Worcestershire sauce
¾	cup red wine vinegar
6	tablespoons olive oil
8	slices bacon, cooked and crumbled
3	green onions, both white and green parts, sliced
18	ounces fresh spinach, washed, drained and dried

Place sugar in pan over high heat. Add Worcestershire sauce to soak sugar. Add vinegar and oil. Mix well until sugar dissolves. Add bacon and onions. Bring to boiling. Pour hot dressing over spinach. Toss and serve immediately.

Serves 6.

Korean Chicken Salad

Marinade:

4	tablespoons soy sauce
2	tablespoons oil
2	tablespoons sherry or white wine
1/2	teaspoon ground ginger
1/2	teaspoon cinnamon
2	cloves garlic, finely chopped

Salad:

10	boneless skinless chicken breast halves
2	cups shredded iceberg lettuce
1	cup thinly sliced cucumber
1	cup thinly sliced carrots
2/3	cup chopped green onion
1	cup bean sprouts
3/4	cup slivered almonds, toasted and salted
2	tablespoons sesame seeds, toasted

Dressing:

1/2	teaspoon ground mustard
1/2	teaspoon salt
1/2	teaspoon Tabasco sauce
1	tablespoon soy sauce
4	teaspoons fresh lemon juice
1/2	cup vegetable or sesame oil

Heat oven to 400°. In tightly covered container, shake marinade ingredients until well blended. Thoroughly coat chicken pieces with marinade. Place chicken in shallow roasting pan. Pour remainder of marinade over top. Cook uncovered 40 minutes, turning after 20 minutes. Cool cooked chicken and cut into thin strips. Place lettuce, cucumber, carrots, onions and bean sprouts in large bowl. The chicken and these 5 salad ingredients may be prepared well in advance.

Blend dressing ingredients in tightly covered container. Shake well and chill. You may refrigerate for up to 1 week. Just before serving toss the salad ingredients adding the chicken, dressing, seeds and almonds.

Serves 10.

Curried Chicken and Grape Salad

10	boneless skinless chicken breast halves or 2 (3-pound) fryers
1	piece fresh gingerroot, sliced
1	small onion, peeled
$1/2$	lemon
1	teaspoon salt
1	pound seedless red grapes, halved
1	cup thinly sliced celery
2	honeydew melons
$1/2$	cup mango chutney (i.e. Major Grey's)
$1/2$	cup golden raisins

Marinade:

$1/4$	cup white wine vinegar
$1/2$	teaspoon salt
$1/2$	teaspoon dried chervil
1	teaspoon dried tarragon
1	tablespoon minced chives
$3/4$	cup extra virgin olive oil

Cracked pepper to taste

Dressing:

1	cup mayonnaise
$1/2$	cup sour cream
2	tablespoons minced parsley
8	green onions with tops, chopped
2	teaspoons curry powder or to taste

Place chicken, ginger, onion, $1/2$ lemon and salt in large pot or Dutch oven. Add enough water to just cover contents. Simmer covered until chicken is very tender, about $1\,1/2$ hours for whole chickens or 20 to 30 minutes for chicken breasts. Remove chicken and cool. If using whole chickens, remove meat from skin and bones. Cube the chicken. Combine all marinade ingredients except the oil in a tightly covered container and shake well to blend. Add olive oil and shake again. Pour over cubed chicken and refrigerate. Add grapes and celery to marinated chicken. Fold curry dressing over all. Taste to adjust seasoning. Chill.

To serve slice and peel 2 ripe honeydew melons to create 8 rings. Spoon generous mound of chicken salad onto each ring. Garnish with chutney and raisins.

Serves 10.

Other salad additions might be cubed avocado, honeydew or cantaloupe melon balls, slivered almonds, artichoke hearts or sliced hearts of palm. Don't be intimidated by the length of the ingredients. Very easy and delicious!

Summer Greens with Grilled Red Potatoes

4	medium red potatoes, boiled whole then quartered
$^1/_3$	cup plus 1 teaspoon olive oil, divided
1	clove garlic, finely minced
1	teaspoon Dijon mustard
$^1/_4$	cup lemon juice
2	tablespoons water
2	teaspoons balsamic vinegar
$^1/_2$	teaspoon freshly ground black pepper
4	cups mixed greens, such as romaine lettuce, spinach or arugula

Prepare grill. Brush potatoes with 1 teaspoon of olive oil. Grill over medium heat on both sides until evenly browned, 8 to 10 minutes. Set aside. In large bowl combine remaining $^1/_3$ cup of olive oil with garlic, mustard, lemon juice, water, vinegar and pepper. Whisk 1 minute. Add potatoes and toss well. Strain out potatoes and place on side dish. Add greens to bowl and toss to coat. Place greens on 6 salad plates and top with warm potatoes. Serve immediately.

Serves 6.

Nice with any grilled entree on a hot summer night.

Fumi Salad

8	tablespoons slivered almonds, toasted
8	tablespoons sunflower seed, unsalted
1	(3-ounce) package chicken flavored ramen noodles
$^1/_4$	cup butter or margarine
1	(16-ounce) package cabbage slaw
8	tablespoons chopped green onion

Dressing:

4	tablespoons sugar
1	teaspoon pepper
2	teaspoons salt
6	tablespoons white vinegar
$^3/_4$	cup vegetable oil
1	tablespoon soy sauce

Combine and shake all dressing ingredients in tightly covered container. Refrigerate up to 1 week.

In medium skillet, brown almonds, sunflower seed and ramen noodles in butter or margarine. Remove from stove and mix in contents of flavor packet from noodles. Refrigerate up to 1 day. In large bowl toss cabbage slaw and onions. Combine with remaining salad ingredients. Pour dressing over cabbage mixture just before serving. Mix well.

Serves 10 to 15.

Salad Elaine

4	cups mixed salad greens containing romaine
1	cup fresh pear slices, cut in half
1	large red apple, chopped
1/2	cup chopped celery
1/2	cup chopped walnuts
1/3	cup crumbled blue cheese

Dressing:

1/2	cup sugar
2	teaspoons celery seed
1	teaspoon ground mustard
1	teaspoon salt
1/3	cup vinegar
1	cup light vegetable oil

Combine all dressing ingredients and mix well in a bowl or tightly covered container. Refrigerate up to 3 weeks. Mix salad ingredients together in large bowl. Toss lightly with just enough dressing to coat. Keep remainder of dressing for other salads.

Serves 6 to 8.

Avocado Salad

1	(10-ounce) package mixed greens
1	large avocado, peeled and chopped
8	green onions, chopped
1/2	pound bacon, chopped and fried until crisp

Dressing:

3/4	cup mayonnaise, Hellmann's preferred
1/4	cup sugar
1/2	teaspoon Dijon Mustard
1	tablespoon fresh lemon juice

At least 4 hours in advance shake all dressing ingredients in tightly covered container. When ready to serve combine first 3 salad ingredients in large bowl and toss with dressing. Sprinkle bacon on top.

Serves 4.

Layered Cauliflower Salad

1	**large head lettuce**
1	**large red onion, chopped**
1	**pound bacon, cut in small pieces and crisply cooked**
1	**large head cauliflower, separated into bite size flowerets**
3/4	**cup sugar**
1/3-1/2	**cup grated Parmesan cheese**
2	**cups mayonnaise**
2	**cups seasoned croutons**

Break up lettuce and put in large bowl. Sprinkle onions over lettuce layer. Sprinkle bacon over onion layer. Place cauliflower flowerets over bacon. Sprinkle sugar and Parmesan cheese evenly over all. Dab on mayonnaise. Do not mix. Cover tightly and refrigerate for up to 12 hours. Just before serving toss with croutons.

Serves 10 to 12.

Rocky Mountain Salad

1/3	**cup chopped onion or to taste**
3	**tablespoons cider vinegar**
2	**teaspoons spicy brown mustard**
1/2	**teaspoon sugar**
1/2	**teaspoon salt**
1/4	**teaspoon freshly ground black pepper**
3/4	**cup olive oil**
2	**heads romaine lettuce, torn into bite-size pieces**
1	**(14-ounce) can water packed artichoke hearts, drained and quartered**
1	**large avocado, peeled, seeded and cut into bite-size pieces**
1/2	**pound bacon, crisply cooked and crumbled**
4	**ounces freshly grated Parmesan cheese**

In food processor or blender combine onion and vinegar. Pulse to puree onion and transfer to medium bowl. Whisk in mustard, sugar, salt and pepper. Gradually add olive oil, whisking constantly until thick.

In large bowl combine lettuce, artichoke hearts, avocado, bacon and cheese. Add enough dressing to coat. Serve immediately.

Serves 6.

Spinach Salad with Dried Cranberries

1   (10-ounce) package fresh spinach
       leaves, torn

$^1/_2$ cup chopped walnuts

$^2/_3$ cup dried cranberries

$^1/_4$ cup sunflower seeds

Dressing:

$^1/_4$ cup raspberry vinegar

2   tablespoons honey

$^1/_2$ teaspoon sugar

1   teaspoon fresh lemon juice

$^1/_4$ teaspoon salt

$^1/_4$ cup vegetable oil

$^1/_4$ cup olive oil

Combine salad ingredients in large bowl. Shake all dressing ingredients in tightly covered container. Just before serving, toss salad ingredients with dressing.

Serves 6.

This makes a nice accompaniment to Pork Tenderloin Stroganoff in the Entrees section.

Best Cranberry Jello Salad

2   (3-ounce) packages strawberry
       gelatin (i.e. Jello brand)

1   cup hot water

1   (28-ounce) can crushed pineapple
       and juice

1   (16-ounce) carton sour cream

1   (16-ounce) can whole cranberry
       sauce

$^1/_2$ cup chopped pecans

Whipping cream, lightly whipped,
       optional

Combine strawberry gelatin with 1 cup hot water, let cool slightly. Stir crushed pineapple and juice into gelatin mixture and set aside. In a separate bowl blend together sour cream and whole cranberry sauce with spoon. When blended stir into gelatin and pineapple mixture. Add $^1/_2$ cup chopped pecans. Pour all ingredients into 13x9-inch pan. Refrigerate until firm. Cut in squares and serve on greens. Top with dollop of whipped cream if desired.

Serves 10 to 12.

Orange, Walnut and Cranberry Salad

6	tablespoons honey
1¹/₂	tablespoons water
³/₄	teaspoon ground allspice
¹/₂	teaspoon salt
¹/₄	heaping teaspoon ground ginger
1	cup walnut halves and pieces
2	teaspoons sugar
³/₄	cup water
³/₄	cup cranberry juice cocktail
¹/₂	cup dried cranberries
8	oranges, peeled and white pith removed, sliced into ¹/₂-inch thick rounds, chilled

Fresh mint sprigs, optional

Heat oven to 325˚. Line baking sheet with parchment paper. Mix first 5 ingredients in large bowl to blend. Add nuts and toss to coat well. Strain nuts, reserving liquid. Transfer nuts to baking sheet and sprinkle with sugar. Bake until golden brown about 17 minutes. Cool completely.

Whisk water, cranberry juice and reserved liquid from nuts in medium saucepan to blend. Stir in dried cranberries. Bring to boil. Reduce heat to medium-low and simmer until cranberries soften and liquid is reduced to thin syrup, about 20 minutes.

Both nuts and cranberry mixture may be prepared up to 3 days in advance. Nuts should be stored in an airtight container at room temperature. Cranberry mixture should be covered and refrigerated.

To serve, arrange oranges on a platter. Spoon cranberry mixture over oranges and sprinkle with nuts. Garnish with mint, if desired.

Serves 8.

Simplicity Salad

4	cups or 1 (16-ounce) bag mixed salad greens
1	clove garlic, cut in half
³/₄	teaspoon seasoned salt
³/₄	teaspoon dry mustard

Freshly ground pepper to taste

¹/₄	cup olive oil
1	tablespoon red wine vinegar
1	cup packaged seasoned croutons

Early in the day, rub cut sides of garlic around edges and bottom of a wooden salad bowl. Place seasoned salt, dry mustard, pepper, oil and vinegar in bowl. Stir to blend. Place greens on top but do not toss. Cover and refrigerate up to 8 hours. Toss greens with dressing just before serving. Add croutons and toss again.

Artichoke hearts, red onion, orange slices and any number of other ingredients may be added to this simple salad. However, it is delicious just as it is and so easy to prepare.

Serves 4.

Marshall Special Salad

1/4	pound bacon, diced and fried until crisp
2	heads romaine, washed, dried and torn into small pieces
1	pint cherry tomatoes, halved
1	cup coarsely grated Swiss cheese
2/3	cup slivered almonds, toasted
1/3	cup freshly grated Parmesan cheese

Dressing:

Juice of 1 lemon

2	small cloves garlic, crushed
1	teaspoon salt
1/4	teaspoon pepper
3/4	cup salad oil
1	cup croutons

Cook bacon and drain on paper towels. Combine bacon with other salad ingredients in a large bowl.

Combine lemon juice, garlic, salt and pepper in a small bowl. Using a whisk add salad oil in a stream. Let dressing stand covered for three hours. Add dressing to salad and toss just before serving. Garnish with croutons.

Serves 8.

This is an all time favorite recipe from a gourmet group that has been together for 24 years!

Spinach-Raspberry Salad

1	(10-ounce) package fresh spinach
1/4	cup vegetable oil
2	tablespoons raspberry vinegar
2	tablespoons seedless raspberry jam
2	tablespoons minced green onions
1/4	teaspoon salt
3	drops Tabasco sauce
1/8	teaspoon pepper
6	ounces fresh raspberries
1	(3 1/2-ounce) jar macadamia nuts, coarsely chopped

Wash and trim greens. Tear into bite size pieces and pat dry. In small bowl combine oil and vinegar. Whisk in jam. Stir in onions, salt, pepper and Tabasco. Dressing may be made up to two days ahead. Toss greens with dressing in large bowl. Arrange on individual plates. Sprinkle with raspberries and nuts.

Serves 8.

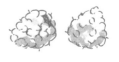

V.I.P. Salad

1	medium head iceberg lettuce or 1 (10-ounce) package mixed greens containing romaine
1	cup raw cauliflower, cut into bite-size flowerets
1/2	medium avocado, peeled and sliced
1	tomato, peeled and sliced
1/2	cup slivered almonds, toasted

Dressing:

4	cloves garlic, quartered
1/2	cup lemon juice
4	teaspoons salt
2	teaspoons paprika
1	teaspoon sugar
1	teaspoon pepper
1/2	teaspoon celery seed
3	teaspoons ground mustard
1 1/4	cups salad oil

Mix all dressing ingredients in bowl or shake in tightly covered container. In large bowl combine all salad ingredients except almonds. Remove garlic from dressing. Toss salad with just enough dressing to coat vegetables. Sprinkle with almonds and serve. Refrigerate remaining dressing for up to 3 weeks.

Serves 8.

To toast almonds and most other nuts, place on baking sheet in 350˚ oven for 5 to 10 minutes or in microwave for 1 to 2 minutes on medium heat.

In 1974, the League of Catholic Women assumed full responsibility for the operation of both the **Girls and Boys Group Homes**. Still contracting with Hennepin County Social Services for a per diem rate, the League maintained the buildings and properties, hired and oversaw professional staff and provided volunteers to interact with and support the residents.

In 1975, the name **Pathway** was adopted as the overall designation for the Girls and Boys Group Homes. In 1982, the former Boys Home merged with the former Girls Home to become a coed facility until 1993 when it was converted into a female residence again.

In 1998, the League decided to close Pathway and began searching for other community involvement to meet to current societal needs. Two new projects have been initiated since 1998. More are scheduled to begin in 2000-2001.

Southern Sweet Potato Salad

6	medium sweet potatoes, peeled and cut into $1/2$-inch cubes
$1^1/_2$	cups chopped celery
3	green onions with tops, sliced
1	cup currants or raisins
1	(20-ounce) can crushed pineapple, drained well
1	cup chopped pecans
1	cup mayonnaise
1	cup sour cream
2	tablespoons cider vinegar
1	tablespoon honey
$1/_2$	teaspoon salt
$1/_8$	teaspoon freshly ground pepper

Bring large pot of salted water to boiling. Add sweet potato cubes. Boil about 5 to 7 minutes just until tender but firm enough to hold their shape. Drain into a colander and rinse under cold water. Drain well. In large bowl gently toss sweet potatoes with celery, green onions, currants or raisins, pineapple and pecans.

In medium bowl mix together mayonnaise, sour cream, vinegar, honey, salt and pepper. Gently toss with sweet potato mixture. Cover and refrigerate until serving time.

Serves 8 to 12.

An interesting alternative to regular potato salad.

The **Northside Breast Feeding Campaign (NBC)**, established in 1998, was an outgrowth of the **Nutrition Education Initiative (NEI)** coordinated and sponsored by the League of Catholic Women on the near northside of Minneapolis. NEI brought representatives from private businesses, public agencies and volunteer organizations to dialogue with women from the near northside area. This broadly-based coalition determined that the first step to good lifetime nutrition was getting the right start through breastfeeding.

In partnership with an Allina Foundation Reach Grant, the League has provided funding, leadership and volunteers for the Northside Breastfeeding Campaign. NBC has accomplished the following:
* Development of a sustainable community support network including peer counselors and a trained lactation educator.
* Breastfeeding education for physicians at North Memorial Clinic and Pilot City clinic and nutritionists in Hennepin County.
* Implementation of a successful media campaign to promote breastfeeding.
* Development of quality breastfeeding materials for clinics, social service agencies, daycare providers and hospital use.
* Funding and support for a breastfeeding center which Pilot City will continue to operate.

Greek Style Pasta Salad

2   cups medium pasta shells or garlic or spinach tortellini

$1/2$ pint cherry tomatoes, stemmed and halved

1   medium green bell pepper, stem and seeds removed, cut into $1/2$-inch pieces

1   medium cucumber, pared, quartered lengthwise, cut into $1/2$-inch cubes

1   small red onion, cut into $1/2$-inch cubes

$1/2$ cup sliced celery

1   ounce feta cheese, cut into $1/2$-inch cubes

$1/4$ cup pitted, split Kalamata olives

1   tablespoon chopped Italian flat leaf parsley

1   tablespoon chopped fresh mint

$1/2$ teaspoon dried oregano

1   (8-ounce) jar marinated artichokes, cut into chunks and liquid reserved

Coarsely ground black pepper to taste

Cook pasta al dente in salted boiling water according to package directions. Drain pasta and plunge into cold water. Drain well. Mix all additional ingredients including reserved artichoke liquid and toss with pasta. Chill until ready to serve. May be prepared 1 day ahead.

Serves 8.

Herb Salad

1	head Boston lettuce, washed and chilled
2	Belgian endive or 1 bunch arugula, separated, washed and chilled (curly endive may be substituted)
2	tablespoons chopped parsley
6-8	sprigs fresh watercress

Dressing:

1/2	cup vegetable oil
1/4	cup tarragon vinegar
1	tablespoon fresh or frozen snipped chives
1	tablespoon fresh snipped dill or 1 teaspoon dried dill weed
1/2	clove garlic, crushed
1	teaspoon sugar
1/2-1	teaspoon salt
1/4	teaspoon coarsely ground pepper

In container with tight fitting lid combine oil, vinegar, chives, dill, garlic, sugar, salt, pepper and shake well. Chill at least one hour. This dressing can be refrigerated up to 1 week.

Wash and dry lettuce and endive. Tear into bite-size pieces and put into large salad bowl or plastic bag. Salad greens may be prepared ahead, covered and refrigerated for up to 6 hours. Just before serving, shake dressing vigorously. Pour over salad greens and toss until well coated.

Serves 6 to 8.

This salad is aromatic and delightfully different. Perfect for the summer season when your herb garden is in bloom.

Curried Waldorf Salad

3	cups unpeeled chopped red apples
1	cup red seedless grape halves
1	(8-ounce) jar apple curry chutney
3/4	cup sliced celery
1/2	cup chopped walnuts
1/4	cup mayonnaise
	Romaine or iceberg lettuce leaves

Combine apples, grapes, chutney, celery, nuts and mayonnaise in medium bowl. Toss well to coat. Refrigerate at least 1 hour and up to 3 hours. Serve on lettuce leaves.

Serves 4.

Pear, Blue Cheese and Walnut Salad

1	cup chopped walnuts or pecans
1/2	cup sugar
2	tablespoons butter
3	medium pears, cored, peeled and sliced
2	tablespoons fresh lemon juice
4-6	cups fresh mixed salad greens or 2 (10-ounce) packages mixed salad greens
2	ounces blue cheese or more to taste

Dressing:

1/3	cup white wine vinegar
1/4	cup vegetable oil or part walnut oil
1/3	cup pear nectar or pear syrup
1	teaspoon Dijon mustard
1/4	teaspoon salt
1/8	teaspoon pepper

Sauté nuts in sugar and butter over low heat in a small skillet, stirring constantly until nuts are coated and candied. When cool, break apart and set aside. Peel, core and slice pears. Coat pears with lemon juice if doing ahead. Wash and tear salad greens and crumble blue cheese.

In tightly covered container combine all dressing ingredients and shake well. Just before serving, toss salad ingredients with dressing and candied nuts. Salad may be arranged on individual plates or served in a bowl as a tossed salad.

Serves 8.

Concerned about the economic, political and social status of women looking for employment in the early 1900's, the League of Catholic Women purchased two buildings located at 1602 and 1608 Hawthorne Avenue. Here they established a residence for single women engaged in or looking for work. Named **St. Mary's Hall**, this facility operated until 1945.

At St. Mary's young women, many from small towns or foreign countries, received practical assistance in the form of cafeteria meals, a reading room, a wide-variety of academic and vocational courses of study and an employment bureau.

Carlis Caesar Salad

1	head romaine lettuce, washed, dried and torn into bite-size pieces
2	tomatoes, cut into wedges
1/4	cup chopped green onion
1/2	pound bacon, fried until crisp and crumbled
1/2	cup freshly grated Parmesan cheese

Bowl Seasoning:

2	tablespoons olive oil
2	large cloves garlic, crushed

Dressing:

1/3	cup olive oil
1/4	teaspoon fresh mint
1/4	teaspoon dried oregano
1/4	teaspoon salt
1/2	teaspoon coarsely ground pepper
1/4	cup fresh lemon juice
1	coddled egg

To a large wooden serving bowl place olive oil and crushed garlic. Let stand for at least 2 hours.

In separate bowl combine dressing ingredients. Blend with mixer or blender until thickened.

Just before serving combine salad ingredients and dressing in prepared serving bowl. Toss lightly.

Serves 6 to 8.

To coddle an egg, bring a small pan of water to boiling. Place egg in its shell into water, cover and remove from heat. Let stand for no longer than 4 minutes. Crack open and add to other dressing ingredients.

The League of Catholic Women operated **Chi Rho Club** from 1958-1969. Young men and women who came to work or attend business or trade schools in the Twin Cities were welcomed at the Downtown Center. A professional group worker assisted a League committee in carrying out the program designed to familiarize young people with cultural, social and religious resources in the Twin Cities. A priest from St. Olaf Catholic Church acted as Spiritual Director and was vitally important to the success on this outreach project. Junior Catholic League members often hosted these activities.

Green Bean Salad

1   **pound fresh green beans, lightly steamed**

2   **tablespoons chopped red pepper**

1   **cup shredded provolone cheese**

1   **hard boiled egg, peeled and chopped**

Dressing:

1/3   **cup vegetable or olive oil**

1 1/2   **tablespoons fresh lemon juice**

1/2   **teaspoon salt**

1/4   **teaspoon dill weed**

2   **teaspoons minced onion**

Combine first 3 ingredients in large bowl. Reserve egg for garnish.

In tightly covered container shake all dressing ingredients together. Toss dressing with all salad ingredients except egg. Chill. Before serving top with chopped hard-boiled egg.

Serves 4 to 6.

"Thyme to Spare" Potato Salad

2   **pounds peeled or unpeeled red potatoes, boiled just until tender and cubed**

1/2   **large red onion, thinly sliced**

3-4   **celery stalks, sliced**

1/2   **medium red pepper, cut into thin strips**

Dressing:

1/2   **cup nonfat Italian dressing**

1/2   **teaspoon paprika**

1/2   **tablespoon minced garlic**

1   **tablespoon bottled basil pesto**

1/2   **teaspoon coarsely ground black pepper**

1   **tablespoon sugar**

1   **tablespoon Dijon mustard**

2   **tablespoons balsamic vinegar**

Toss all salad ingredients together in large bowl. Combine dressing ingredients in tightly covered container and shake well. Just before serving toss salad ingredients with dressing. Shredded carrots and or bacon bits may be added if desired.

Serves 8 to 10.

An original recipe from David Kennedy of "Thyme to Spare" Catering. It was served at the LCW annual golf outing in 1998.

During Christmas...

Our family treasures a special time at Christmas Eve when there are only lighted candles, Christmas tree lights and quiet Christmas music. Everyone relaxes and shares their hopes and dreams for the next year.

Every Christmas Eve we have a leisurely meal of beef fondue. It is not only easy and delicious fare but it seems to encourage good conversation. When the children were small we had our fondue around a big coffee table in front of the fireplace. Recently one of our grown sons proposed to his girlfriend over Christmas Eve fondue and both adult children put fondue pots on their wedding gift lists!

In our family we have tried the following method of limiting an excess of Christmas presents for our young children. We explain to them that since Jesus received three gifts from the Wise Men, they too will receive three gifts on His birthday. So far everyone is benefiting from this tradition!

When our children were young we always had a birthday party for Baby Jesus on Christmas Eve. We baked a special cake and each child put a candle on it. We lit the candles and sang "Happy Birthday, Dear Jesus" and then, one at a time, they blew out their candle and made a wish they thought Jesus might want to make. Our married children have continued this tradition. It helps remind our whole family of exactly whose birthday we are celebrating on December 25.

Soups

Chinese Chicken Soup

8	cups canned or homemade chicken broth
3	tablespoons soy sauce
2	tablespoons dry sherry
$1/8$	teaspoon ground ginger
1	whole boneless, skinless chicken breast, cut into small pieces
$1/4$	pound fresh or frozen shrimp, shelled and deveined, optional
1	bunch washed fresh spinach, torn into pieces
$1/2$	pound sliced mushrooms
2-3	green onions, sliced
1	hard cooked egg, cut into six slices

In large pan heat broth, soy sauce, sherry and ginger to boiling. Add chicken, shrimp (if desired), spinach and mushrooms. Cook over medium high heat 5 minutes until chicken and shrimp are tender. Ladle soup into bowls. Top with green onions and an egg slice.

Serves 6.

Christmas Wild Rice Soup

1	cup uncooked wild rice
1	(1.8-ounce) dry vegetable soup mix (i.e. Knorr)
1	pound fresh mushrooms, chopped
1	large onion, chopped
3-4	celery stalks, chopped
$1^1/2$	tablespoons olive oil
3	($10^3/4$-ounce) cans cream of potato with roasted garlic soup
$2^1/2$	cups skim milk
$3/4$	pound bacon, cooked and crumbled, optional
2	cups Cheddar cheese, shredded

Salt and pepper to taste

Water, if needed

Heat oven to 350°. Wash rice. Mix with 3 cups water and add vegetable soup mix. Cook covered in oven for 1 hour or on stove, bringing to boil and turning down to simmer, about 1 hour or until water is fully absorbed.

In large saucepan sauté chopped mushrooms, onion and celery in olive oil. Add cooked rice, potato soup, milk and bacon, if desired. Bring to a simmer, stirring frequently. Soup scorches easily. Add cheese, salt and pepper to taste. Reduce heat and simmer. Add water if soup becomes too thick.

Serves 8.

A traditional Christmas Eve favorite in this contributor's family.

Beef and Vegetable Soup

3	pounds lean boneless beef, cut into small pieces
6	cups water
2	teaspoons salt
$1/2$	teaspoon black pepper
2	cloves garlic, minced
1	whole bay leaf
$1/3$	cup pearl barley or rice
1	quart chopped tomatoes, canned or fresh
4	stalks celery, sliced
4	large carrots, sliced
2	medium onions, cut into wedges
$1/2$	small head of cabbage, coarsely shredded
2	$15^1/2$-ounce cans red kidney beans

Combine meat, water, salt and pepper in Dutch oven or large saucepan. Bring slowly to boiling. Spoon off foam that rises to top. Add garlic and bay leaf. Cover and simmer gently until the meat is tender, about $1^1/4$ hours.

Add barley or rice, tomatoes with liquid, celery, carrots, onion and cabbage. Cover and simmer until vegetables are tender, about 20 minutes. Add beans with liquid. Adjust seasonings. Serve hot. Offer sour cream at the table.

Serves 8 to 10 generously.

Clam Chowder

$1/4$	cup diced onion
10	tablespoons butter or half butter, half margarine
10	tablespoons all-purpose flour
3	cups milk, heated
1	pint clams and liquid
3	cups diced potatoes, cooked in water to cover
$1^1/2$	teaspoons seasoned salt

Sauté diced onion in butter in medium saucepan. Whisk in flour. When smooth add hot milk and stir constantly. Heat clams and liquid in separate saucepan. When flour mixture has thickened to cream sauce add clams with liquid. Add warm potatoes and hot cooking water along with seasoned salt. Bring just to boiling point and serve.

Makes 2 quarts.

This is one of the most popular recipes created by Harold Lindberg, chef at the Boulevard Twins Restaurant, popular in the 1950's.

Tomato and Tortellini Soup

1	teaspoon olive oil
1	large onion, chopped
1	teaspoon bottled minced garlic
8	ounces fresh mushrooms, sliced
2	($14\frac{1}{2}$-ounce) cans low-fat chicken broth
1	($14\frac{1}{2}$-ounce) can seasoned diced tomatoes with garlic and onion
1	teaspoon Worcestershire sauce
$\frac{1}{2}$	teaspoon dried basil
1	(14-ounce) bag frozen cheese tortellini

Grated Parmesan cheese to taste

Over medium heat warm olive oil in Dutch oven or large saucepan. Sauté onion and garlic and cook until tender, about 3 minutes. Add mushrooms and cook 2 minutes more. Add broth and undrained tomatoes. Raise heat to high. Cover and bring soup to boiling. Add Worcestershire and basil. Add tortellini when broth comes to a rolling boil. Bring to a boil again. Cook 3 to 4 minutes or until tortellini is tender. Ladle into bowls. Serve with Parmesan cheese.

Serves 6.

Harbor View Cucumber Soup

6	cups chicken stock or canned chicken broth
$\frac{1}{4}$	cup minced white onion
$\frac{1}{4}$	cup minced garlic or less to taste
$\frac{1}{2}$	cup (1 stick) butter, divided
$\frac{1}{2}$	cup all-purpose flour
2	large cucumbers, peeled and chopped
2	tablespoons minced garlic
$\frac{1}{2}$	cup sour cream

Tabasco sauce to taste

Salt and pepper to taste

Dill pickle juice to thin

Cucumber slices and fresh dill for garnish

Heat chicken stock or broth to simmering. In small skillet sauté onion and $\frac{1}{4}$ cup garlic in $\frac{1}{4}$ cup butter until softened. Add to simmering stock. In same skillet make a roux by cooking flour with remaining butter until bubbly. Whisk roux into simmering stock. Stir constantly until thickened. Cool several hours or overnight.

When completely chilled puree soup-base, cucumbers, sour cream and garlic in blender. Season with Tabasco, salt and pepper to taste. Thin to desired consistency with pickle juice. Serve in chilled soup cups and garnish with cucumber slices and fresh dill.

Serves 10 to 12.

Our thanks to the Harbor View Café in Pepin, Wisconsin and to owner/chef Paul Hinderle.

Senator Lodge's Family Bean Soup

4-5   **quarts water**

2   **cups (1 pound) dried small white beans**

1   **large onion, peeled and pierced with 3 whole cloves**

4   **sprigs fresh parsley and 1 bay leaf tied together with string**

2   **tablespoon salt**

2   **(1 pound) smoked ham hocks**

1½   **cups finely chopped onion**

1   **cup finely chopped celery**

¼   **cup finely chopped fresh parsley**

1   **teaspoon finely chopped garlic**

½   **teaspoon fresh ground pepper**

Salt to taste

In heavy large pot bring 2 quarts water to boiling over high heat. Drop in beans and boil 2 minutes. Water should cover the beans by at least 2 inches. Turn off heat and allow beans to soak 1 hour. Add clove pierced onion, parsley, bay leaf and 2 teaspoons salt. Bring to boiling again. Reduce heat to low and simmer, partially covered, 1 hour or until beans are tender. Beans should be covered with water at all times. Keep kettle of boiling water at hand. Remove onion, bay leaf and parsley. Drain beans over bowl or pot. Measure cooking liquid and add enough water to make 3 quarts. Return liquid and beans to pot. Add ham hocks and bring to boiling over high heat. Return to low and simmer, partially covered, for 2 hours. Stir in chopped onion, celery, parsley, garlic, pepper and ½ teaspoon salt to taste. Use less salt if desired. Continue to simmer, partially covered, 45 minutes. Take out hocks, skin and bone. Cut meat into small pieces. Return ham to soup. Ladle into soup bowls.

Serves 8 to 10.

Best bean soup ever! From the kitchen of Henry Cabot Lodge's famous Boston family.

After completely redesigning, remodeling and decorating the Downtown Center in 1962, plans were made for the League of Catholic Women's first **Biennial Exhibition of Liturgical and Sacred Art** which opened in the winter of 1963. It brought to the attention of the public the best work of local artists expressing spiritual concepts in new ways following Vatican II. The League purchased Paul Granlund's beautiful bronze, "Father Damien," after the 1963 exhibit. This sculpture is currently displayed at the LCW Downtown Center. In the 1980's several local artists exhibited their work at the League. There have also been exhibitions centered around the work of LCW members.

Warm Heart Chicken Soup

2	whole boneless, skinless chicken breasts, chopped
$1/4$	cup chopped onion
$1/2$	cup sliced fresh mushrooms, optional
1	medium clove garlic, minced
$2^{1}/4$	cups chicken stock or broth, divided
1	tablespoon chopped fresh rosemary
1	cup chopped carrots
1	cup chopped celery
1	cup slightly cooked noodles
2	tablespoons chopped fresh Italian parsley or cilantro

Salt and pepper to taste

$1/2$	teaspoon ground sage

In large saucepan cook chicken, onion, mushrooms and garlic in $1/4$ cup chicken broth until tender. Add rosemary, 2 cups chicken broth, carrots and celery. Simmer 10 minutes. Add noodles, Italian parsley or cilantro, salt, pepper and sage. Simmer 30 minutes. Do not boil. Ladle into bowls.

Serves 3 to 4.

*This recipe is from Bonnie Dehn's kitchen. Bonnie is the owner of Dehn's Garden, author of **Herbs in a Minnesota Kitchen** and frequent volunteer and chef for the Aids Ministry of the League of Catholic Women.*

Stilton and Pear Soup

$1/4$	cup ($1/2$ stick) butter
2	stalks celery, minced
1	large onion, minced
2	leeks, bulbs only, minced
$1/2$	cup all-purpose flour
4	cups chicken stock or broth, divided
$1/4$	pound Monterey Jack cheese, grated
2	cups whipping cream
$1/4$	pound Stilton cheese, diced
3	ripe pears, peeled, cored and diced

Melt butter in large stockpot. Add celery, onion and leeks. Sauté until vegetables are soft. Sprinkle in flour and cook 2 minutes, stirring occasionally. Gradually add 2 cups chicken stock, stirring constantly.

Transfer mixture to food processor or blender and puree. Return to pot and add remaining stock, Monterey Jack cheese and cream. Heat thoroughly. Soup may be served chilled. Divide Stilton cheese and pears in individual bowls. Ladle hot or cold soup into bowls.

Serves 8.

Chili Blanco

1	pound dry white beans, rinsed
6	cups chicken broth
2	medium onions, chopped
1	tablespoon oil
6-8	cloves garlic, minced
1	(7-ounce) can diced green chilies
2-3	teaspoons ground cumin
2	teaspoons dried oregano
1	teaspoon ground cayenne pepper
4	cups cooked chicken, diced
1	cup sour cream
3	cups shredded Monterey Jack cheese

Toppings:

1	cup sour cream
1/2	cup chopped green onion
1/4	cup chopped cilantro
1	cup chopped tomatoes

Combine beans and broth in large pot. Cover and simmer 2 hours. Sauté onion in oil until golden. Add onion, garlic, green chilies, cumin, oregano, cayenne pepper and chicken to bean mixture. Simmer 30 minutes. Add sour cream and cheese. Heat until cheese melts. Do not boil! Soup may break down if boiled.

Serve topped with sour cream, green onion, cilantro and tomatoes.

Serves 4 to 6.

Cold Strawberry Soup

6	cups fresh strawberries, washed and stems removed
2	cups orange juice
1/4	cup Grand Marnier liqueur
1	cup sour cream or plain yogurt
	Mint sprigs, optional

Puree all but 12 strawberries in blender or food processor. Transfer puree to large pitcher or bowl. Whisk in other ingredients until well blended. Cover and refrigerate 6 hours to 24 hours.

Serve in 8 chilled shallow soup bowls. Slice reserved strawberries lengthwise in 1/4-inch slices. Arrange slices on top of each portion making a star pattern and garnish with mint.

Serves 8.

Mulligatawny Soup

1/4   **cup finely chopped onion**

1/2   **teaspoon curry powder**

2   **tablespoons vegetable oil**

1   **tart apple, peeled, cored and chopped**

1/4   **cup chopped carrot**

1/4   **cup chopped celery**

2   **tablespoons chopped green pepper**

3   **tablespoons all-purpose flour**

4   **cups chicken broth**

1   **(16-ounce) can chopped tomatoes, drained**

1   **tablespoon chopped parsley**

2   **teaspoons fresh lemon juice**

1   **teaspoon sugar**

2   **whole cloves**

1/4   **teaspoon salt**

1/8   **teaspoon pepper**

1   **cup diced, cooked chicken**

In large saucepan, cook onion and curry powder in vegetable oil until onion is tender. Stir in chopped apple, carrot, celery and green pepper. Cook, stirring occasionally, until vegetables are crisp tender, about 5 minutes. Sprinkle flour over vegetable mixture, stirring to mix well. Add broth, drained tomatoes, parsley, lemon juice, sugar, cloves, salt and pepper. Bring to boiling before adding chicken. Reduce heat, simmer, stirring occasionally, 30 minutes. Remove cloves. Ladle into bowls while hot.

Serves 6.

Cardinal Cup

3   **(10 3/4-ounce) cans beef bouillon**

4 1/2   **cups tomato juice**

1   **tablespoon lemon juice**

1   **tablespoon prepared horseradish**

1   **tablespoon Worcestershire sauce**

Mix all ingredients in medium saucepan. Heat thoroughly, but do not boil. Serve hot or cold.

Serves 8.

Keeps well in the refrigerator. A great "pick me up".

Crème de Brie Soup

¼	cup (½ stick) butter
1	pound onions, diced
1	pint fresh mushrooms, sliced
4	teaspoons minced garlic
1	cup dry white wine
¼	cup all purpose flour
3½	cups chicken broth, homemade or canned
1	whole bay leaf
1¼	pints whipping cream
1	tablespoon fresh chopped thyme
6	ounces Brie, rind removed and cut into 1 ounce slices
1	tablespoon dry sherry

Salt and pepper to taste

12	rounds of sliced French bread, toasted
4	ounces Brie, cut into 12 slices

Melt butter in heavy medium saucepan. Sauté onion, mushrooms and garlic. Add wine. Cook until almost all the wine has evaporated. Add flour to mixture in pan and stir until thoroughly blended. Add chicken broth and bay leaf. Heat to boiling. Reduce heat and simmer until fairly thick. Add whipping cream and thyme. Blend completely. Strain through sieve if you wish smoother consistency. Return to pan. Add cut up Brie and blend in slowly with a whisk. Whip until cheese melts. Add sherry, salt and pepper to taste.

Ladle hot soup into 6 ovenproof bowls. Place 2 toasted bread rounds on top of soup. Cover bread with Brie slices. Brown under broiler just until cheese begins to bubble.

Serves 6.

Women/Becoming, an outreach service of the League of Catholic Women, made its debut in 1977. Initially it was established to aid in the intervention, treatment and aftercare of women with chemical dependency problems of their own or a family member. Gradually **W/B** began to concentrate on providing women with a variety of opportunities to develop personal and spiritual awareness and self-confidence, making them less likely to become either dependent or co-dependent. Several programs are offered each year.

In 1997, Women/Becoming took a major role in founding **WomenSpirit**, an inter-faith forum on women's spirituality. WomenSpirit sponsors two or three programs a year at various sites throughout the Twin Cities.

Both Women/Becoming and WomenSpirit are open to all. For more information on their program offerings, call 612-332-2649.

Tuscan Bean and Cabbage Soup with Parmesan Croutons

1	tablespoon butter
2	tablespoons olive oil
1	medium onion, coarsely chopped
2	celery stalks, diced
3	cloves garlic, finely chopped
1½	pounds green cabbage, chopped
6	cups chicken stock or canned reduced-sodium broth
1	(28-ounce) can Italian plum tomatoes, drained and chopped
2	cups canned cannellini beans, drained
1	smoked ham bone or smoked ham hock
¼	cup chopped fresh basil or 1 heaping tablespoon prepared pesto sauce

Salt and freshly ground pepper

Croutons:

16	½-inch-thick French bread baguette slices
1	cup freshly grated Parmesan cheese
1	teaspoon dried oregano, crumbled

Olive oil

Melt butter with oil in large heavy pot over medium heat. Add onion, celery and garlic. Cook 5 minutes, stirring frequently. Add cabbage and cook 5 minutes, stirring occasionally. Add chicken stock or broth, tomatoes, beans, ham bone, basil or pesto, salt and pepper. Bring to boiling. Reduce heat and simmer 45 minutes, stirring occasionally. Taste and adjust seasoning. Discard bone. Cool, cover and refrigerate. May be prepared 1 day ahead. Bring soup to simmering point before continuing.

Heat oven to 375°. Arrange bread slices on baking sheet. Sprinkle cheese and oregano on bread slices. Drizzle with olive oil. Bake until bread is crisp and cheese melts, about 5 minutes.

Ladle soup into bowls. Top each serving with 2 croutons. Pass remaining croutons.

Serves 8.

Turkey-White Bean Chili with Queso Fresco and Grilled Onions

2	ounces clarified butter
3/4	pound yellow onions, minced
3/4	pound carrots, minced
3/4	pound celery, minced
6	cloves garlic, minced
2	pounds ground turkey
2	tablespoons ground cumin
1	tablespoon chili powder
1	tablespoon ground coriander
2	tablespoons salt
1	tablespoon black pepper
2	medium red jalapeno peppers
2	medium green jalapeno peppers
8	cups chicken stock or broth
1	pound ground Great Northern beans, cooked
1	cup Masa Harina*
1	medium red onion, thinly sliced
1	medium tomato, diced
2	ounces Queso Fresco* (Mexican fresh cheese)

In very large saucepan or soup pot, heat clarified butter. Sauté yellow onion until golden brown. Add carrots, celery and garlic. Cook 5 minutes. Add turkey, 5 dry spices, red and green jalapenos. Cook until turkey is well browned. Add chicken stock or broth and cooked white beans. Cook until liquid is reduced by one-third. Stir in Masa Harina. Sauté sliced red onions in small non-stick skillet until translucent.

Ladle 8 ounces of chili into each bowl. Top with diced tomato, Queso Fresco and sautéed red onion, tomato and Queso Fresco.

Serves 6.

To make clarified, sometimes known as "drawn" butter, place butter in saucepan at low heat until completely melted. Remove all foam that rises to top of liquid. Remove pan from heat and let contents stand until all milk solids have fallen to bottom of pan. With a ladle, remove all clear oil and store clarified butter for future use. Half margarine and half butter make the best clarified mixture for cooking. The margarine will increase the smoke point temperature, allowing liquid to be heated to higher temperature without burning.

One pound butter makes 1 1/2 cups (12 ounces) clarified butter.

* Items may be purchased at Mexican grocery stores and some specialty shops.

Tejas Beef Chili

1¹⁄₂	pounds tomatoes, cored and quartered
1	pound onions, sliced 1 inch thick
2¹⁄₂	teaspoons corn oil
4	pounds beef sirloin, cut into ¹⁄₂-inch cubes
3¹⁄₂	teaspoons unsweetened cocoa powder
2¹⁄₂	teaspoons ground cumin
2¹⁄₂	teaspoons Pasilla Chile powder*
¹⁄₂	teaspoon ground cayenne pepper
¹⁄₂	teaspoon ground coriander
2¹⁄₂	teaspoons salt
³⁄₄	teaspoon black pepper
3	tablespoons Ancho Puree*
5	teaspoons tomato paste
2	cloves garlic, minced
14	ounces veal or beef broth
1	teaspoon Masa Harina* dissolved in ¹⁄₂ cup water
2¹⁄₂	teaspoons fresh thyme leaves

On outdoor grill or under broiler, grill tomatoes and onions until blackened. Heat corn oil in large heavy skillet or soup pot. Sear beef over high heat until well browned. Stir in 7 dry spices until well mixed with meat. Stir in Ancho Puree and tomato paste. Mix well. Add garlic, blackened tomatoes, onions and broth. Bring chili to simmer. Do not boil! Simmer 90 minutes. Chili may also be covered and cooked in 350° oven about 90 minutes. Just before serving stir in Masa Harina mixture and thyme.

Serves 10 to 12.

This often requested recipe is from James Foley, master chef at Tejas Restaurant in Edina, Minnesota.

*Special Mexican ingredients are available at Mexican grocery stores.

When the Boys Group Home merged with the Girls Group Home in 1982, their residence on 13th Avenue was available for a new purpose. In 1983, the League of Catholic Women opened **Emergency House,** a transitional housing facility for homeless women and children.

With the help of per diem funding from Hennepin County Social Services, the LCW managed and operated Emergency House for 12 years, attempting to give clients access to job opportunities and permanent housing.

Hot or Cold Summer Soup

1/4	cup (1/2 stick) butter or margarine
1	cup chopped onion
4	tablespoons flour
4	cups fresh tomatoes, peeled, seeded and chopped
4	cups cucumbers, peeled and seeded
1/2	cup minced green pepper
1/2	teaspoon salt
1/4	teaspoon white pepper
5	cups chicken broth
2	ripe avocados, peeled and finely diced
1	cup whipping cream

In large soup kettle melt butter or margarine. Add onion. Sauté 3 to 4 minutes. Add flour and mix well. Add tomatoes, cucumbers, green pepper, salt and pepper. Stir briskly. Stir in broth and simmer 30 minutes. Cool. Puree in blender in batches. Chill to serve cold. To serve hot, return soup to stove and heat thoroughly. Before serving hot or cold, peel and finely dice avocados. Add to soup, stirring briskly. Stir in cream. Ladle into warmed or chilled bowls.

Serves 6 to 8.

This soup should be served very hot or very cold. Either way, it takes full advantage of the summer harvest of avocado, tomato and cucumber.

Cold and Creamy Cranberry Soup

2	oranges
1	tablespoon butter
1 1/4	cups granulated sugar
1	cup sherry wine
1	pound fresh or frozen cranberries
1	cup dry Sauterne or other dry white wine
1	cup light cream
1	cup sour cream
1	cup club soda or champagne
1	cup crème fraiche
16	pecan halves

Peel rind from oranges with potato peeler. Cut rind in julienne strips. Reserve oranges for juice. Melt butter in medium saucepan. Do not brown. Sauté rind in butter. Add sugar, sherry and juice from reserved oranges. Boil 2 minutes. Add cranberries. Cover and cook 3 minutes. Chill overnight.

Place chilled mixture in blender. Add white wine. Blend at moderate speed 1 minute. Add cream and sour cream. Blend 1 minute more. Strain orange rind and cranberry seeds from mixture. Before serving add club soda and mix well. Serve cold garnished with crème fraiche and 2 pecan halves.

Serves 8.

Rolf Gahlin, a very fine Swedish chef, has retired from the kitchen but his recipes, like this one, will endure for years.

Seafood Curry Soup

8	cups chicken stock or broth
1	teaspoon curry powder
2½	red Delicious apples, diced
2½	pears, diced
½	fresh pineapple, diced
½	cup raisins
½	cup coconut
½	teaspoon anise seeds
½	cup sugar
½	teaspoon ground nutmeg
1	teaspoon ground allspice
½	teaspoon ground cinnamon
3	tablespoons butter
3	tablespoons all-purpose flour
1	pint whipping cream
½	cup sherry
1	cup thawed frozen peas
½	pound shrimp, cleaned and washed
½	pound scallops, cleaned and washed
½	pound crab, cleaned and washed
2	tablespoons butter

Garnish with toasted coconut and almond slices

Place first 12 ingredients in large kettle. Bring to boiling and turn heat to low. Simmer 2 hours. Strain and save only stock. Place cooked, strained stock back in kettle. Boil until reduced to half, about 1 quart.

In medium saucepan melt 3 tablespoons butter. Add flour. Cook and stir 3 to 5 minutes until well blended. Add to reduced stock in kettle. Add cream, sherry and thawed green peas.

In large skillet sauté cleaned shrimp, scallops and crab in 2 tablespoons butter until done. Add to stock mixture. Soup may be served hot or cold. It is delightful either way.

Makes 1½ quarts.

Fresh Tomato Soup with Basil Aioli

Aioli:

2   **cloves garlic, peeled**

1/3   **cup packed coarsely chopped fresh basil leaves or tarragon**

1   **teaspoon fresh lemon juice**

1/4   **cup reduced-fat mayonnaise**

Soup:

1   **tablespoon olive oil**

1   **cup sliced onion**

1   **inner celery stalk with leaves, thinly sliced diagonally**

1   **small clove garlic, minced**

1   **large fresh basil sprig or 1/2 teaspoon dried**

3   **pounds tomatoes, peeled and halved**

2   **cups chicken stock or canned reduced-sodium broth**

To make aioli finely chop garlic in food processor or by hand. Add basil or tarragon and lemon juice. Chop finely. Add mayonnaise and blend. May be prepared 1 day ahead. Cover and refrigerate.

Heat oil in heavy medium saucepan over low heat. Add onion, celery, garlic and basil. Cover and cook until vegetables are very tender, stirring frequently, about 25 minutes.

Place large strainer over bowl. Working over strainer squeeze seeds and juice from tomatoes. Chop tomatoes and add to vegetables in saucepan. Using rubber spatula, press on tomato seeds and pulp in strainer to extract as much juice as possible. Add strained juice to saucepan. Add chicken stock and simmer over medium-low heat. Discard basil sprig. Ladle soup into bowls. Drizzle with aioli.

Serves 4.

Aioli is a garlic mayonnaise from Provence that is served with a wide variety of dishes. It is delicious drizzled over this soup which is served hot or cold. It also makes a nice veggie dip.

Apple Stilton Soup

1/4   **cup (1/2 stick) butter**

2   **cups chopped apples**

1/4   **cup chopped shallots**

1/4   **cup chopped parsley**

1   **teaspoon fresh basil**

1/4   **teaspoon dried sage**

3   **cups chicken broth**

1   **cup crumbled Stilton cheese**

Freshly ground pepper to taste

Melt butter in heavy medium saucepan. Add apples, shallots, parsley, basil and sage. Cover and cook over low heat until apples are soft. Add chicken broth. Simmer gently 10 minutes. Process in food processor until smooth. Return to pan. Add cheese. Cook over low heat until cheese is melted and soup is smooth. Add pepper to taste.

Serves 6.

This soup is very thin and the blue cheese is quite delicate. Attractive served in demitasse cups before dinner.

Carrot Soup

2¾   cups chicken stock or broth

1   pound carrots, sliced

1   medium onion, chopped

½   teaspoon dried thyme

½   teaspoon ground nutmeg

1   teaspoon curry powder, optional

1   teaspoon red chili powder

1   clove garlic, minced

1   bay leaf

1   cup milk

1   (3-ounce) package cream cheese, cubed and softened

1   teaspoon grated fresh orange zest

Salt and white pepper to taste

½   cup chopped parsley

Toasted almonds for garnish

Combine first 9 ingredients in medium saucepan. Cover and simmer until carrots are tender. Remove bay leaf. Run soup through blender. This can be done ahead. Refrigerate.

Return soup to saucepan. Add milk. Heat soup to simmering. Add cream cheese and stir until melted. Add orange zest, salt and pepper to taste. Garnish with toasted almonds and chopped parsley.

Serves 4.

Nicely Iced Melon Soup

2   cups orange juice

3   cups finely chopped peeled cantaloupe

⅓   cup freshly squeezed lime juice

¼   cup honey

2   tablespoons sugar

2   tablespoons minced mint or 1 teaspoon dried, crumbled

2   cups sparkling white wine

Fresh mint and watermelon balls for garnish

Puree orange juice, cantaloupe and lime juice in processor. Mix in honey, sugar and mint. Pour puree into non-metal container. Add wine and stir gently. Cover and refrigerate several hours or overnight. Ladle into bowls. Garnish each serving with fresh mint sprigs and watermelon balls.

Serves 6.

Lemon Soup

1   **quart chicken broth**

$\frac{1}{4}$ **cup orzo (rice size pasta) uncooked**

3   **eggs**

$\frac{1}{4}$ **cup fresh lemon juice**

$\frac{1}{4}$ **cup fresh dill**

Black pepper to taste

4-6   **fresh dill sprigs**

2   **tablespoons shaved lemon rind**

Heat chicken broth to boiling. Add orzo to chicken broth. Remove from heat. Let broth and pasta cool.

Beat eggs well. Add lemon juice and mix. Stir chopped dill and black pepper together. Add to egg and lemon mixture.

When chicken broth is completely cooled, add egg and lemon liquid mixture to broth. Put combined mixture over low heat. Stir until mixture heats up. Do not let soup boil!

Ladle into soup bowls garnished with a few sprigs of dill, lemon shavings and a little black pepper.

Serves 4 to 6.

"This is a traditional soup served in Greek kitchens. It might best be accompanied by a lovely bread (pita brushed with melted butter and garlic spread would do nicely), a plate of Greek olives, red tomatoes, marinated artichoke hearts and sprigs of fresh parsley, sprinkled with crumbled feta cheese. And yes, it goes without saying that a glass of fine Greek Retsina wine would make the lemon soup a culinary treat worthy of any Greek god, goddess or mere mortal."

Our thanks to Father Joseph Gillespie, Vicar of the Basilica of Saint Mary, for his recipe and his remarks!

Begun in 1994, **By Your Side** is a League of Catholic Women sponsored project that links League members with students from the College of St. Catherine, Minneapolis campus, in a supportive mentoring program. By Your Side participants meet together at least twice a year and students and LCW volunteers stay connected through telephone calls, letters and personal visits.

Easy Chili

2	pounds lean ground beef
1	teaspoon oil
6	stalks celery, minced
1/2	green pepper, minced
1	large onion, minced
8	cups chopped tomatoes, fresh or canned
1	(6-ounce) can tomato paste
2	tablespoons chili powder
2	(15.5-ounce) cans kidney beans
2	(15.5-ounce) cans hot chili beans
1/4	cup sugar
Salt and pepper to taste	
1	pint mushrooms, sliced

In large stockpot brown ground beef in 1 teaspoon oil. Add remaining ingredients. Simmer slowly over low heat 2 hours. To cook in oven put chili in covered casserole and bake in a 350° oven for 2 hours.

Serves 8.

Our thanks to Fr. Ambrose Mahon, retired pastor of St. Patrick's Church in Edina, for his "famous" chili recipe.

To save calories when browning meat, sprinkle heavy skillet with salt, place pan over high heat until very hot. Add ground beef and cook, stirring until browned. No oil or butter is needed.

Soupe au Potiron

1	(1 pound) pumpkin
1	onion, sliced
6	cups salted water
1 3/4	cups milk
1/4	cup cream or half-and-half
Salt and pepper to taste	
2	eggs, beaten
1/4	cup (1/2 stick) butter

Puncture whole pumpkin with sharp fork. Microwave for 3 minutes to soften slightly. Cut pumpkin into pieces, remove pulp and peel. Put pumpkin pieces into soup kettle with sliced onion and salted water. Cover kettle and boil pumpkin 15 minutes or until soft. Drain water and reserve. Puree cooked pumpkin in blender. Put puree in top of double boiler. Add milk and cream. If soup seems too thick, dilute with some reserve water. Add salt and pepper to taste. Cook over simmering water 20 minutes. Mix a few spoonfuls of soup with beaten eggs. Add mixture to soup gradually, stirring constantly until thickened. Just before serving, stir in butter.

Serves 4.

This contributor picked up this recipe while living in Switzerland.

Grilled Late Season Tomato Soup with Bacon, Garlic and Croutons

8	large tomatoes
2	leeks, diced
1	medium yellow onion, diced
6	cloves garlic, sliced
2	tablespoons olive oil
2¼	cups chicken broth, heated
2	ounces thinly sliced smoked bacon
½	cup dry red wine

Pinch of cayenne pepper or more to taste

½	teaspoon red wine vinegar
¼	teaspoon salt
6	slices sourdough bread, cut ½-inch thick and brushed with olive oil
1	clove garlic, peeled

Prepare grill. Grill whole uncored tomatoes over moderately hot fire. Allow them to take as much smoke as possible. Let skins get fairly dark. Tomatoes should feel soft all over. If skins remain intact they will begin to bubble and release little puffs of steam, an indication that heat has penetrated to center. Carefully transfer tomatoes to platter and let cool.

While tomatoes are grilling cook leeks, onion and garlic in olive oil in covered soup pot until they release their juices and begin to soften. Remove lid. Raise heat and let brown. Pour hot chicken broth over vegetables and heat just to boiling. Turn off heat. Cover pot.

Over a bowl remove cores and as much of skin as possible from tomatoes. Break tomatoes into rough pieces by hand. Let juice and pulp fall into bowl. Add tomatoes and juice to pot. Slice bacon crosswise into small pieces. In small pan simmer bacon and red wine together for 5 minutes. Add to soup. Add cayenne, vinegar and salt. Turn heat on very low.

While soup is warming grill bread over fire until nicely browned on both sides. Rub bread on one side with garlic clove. Put one slice of bread in each warm bowl. Ladle the hot soup over it. Serve immediately.

Serves 6.

This soup is a delicious way to use the last tomatoes on the vine. Its hearty flavor makes it a good transition into fall.

Sweet Corn Chowder

6	slices bacon
1	large onion, chopped
1	stalk celery, chopped
1/4	cup all-purpose flour
2	medium potatoes, peeled and diced
2	cups homemade chicken stock or reduced-sodium canned broth
1	bay leaf
2	cups whole milk
1/2	red pepper, cored, seeded and chopped
1/2	green pepper, cored, seeded and chopped
3	cups kernels from 4 to 5 fresh corn cobs, reserve cobs

Salt and freshly ground pepper to taste

Chopped fresh parsley for garnish

In large saucepan, sauté bacon until crisp. Remove and drain on paper towels. Chop. Add onion and celery to pan. Sauté in bacon fat until soft. Sprinkle with flour and cook, stirring, for 3 to 4 minutes. Add potatoes, chicken stock, bay leaf and reserved corn cobs. Bring mixture to boiling. Reduce heat and simmer until potatoes are soft, about 20 minutes. Remove corncobs. Add milk, chopped peppers, and corn kernels. Do not let soup boil again. Ladle into bowls and sprinkle with parsley and bacon bits.

Serves 8 to 10

The contributor credits this original recipe to Lucia Watson.

Fresh corn is essential for this chowder. The cobs give it a fuller flavor.

From its early days until 1973, the League of Catholic Women maintained a Senior and Junior division. For nearly 50 years, **Junior Catholic League** members were active in organizing social events and initiating service projects, especially for young people.

Under professional direction, the JCL also staged a series of "**Top Hat Reviews**" over the years. Dear to the hearts of its talented performers and well-received by audiences, these musicals provided needed funds to support the League's social services.

Spinach and Tortellini Soup

3/4	**pound fresh spinach**
3	**(49$\frac{1}{2}$-ounce) cans chicken broth**
1	**(8-ounce) package fresh cheese-filled spinach tortellini**
2	**whole boneless skinless chicken breasts, cut into $\frac{1}{2}$-inch pieces**
1	**pint fresh mushrooms, sliced**
1	**medium size red bell pepper, seeded and diced**
1	**cup cooked white rice**
2	**teaspoons dried tarragon**

Salt and freshly ground pepper to taste

1	**cup chopped red pepper**
1	**cup freshly grated Parmesan cheese**

Rinse and chop spinach. Set aside. Bring broth to boiling over high heat in large soup pot. Add tortellini and boil gently until pasta is al dente, 6 to 8 minutes. Add spinach, chicken, mushrooms, bell pepper, rice and tarragon to broth. Bring to boiling over high heat. Reduce heat to simmer. Cover and cook until chicken is no longer pink in center, about 2 minutes. Ladle soup into large bowls. Garnish with chopped red pepper and cheese.

Makes 5 quarts or 10 to 12 servings.

This is a great dish for a big crowd. It can be made in any amounts you wish and it freezes well.

Easy Asparagus Soup

1	**(10$\frac{3}{4}$-ounce) can cream of asparagus soup**
1	**cup sour cream**
1	**cup crushed ice**
$\frac{1}{2}$	**teaspoon salt**

Tabasco sauce to taste

$\frac{1}{2}$	**cucumber, finely chopped**
$\frac{1}{8}$	**teaspoon Beau Monde seasoning or to taste**
1	**avocado, thinly sliced for garnish**

Coarse ground black pepper for garnish

Combine soup, sour cream, ice, salt, Tabasco, cucumber and Beau Monde in blender. Process until smooth. Garnish with the avocado and pepper. Serve hot or cold.

Serves 4.

Cold Asparagus Soup

2	cups chopped onion
4	cloves garlic, minced
1/4	cup (1/2 stick) butter
6	cups chicken broth
1	cup fresh chopped parsley
8	large fresh basil leaves, washed and dried
1	tablespoon dried tarragon
1	teaspoon salt
1	teaspoon ground pepper
3	pounds fresh asparagus, cut in 1-inch pieces
2	medium carrots, cut in 1-inch pieces

Pinch of cayenne pepper or more to taste

3/4	cup sour cream for garnish
1/2	cup chopped tomatoes for garnish

In large heavy saucepan sauté onions and garlic in butter. Add broth, parsley, basil, tarragon, salt and pepper. Bring to a boil. Add asparagus and carrots. Simmer 35 to 40 minutes. Cool 30 minutes. Add cayenne. Put in blender or food processor. Puree until smooth. Strain. Ladle into bowls and garnish with sour cream and tomatoes.

Serves 8.

In 1963, the League of Catholic Women opened **The Switching Post (S/P)**, a consignment shop at 2015 Aldrich Avenue South. Records indicate that the S/P was perhaps the first consignment shop to open in Minneapolis. For the League this innovation replaced a series of annual rummage sales. In addition to selling used furniture, household goods and clothing at the Switching Post, the League began training S/P volunteers to conduct estate sales.

To date, highly skilled LCW members have operated hundreds of estate sales throughout the metropolitan area. This League service benefits bargain hunters as well as those who wish to settle an estate or "downsize" by selling household goods. The profits from estate sales help fund LCW social services.

The Switching Post was sold in 1990 but its estate sales branch continues under the name **At Your Service (AYS)**. AYS may be contacted by calling (612) 332-7830.

Shrimp Bog

½	pound bacon, finely diced
2	medium onions, finely chopped
1½	cups uncooked long grain rice
3¼	cups low-fat chicken broth, divided
1½	cups peeled and chopped tomatoes with juice
2	teaspoons fresh lemon juice
1½	teaspoons Worcestershire sauce
1	teaspoon salt
¾	teaspoon ground nutmeg
¼	teaspoon cayenne
¼	teaspoon black pepper
2	pounds fresh medium shrimp (26 to 30 per pound), clean and deveined
¼	cup chopped fresh parsley

In 3-quart saucepan fry bacon over medium heat. Drain and set a side. Pour off all but 3 tablespoons fat. Add onion. Cook 3 to 4 minutes, stirring well. Add rice, 2½ cups broth, tomatoes with juice, lemon juice, Worcestershire sauce, salt, nutmeg, cayenne and black pepper. Bring to a low simmer. Cover. Cook 20 minutes. Stir in bacon, shrimp and remaining cup of broth. Continue cooking uncovered 10 minutes. Stir with fork. Adjust seasoning as desired and garnish with parsley. Ladle into shallow bowls.

Serves 6 to 8.

This dish resembles a Creole stew.

White Gazpacho

2	cups chopped, peeled, seeded cucumber
1	cup low-fat, sodium-reduced chicken broth
1½	tablespoons white wine vinegar
⅛	teaspoon salt
1	(16-ounce) container low-fat sour cream
1	clove garlic, crushed
1	cup diced tomato
½	cup chopped green onions

Place first 6 ingredients in blender or cuisinart. Pulse 3 to 4 times until coarsely chopped. Put soup into container and refrigerate at least 3 hours or overnight. Ladle soup into bowls and top with chopped tomatoes and green onions.

Serves 4.

Full-Meal Italian Pasta Soup

1/2	cup sherry, white wine or unsweetened apple juice
2	teaspoons olive oil
2	tablespoons minced fresh garlic
1	medium yellow onion, diced
1	large carrot, diced
1	rib celery with leaves, diced
1	medium parsnip, diced
1	small zucchini, diced
4	sun-dried tomatoes, not packed in oil, chopped
2	bay leaves
1	tablespoon dried basil
1	teaspoon dried marjoram
2	cups canned peeled Italian tomatoes with juice
1/2	cup orzo (rice-size pasta), uncooked
8	cups chicken, vegetable or beef broth
1/3	cup chopped Italian parsley
	Salt and pepper to taste

Combine sherry and olive oil in large soup pot over medium-high heat. Heat to simmering. Stir in garlic. Cook 3 minutes. Add onion, carrot, celery, parsnip, zucchini and dried tomatoes. Cook over medium heat stirring frequently for 5 to 6 minutes or until vegetables soften. Add bay leaves, basil, marjoram, tomatoes with juice, broth and orzo. Bring soup to boiling, stirring 10 minutes or until pasta is tender. Remove from heat. Add parsley and season to taste.

Serves 6 to 8

Keep a copy of this recipe handy as guests often request one. Prepare soup a day ahead to allow flavors to blend.

The League owned and operated the **Margaret Barry House** for fifty years, the longest community service in LCW history. Its operating budget was provided by United Fund. In 1963, the planning division of United Fund recommended that Margaret Barry House merge with Northeast Neighborhood House and the League gave the Margaret Barry House property at 279 Pierce Street, N.E. to the successor agency, Eastside Neighborhood Services, Inc. League members served on the Eastside Board for many years.

Creamy Beer Cheese Soup

1	green pepper, minced
¹/₂	cup minced carrot
¹/₄	cup minced celery
2	tablespoons minced onion
¹/₄	cup butter
¹/₄	cup flour
2	tablespoons instant granulated chicken broth

Freshly ground pepper to taste

4	cups milk
1	cup beer
1	cup freshly shredded extra-sharp Cheddar cheese
¹/₂	cup chopped chives, optional

In a large saucepan sauté green pepper, carrot, celery and onion in butter. Blend in flour and instant chicken broth. Add pepper, milk and beer. Heat thoroughly. Add cheese and stir until it melts. Ladle into bowls and sprinkle with more shredded Cheddar and chopped chives if desired.

Serves 4 to 6.

Cheesy Cream of Vegetable Soup

2	tablespoons chopped onion
1	tablespoon butter
1	cup fresh corn kernels
¹/₂	cup chopped broccoli
¹/₄	cup shredded carrot
¹/₄	cup water
1	(10³/₄-ounce) can condensed cream of potato soup
1	cup milk
¹/₄	cup (1-ounce) freshly shredded Cheddar cheese
1	ounce provolone cheese, cut up

Pepper to taste

In large saucepan sauté onion in butter or margarine until tender but not brown. Add corn, broccoli, carrot and water. Bring to boil. Reduce heat. Cover and simmer 10 minutes or until vegetables are tender. Stir in soup, milk, cheeses and pepper. Cook and stir over medium heat until cheeses are melted and mixture is heated through.

Serves 3 to 4.

Thanksgiving at the Lake...

Our family has a post-Thanksgiving dinner at our cabin in northern Minnesota. Because our married children have obligations to their spouses' families on Thanksgiving Day, we gather at the cabin to enjoy a leisurely, casual dinner on the day after the holiday. We plan lots of outdoor activities like building snowmen and cross-country skiing and we always end the day by searching for the "perfect" Christmas tree to cut down and bring home.

At Eastertime...

At our house the Easter egg hunt is for the whole family. Each dyed egg, Easter basket or plastic egg filled with coins has the name of one family member on it. If someone spies another person's "goodies," he or she must keep it a secret until the owner discovers it. The adult eggs are hidden above the waist in hard-to-find places. The children's eggs are hidden below the waist in easier spots. Some hunts have lasted 45 minutes...a good opportunity for the cook to prepare brunch!

Breads
& Brunches

Overnight Easy Caramel-Pecan Sticky Rolls

12-18 frozen white bread rolls

$1/2$ **cup chopped pecans**

1   **(3-ounce) package regular, not instant, butterscotch pudding**

$1/2$ **cup (1 stick) butter or margarine**

$1/2$ **cup brown sugar**

1   **tablespoon ground cinnamon**

Heat oven to 350˚. Grease bundt or tube cake pan. Place 12 to 18 frozen white rolls in pan. Sprinkle pecans on top. Sprinkle pudding mix over nuts. Melt butter. Mix with brown sugar and cinnamon. Pour over rolls.

Cover with wax paper or tea towel. Let rise at room temperature overnight but no more than 10 hours.

Bake 30 minutes. Flip onto serving tray immediately and serve warm.

Serves 12 to 18.

A treat for a special family breakfast and easy for the cook to prepare the night before.

Dilly Casserole Bread

1   **package (1 tablespoon) dry yeast**

$1/4$ **cup warm water**

1   **cup cottage cheese**

2   **tablespoons sugar**

1   **tablespoon instant minced onion**

2   **teaspoons dried dill weed**

1   **teaspoon salt**

$1/4$ **teaspoon baking soda**

1   **egg**

$2^{1}/_{4}$- $2^{1}/_{2}$ **cups all-purpose flour**

1   **tablespoon butter**

Coarse or Kosher salt for topping

Heat oven to 350˚. Soften yeast in $1/4$ cup warm water. Combine cheese, sugar, onion, dill weed, salt, soda, egg and yeast in large bowl. Gradually add flour. Beat well after each addition to form stiff dough. Cover. Let rest until dough has doubled in size, about 1 hour. Stir dough with spoon. Place in greased 8-inch round pan or $1^{1}/_{2}$-quart casserole. Let rise until double in size about 40 minutes. Bake 40 to 50 minutes or until deep brown. Rub with butter and coarse salt.

Depending on room temperature dough may take longer to rise. It is important that it doubles in size during first and second stages.

Makes 1 large loaf.

Food Processor French Bread

3   **cups unbleached all-purpose flour, divided**

1   **envelope (1 tablespoon) dry yeast**

1   **teaspoon salt**

1¼   **cups tepid water, 70 to 75°**

Heat oven to 450°. In food processor with steel blade, place 1 cup flour, yeast and salt. Mix for 2 seconds. Add 1¼ cups tepid water and run for 15 seconds. Let rest 1 minute. Add remaining flour ½ cup at a time through feeding tube with machine running. Dough will gradually mass together. After all flour is added, let dough run for 25 pulses or about 15 to 20 seconds.

Turn off processor and remove dough. Knead on floured surface by hand 2 minutes. Add a little flour if dough is too sticky. Place dough in large lightly greased bowl, cover and let rise in warm place 1 hour or until double in size. Punch down and let rise again until double.

Remove from bowl to lightly floured surface. Flatten and divide into two pieces. Let rest 5 minutes and roll to length of 12 to 15 inches. Roll up starting with 15-inch edge. Place each loaf seam side down in lightly greased French bread or large size pan. Use double baguette pan for two loaves. Cover with towel and let double in size, about 40 minutes. Make diagonal slashes on top when ready to put in oven.

Place pan in oven and spray loaves and sides of pan with cold water. Be careful not to spray the oven light. Repeat this spraying process 3 times every 3 minutes, totaling 9 minutes baking time. Turn temperature down to 375° and continue baking 15 minutes. Check to see if loaves are nicely browned and sound hollow when tapped. Remove from pan to cool.

Eat immediately or freeze. To warm thawed bread, run unwrapped loaf quickly under water and place in oven at 350° for 3 to 5 minutes or until heated thoroughly.

Makes 2 baguettes.

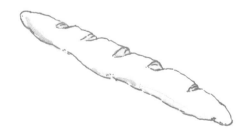

Baked Baguette with Lemon-Garlic Butter

1/2	cup (1 stick) butter, softened
2	tablespoons chopped fresh parsley
3	cloves garlic, pressed
1	teaspoon grated lemon zest
1	French bread baguette cut crosswise into 1-inch thick slices

Heat oven to 300˚. Mix butter, chopped parsley, garlic and grated lemon zest in small bowl to blend. Season lemon-garlic butter with salt and pepper to taste. Spread evenly over one side of each bread slice. Reassemble bread slices and wrap in foil. Place on baking sheet. May be made 8 hours ahead and chilled.

Bake wrapped bread until heated through about 20 minutes. Serve warm.

Serves 6 generously.

Don't leave out the lemon zest! It makes all the difference.

Tea Shoppe Poppy Seed Muffins

3	cups all-purpose flour
2 1/2	cups sugar
1 1/2	teaspoons baking powder
1 1/2	teaspoons salt
3	eggs
1 1/2	cups milk
1 1/8	cups vegetable oil
1 1/2	tablespoons poppy seed
1 1/2	teaspoons vanilla
1 1/2	teaspoons almond flavoring
1 1/2	teaspoons butter flavoring

Glaze:

3/4	cup granulated sugar
1/4	cup orange juice
1/2	teaspoon vanilla
1/2	teaspoon almond flavoring
1/2	teaspoon butter flavoring

Heat oven to 350˚. Combine all muffin ingredients in large bowl. Mix with electric mixer 2 minutes at medium speed. Pour batter into greased or paper-lined muffin cups. Bake 30 to 40 minutes for large muffins, 15 to 20 for small muffins or until tester comes out clean.

Combine all glaze ingredients in small bowl. Blend well. With a pastry brush apply glaze to tops of warm muffins.

Makes 18 to 20 large muffins or 20 to 36 small muffins.

Cheese Puffs

1	**cup milk**
¼	**cup (½ stick) butter or margarine**
½	**teaspoon salt**
⅛	**teaspoon pepper**
1	**cup all-purpose flour**
4	**eggs**
1	**cup shredded Swiss or Gruyère cheese, divided**

Heat oven to 375°. Heat milk and butter in medium saucepan. Add salt and pepper. Bring to full boil. Add flour all at once, stirring over medium heat about 1 minute or until mixture leaves side of pan and forms a ball. Remove pan from heat. By hand beat in 4 eggs one at a time until mixture is smooth and well blended. Beat in ¼ cup of cheese. Using a large spoon make 6 to 8 equal sized mounds of dough in a circle on lightly greased baking sheet using about ¾ of dough. Each mound should just touch the next one. Place small amount of remaining dough on top of each large mound. Sprinkle with remaining ½ cup cheese.

Bake on center shelf of oven 55 minutes or until puffs are lightly browned and crisp. Serve hot with or without butter.

Serves 6 to 8.

The French name for this recipe is Gougère. They are so delicious, count on at least two per person. Do not double recipe, make separate batches. They are also good cold, split and filled with ham, turkey or chicken salad.

Orange Honey Muffins

1	**cup all-purpose flour**
3	**teaspoons baking powder**
½	**teaspoon salt**
½	**teaspoon baking soda**
1	**cup quick cooking rolled oats**
1	**cup orange juice**
⅓	**cup honey**
1	**egg**
2	**tablespoons vegetable oil**
1	**tablespoon grated fresh orange zest**

Heat oven to 400°. In large bowl sift together flour, baking powder, salt and baking soda. Stir in oats. Combine orange juice, honey, egg and oil. Mix with dry ingredients just until blended. Add grated orange zest. Batter will be thin. Fill greased or paper-lined large or small muffin cups ⅔ full.

Bake until golden brown, 15 to 20 minutes for large muffins, about 10 minutes for small muffins or until tester comes out clean.

Makes 12 large muffins or 24 small muffins.

Scones

1³/₄	cups all-purpose flour
3	tablespoons sugar
2¹/₂	teaspoons baking powder
¹/₂	teaspoon salt
¹/₃	cup butter
1	egg, beaten
¹/₂	cup currants or raisins
4-6	tablespoons half-and-half cream or 2% milk
1	egg, beaten
2	tablespoons sugar
1	teaspoon ground cinnamon

Heat oven to 400°. By hand blend together flour, sugar, baking powder and salt in large bowl. Cut butter into flour mixture with pastry blender until mixture resembles fine crumbs. Stir in egg and mix very lightly. Add currants and just enough cream to make dough come away from sides of bowl. Turn dough onto lightly floured surface. Knead gently about 10 times. Roll or pat to ¹/₂-inch thick. Cut with floured 2-inch round cutter or cut into diamond shapes.

Place scones on ungreased baking sheet. Mix cinnamon and sugar. Brush dough with 1 beaten egg and sprinkle with cinnamon and sugar. Bake until golden brown, about 10 to12 minutes. Remove immediately from cookie sheet. Do not overcook or they will be dry.

Split scones and serve with Devonshire cream and strawberry jam or lemon curd in Complements section.

Yield 15 scones.

It is very important to mix scones by hand and as lightly as possible. A light hand makes all the difference.

For years these scones were the highlight of Spring Tea given by the Friends of the Basilica in the Rector's Dining Room.

During the 1970's, the League of Catholic Women's Downtown Center served as a place where mothers could come for one-to-one counseling with Hennepin County Social Service workers. During these sessions LCW volunteers saw to it that the young children of these clients were well cared for. From 1970-78, this service, called **Project St. Francis**, also stocked and operated a maternity loan closet on the premises.

Best Blueberry Muffins

1	egg
1	cup sugar
1	cup sour cream
$1/4$	cup ($1/2$ stick) butter, softened
1	scant teaspoon baking soda
$1/4$	teaspoon salt
$1^3/4$	cups all-purpose flour
1	cup fresh blueberries

Heat oven to 350°. Beat egg and sugar by hand in large bowl until well blended. In separate bowl, mix sour cream with butter and add egg and sugar. Blend baking soda, salt and flour and add to egg, sugar, sour cream and butter mixture. Stir until blended. Add blueberries and fold in lightly being careful not to smash the berries.

Divide muffin dough into greased or paper lined large or small muffin cups. Bake 40 minutes for large muffins, 20 minutes for small or until tester comes out clean.

Makes 24 large or 48 small muffins.

This is a very old family recipe handed down for at least four generations. May substitute raspberries or cranberries for blueberries.

Fresh Rhubarb Coffee Cake

$1/2$	cup sugar
1	cup brown sugar
$2/3$	cup oil
1	egg
1	cup buttermilk
$2^1/2$	cups all-purpose flour
1	teaspoon baking soda
1	teaspoon salt
2	cups chopped rhubarb
$1/2$	cup chopped nuts
1	teaspoon vanilla
$1/2$	cup (1 stick) melted butter
$1/3$	cup sugar

Heat oven to 325°. Combine sugars, oil, egg and buttermilk in large bowl. In separate bowl combine sifted flour with soda and salt. Add to egg mixture. Add rhubarb, nuts and vanilla. Pour into greased 13x9-inch pan.

Drizzle melted butter over batter. Sprinkle with sugar. Bake 35 to 40 minutes or until tester comes out clean.

Serves 10.

Rhubarb Bread

1½   cups brown sugar

⅔   cup oil

1   egg

1   cup sour cream

1   teaspoon each salt

1   teaspoon soda

1   teaspoon vanilla

2½   cups all-purpose flour

1½   cups diced rhubarb

½   cup chopped pecans

Topping:

½   cup sugar

1   tablespoon butter or margarine, softened

Heat oven to 325˚. Combine all bread ingredients in large bowl and blend well. Pour into 2 greased 9x5-inch loaf pans. Mix topping ingredients and sprinkle on top of bread loaves. Bake 1 hour or until tester comes out clean.

Makes 2 loaves.

Batter for one loaf of most quick breads may be used to fill 3 to 4 small 6x3-inch aluminum foil pans. Reduce baking time by about half or until tester comes out clean. Smaller breads bake evenly, slice well and make convenient hostess gifts.

Lemon Loaf

½   cup butter or margarine, softened

1   cup sugar

2   eggs

1½   cups all-purpose flour

1   teaspoon baking powder

½   teaspoon salt

½   cup milk

2   teaspoons freshly grated lemon zest

Glaze:

Juice of 1 lemon, about ¼ cup

¼   cup sugar

Heat oven to 350˚. Grease and flour one 9x5-inch loaf pan or three 6x3-inch pans. Cream butter or margarine and sugar until fluffy. Beat in eggs. Sift flour, baking powder and salt. Add flour mixture to creamed sugar mixture a small amount at a time alternating with milk. Stir in lemon zest.

Pour batter into prepared loaf pans. Bake 50 to 55 minutes for large loaf, or 30 to 40 minutes for small loaves or until tester comes out clean. Let cool slightly. Turn out upright on to aluminum foil.

Combine lemon juice and sugar in small bowl. Mix well. Pour glaze over slightly cooled bread, slowly covering top and sides.

Makes 1 large loaf or 3 small loaves.

Cherry Nut Bran Bread

2½   cups all-purpose flour

1   teaspoon salt

4   teaspoons baking powder

¾   cup sugar

1¼   cups milk

1   egg

2   tablespoons melted shortening or oil

1   cup bran cereal (i.e. All-Bran)

½   cup chopped candied cherries

1   cup chopped walnuts

Cherry Nut Topping:

1   tablespoon butter or margarine, softened

¼   cup brown sugar

½   cup chopped candied cherries

¼   cup chopped walnuts

Heat oven to 350°. In medium bowl sift flour, salt, baking powder and sugar together. Set aside. Combine milk, egg and melted shortening or oil in large bowl. Add flour mixture all at once to egg mixture. Stir just until dry ingredients are moistened. Stir in bran, cherries and walnuts. Turn batter into 9x5-inch or three 6x3-inch greased and floured loaf pans.

Combine softened butter, brown sugar, cherries and walnuts. Sprinkle over batter. Bake 1 hour for large loaf or 40 to 45 minutes for small loaves or until tester comes out clean.

Makes 1 large loaf or 3 small loaves.

Kristen's Banana Bread

½   cup butter

1   cup sugar

2   eggs, beaten

3   bananas, mashed

3   tablespoons milk mixed with 1 teaspoon lemon juice

2   cups sifted all-purpose flour

1   teaspoon soda

½   teaspoon salt

½   cup chopped walnuts or other nuts

Heat oven to 325°. Cream butter and sugar in large bowl. Add beaten eggs and blend well. Add mashed bananas. Mix well. Add soured milk. Combine flour, soda and salt in separate bowl. Add to banana mixture. Stir in nuts. Pour into one 9x5-inch or three 6x3-inch greased loaf pans.

Bake 55 minutes for large loaf, 35 for small loaves or until tester comes out clean.

1 large loaf or 3 small loaves.

Of all the banana bread recipes submitted, League testers and tasters gave this one the highest marks.

Swedish Almond Coffee Cake

Crust:

1/2	cup (1 stick) butter
1	cup all-purpose flour
1	tablespoon water

Filling:

1	cup water
1/2	cup (1 stick) butter
1	cup flour
3	eggs
1/2	teaspoon almond extract or more to taste

Frosting:

1	cup powdered sugar
1	tablespoon butter, room temperature
1/2	teaspoon almond extract
1/2-1	cup sliced and toasted almonds, if desired

Heat oven to 350°. In small bowl, cut butter into flour with fork until mixture resembles coarse meal. Gently stir in water and mix together until it forms ball. Divide ball in half. Roll or pat each half into two strips, 12x3 inches and about 1/4-inch thick. Place strips 3 inches apart on ungreased baking sheet.

Place water in large saucepan. Add butter and bring water to boiling. Remove from heat. Add flour and stir until smooth. Stir in eggs, one at a time. Beat well after adding each egg. Add almond extract. Spread filling equally over each strip of crust.

Bake 55 to 60 minutes. Cool slightly.

Cream powdered sugar, butter and almond extract until smooth. Spread frosting on top of filling on slightly cooled coffeecake. Sprinkle with sliced almonds or serve plain.

Serves 12.

Do not prepare ahead. Serve soon after baking. This pastry was standard fare at "Koffee Klatches" in the 1950's.

In addition to performing community service, the League of Catholic Women provides its members with opportunities for personal enrichment. **Monthly programs** feature speakers on topics of current interest. An **Autumn Retreat** as well as **Advent and Lenten Series** explore the life of the spirit. The **Fall Luncheon, Annual Benefit Ball** and **May Annual Meeting** bring members together to celebrate. The **Book Club, Antique Group, Art Tours, Bridge Lessons, Spring Bridge Marathon, Golf Tournament, Garden Tours** and a host of other events promote and cement friendships.

Blueberry Breakfast Cake

3/4	cup sugar
1/4	cup (1/2 stick) butter, softened
1	egg
2	cups all-purpose flour
2	teaspoons baking powder
1/2	teaspoon salt
1/2	cup milk
2	cups fresh blueberries

Topping:

1/2	cup sugar
1/3	cup all-purpose flour
1	teaspoon cinnamon
1/4	cup (1/2 stick) butter, softened

Heat oven to 350°. Cream sugar, butter and egg in large bowl. Set aside. Mix flour with baking powder and salt. Add to creamed mixture, alternating with milk. Gently fold in blueberries. Pour batter into greased 9-inch square pan.

In medium bowl, mix topping ingredients together until crumbly. Sprinkle over batter. Bake 35 minutes or until tester comes out clean.

Serves 10.

Oatmeal Bread

1	cup whole wheat flour
1	cup rye flour
1	teaspoon baking powder
1	teaspoon baking soda
1	teaspoon salt
1	cup rolled oats
1 1/4	cups plain yogurt
2	tablespoons honey
1/4	cup light molasses or part honey if lighter taste is preferred
1	cup raisins

Heat oven to 350°. Sift two flours, baking powder, baking soda and salt in large bowl. Stir in rolled oats. In separate bowl, beat yogurt and honey into molasses until blended and smooth. Add honey, yogurt and molasses mixture to flour mixture. Mix until combined. Stir in raisins.

Pour into greased 9x5-inch loaf pan. Let stand 20 minutes before baking. Bake for about one hour or until deep brown.

Serves 12.

Wonderful served warm with cream cheese.

Kathy's Healthy Bran Muffins

5	cups whole wheat flour
2½	cups oat bran
1	cup sesame seed
2	teaspoons salt
1	cup honey
1	cup vegetable oil
1	quart buttermilk
2	cups wheat germ
2	cups brown sugar
5	teaspoons baking soda
1	cup molasses
4	eggs or 1 cup egg substitute
2	cups boiling water

Topping:

1	cup sugar mixed with 2 tablespoons cinnamon

Heat oven to 375°. Combine flour, oat bran, sesame seed and salt in very large bowl or soup kettle. Combine next nine ingredients and add to flour mixture. Spoon into greased or paper-lined large or small muffin cups. Top with a little sugar and cinnamon. Bake 20 minutes for large muffins, 12 minutes for small or until tester comes out clean.

Makes 5 to 6 dozen large muffins or 100 small.

This is an old family recipe that can easily be reduced. Batter may be frozen up to one month. Baked muffins may also be frozen and reheated.

Popovers

4	eggs
1	cup milk
1	cup all-purpose flour
1	teaspoon salt
¼	cup (½ stick) butter, softened, for preparing custard cups

Beat eggs slightly with fork. Add milk and flour mixed with salt. Mix just until blended. Do not over beat. Batter should remain lumpy.

Butter 12 (6-ounce) custard cups including rims with softened butter. Fill cups half full of popover mixture. Set cups on baking sheet. Place on center rack of cold oven.

Set oven at 450° and turn on. Bake 30 minutes. Reduce heat to 300°. Bake 5 to 8 minutes more.

Serves 12.

Do not open oven door while baking. Popovers may collapse. Recipe may be doubled.

Cottage Plantation Biscuits

2¹/₂   cups all-purpose flour

3   tablespoons sugar

1¹/₂   tablespoons baking powder

¹/₂   teaspoon salt

³/₄   cup shortening (i.e. Crisco)

²/₃   cup milk, approximately

Heat oven to 450˚. Mix flour, sugar, baking powder and salt very well. Cut in shortening until mixture resembles fine crumbs. Add enough milk to hold dough together about ²/₃ cup. Put mixture on floured board. Knead a couple of times. Roll to ³/₄-inch thickness and no thinner. Cut with 2-inch round biscuit cutter or jelly glass. Place on ungreased baking pan. Bake for approximately 20 minutes or until golden brown.

Makes 15 biscuits.

These biscuits are better than anything you can buy and are nearly as easy. Nice with chili or soup.

Laura Ingall's Gingerbread

1   cup brown sugar

¹/₂   cup (¹/₄ stick) butter or vegetable shortening (i.e. Crisco)

1   cup molasses

2   teaspoons baking soda

1   cup boiling water

3   cups all-purpose flour

3   teaspoons ground ginger

3   teaspoons ground cinnamon

3   teaspoons ground allspice

3   teaspoons ground nutmeg

3   teaspoons ground cloves

¹/₂   teaspoon salt

Heat oven to 350˚. Blend brown sugar and butter by hand or electric mixer in large bowl. Set aside. Stir molasses and baking soda into 1 cup boiling water until dissolved. Add to brown sugar mixture. Set aside. In separate bowl, mix flour with the five spices and salt. Stir flour into sugar mixture and blend well.

Pour batter into greased 8x8-inch pan. Bake 30 minutes or until tester comes out clean. Dust with powdered sugar

Serves 8.

Children who love Laura Ingall Wilder's books will enjoy making "her" gingerbread.

Breakfast Pizza

1	**pound bulk pork sausage**
1	**(8-ounce) package refrigerated crescent rolls**
1	**cup frozen hash brown potatoes, thawed**
1	**cup (4 ounces) shredded sharp Cheddar cheese**
5	**eggs**
$1/4$	**cup milk**
$1/2$	**teaspoon salt**
$1/8$	**teaspoon pepper**
2	**tablespoons grated Parmesan cheese**

Heat oven to 375°. Cook sausage in skillet until browned. Drain fat. Separate crescent dough into 8 triangles. Place dough in an ungreased 12-inch pizza pan, with points towards the center. Press over bottom and up sides to form crust. Seal perforations. Spoon sausage over crust. Sprinkle with potatoes. Top with cheddar cheese.

Beat together eggs, milk, salt and pepper in bowl. Pour into crust. Sprinkle Parmesan cheese over all. Bake 25 to 30 minutes.

Serves 4 to 6.

If 13x9-inch or 14x11-inch pans are used, bake 1 hour. Best made with frozen squares of hash browns.

Baked Eggs on Artichoke Bottoms

4	**large artichokes**
2	**tablespoons sour cream**
4	**slices prosciutto ham**
4	**eggs**
$1/4$	**cup freshly grated Parmesan cheese**
1	**teaspoon freshly ground black pepper**
1	**tablespoon chopped fresh cilantro**

Heat oven to 375°. Place artichokes in large saucepan and add 1 inch water. Bring to boil, reduce heat and cover. Cook until artichokes are tender about 45 minutes. Remove from pot and set aside to drain and cool.

Peel away artichoke leaves, remove chokes leaving bottoms intact. Set leaves aside.

Place artichoke bottoms on a baking sheet. Spread $1^{1}/_{2}$ teaspoons sour cream on each bottom. Top with folded slice of prosciutto ham. Break an egg on top of each artichoke bottom. Sprinkle with cheese, pepper and cilantro. Bake eggs until done to your liking about 15-20 minutes.

Serve immediately surrounded by artichoke leaves. Dip leaves in egg yolks.

Serves 4.

French Toast Fingers

2   **eggs**

$1/4$ **cup milk**

$1/4$ **teaspoon salt**

8   **slices day-old white bread**

$1/2$ **cup strawberry preserves**

Powdered sugar, optional

In small bowl beat eggs, milk and salt. Set aside. Spread preserves on four bread slices. Top with remaining bread. Trim crusts and cut each sandwich into three strips. Dip both sides in egg mixture. Cook on lightly greased hot griddle 2 minutes on each side or until golden brown. Dust with powdered sugar, if desired.

Use softened butter with cinnamon and sugar as an alternate filling to jam. Both are tasty.

Serves 4.

Baked in a 350˚ oven in big batches these might be a big hit with the little ones attending the League's Annual Breakfast with St. Nicholas.

Oven French Toast

24   **slices day-old French bread ($3/4$-inch-thick)**

12   **thick slices cooked ham**

12   **thin slices cooked turkey**

1-2   **medium tart apples, peeled and thinly sliced**

12   **thin slices provolone or mozzarella cheese**

4   **eggs**

1   **cup milk**

$1/4$ **teaspoon ground nutmeg**

Apple Cranberry Sauce:

2   **tablespoons cornstarch**

$1^{1}/2$ **cups cranberry juice**

1   **tablespoon brown sugar**

1   **teaspoon orange zest**

$1/8$ **teaspoon ground cinnamon**

1   **medium tart apple, peeled and finely chopped**

Place half the bread in greased 13x9-inch baking dish. Top each half with slice of ham, turkey, two or three apple slices and a piece of cheese. Cut or fold meat and cheese to fit bread. Top with remaining bread. In small bowl, beat eggs, milk and nutmeg. Pour over bread. Cover and chill 6 hours or overnight. Remove from refrigerator 30 minutes before baking.

Heat oven to 350˚. Bake uncovered 30 minutes or until knife inserted near center comes out clean. Let stand 10 minutes.

In small saucepan combine first five sauce ingredients. Cook and stir over medium heat until thickened. Cook and stir 2 minutes longer. Mix in chopped apples. Serve warm over French toast.

Serves 12.

Wild Rice and Bacon Scramble

6 tablespoons butter or margarine, divided

3 tablespoons all-purpose flour

1/2 teaspoon salt

1/4 teaspoon pepper

2 cups skim milk

6 ounces (1 1/2 cups) shredded regular or low-fat Cheddar cheese

1 1/2 cups chopped Canadian bacon

1/4 cup chopped green onions

16 eggs or 6 eggs and 2 1/2 cups eggbeaters, beaten

1/4 pound fresh mushrooms, thinly sliced

3 cups cooked wild rice

Heat oven to 350°. In medium saucepan or double boiler, melt 3 tablespoons butter. Blend in flour, salt, pepper and milk. Cook until thickened, stirring constantly. Stir in cheese until melted. Set aside.

Sauté bacon and onions in 3 tablespoons butter in large skillet. Add beaten eggs and scramble until eggs are slightly set but still moist. Fold in cheese sauce and mushrooms.

Pour into buttered 13x9-inch baking dish. Sprinkle wild rice over filling and press in lightly. May be assembled day before serving. Cover and refrigerate until one hour before baking.

Bake casserole for 45 minutes or until heated through and bubbly.

Serves 12.

A wonderful hearty brunch dish. Serve with fresh fruit and a great bread or muffin.

Asparagus and Egg Casserole

6 tablespoons butter

1/4 cup all-purpose flour

1 teaspoon ground mustard

3 cups milk

1 teaspoon salt

1/4 teaspoon pepper

1/8 teaspoon celery salt or to taste

2 cups crumbled potato chips, divided

6 hard-boiled eggs, sliced

2 (10 1/2-ounce) cans small green asparagus tips, drained or 1 pound fresh asparagus, steamed slightly and cut in 1 1/4-inch lengths

Heat oven to 350°. Melt butter over low heat in small saucepan. Blend in flour and mustard and add milk gradually. Cook over low heat and stir constantly until thickened. Season with salt, pepper and celery salt. Reserve 1/2 cup potato chips. Arrange alternate layers of egg, 1 1/2 cups potato chips and asparagus in individual casseroles or 2-quart casserole. Pour sauce over all and top with reserved potato chips.

Bake 20 minutes.

Serves 6.

To avoid burning any cream style sauce prepare in top of double boiler over hot to boiling water, stirring frequently.

Sausage and Tomato Tart

1	**(9-inch) prepared piecrust**
1	**teaspoon prepared mustard**
2	**Polish sausages (¹/₄ pound each)**
1	**medium ripe tomato, cored and thickly sliced**
1	**tablespoon chopped fresh basil or ¹/₂ teaspoon dried**
1	**tablespoon snipped fresh chives**
2¹/₂	**cups (10-ounces) grated Monterey jack cheese**
²/₃	**cup mayonnaise**

Heat oven to 425˚. Immediately reduce oven temperature to 400˚. Bake pastry shell 10 to 12 minutes or until very lightly browned but not quite done. Remove from oven. Spread bottom of hot shell with mustard. Bake shell 3 more minutes. Remove and cool slightly while preparing filling.

Reduce oven temperature to 350˚.

Coarsely chop sausages. Cook in small skillet over low heat until some fat is released. Increase heat and sauté until cooked thoroughly. Drain on paper towels and cool. Sprinkle sausage over cooked pastry. Cover with tomato slices. Combine herbs, cheese and mayonnaise and distribute over tomatoes. Using back of spoon gently spread cheese mixture to edges and fill surface gaps.

Bake 35 minutes or until cheese is thoroughly melted. Cool at least 5 minutes before cutting into wedges. Serve hot or at room temperature.

Serves 4 to 6.

To save time use a ready-made pie shell. For variety, substitute ¹/₄ cup chopped fresh parsley and 2 tablespoons chopped fresh dill for chives and basil.

Goat Cheese, Artichoke and Smoked Ham Strata

2	cups whole milk
1/4	cup olive oil
8	cups sourdough bread, crusts removed and cut into 1-inch cubes
1 1/2	cups whipping cream
5	large eggs
1	tablespoon chopped garlic
1	teaspoon salt
3/4	teaspoon black pepper
1/2	teaspoon ground nutmeg
3	cups (12 ounces) fresh goat cheese such as Montrachet, crumbled
2	tablespoons chopped fresh sage
1	tablespoon chopped fresh thyme
1 1/2	teaspoon herbs de Provence
12	ounces smoked ham, chopped and divided
3	(6 1/2-ounce) jars marinated artichoke hearts, drained and halved lengthwise, divided
1	cup grated Fontina cheese, packed and divided
1 1/2	cups grated Parmesan cheese, packed and divided

Heat oven to 350˚. Whisk milk and oil in large bowl. Stir in bread. Let stand until liquid is absorbed about 10 minutes. Whisk cream and next 5 ingredients in another large bowl to blend. Add goat cheese. Mix herbs in separate small bowl.

Place half of bread mixture in buttered 13x9-inch dish. Top with half of ham, artichoke hearts, herbs and cheeses. Pour half of cream mixture over ingredients in prepared dish. Repeat layering. May be made one day ahead, covered and refrigerated.

Bake strata uncovered until firm in center and brown around edges about one hour.

Serves 8.

This is tasty served with Orange, Walnut and Cranberry salad in Salads section.

Herbs de Provence is a dried herb mixture available at specialty food stores and some supermarkets. A combination of dried basil, savory and fennel seeds can be substituted.

Spinach Quiche

1	(10-inch) pie shell, homemade or store bought
1/4	cup freshly grated Parmesan cheese, divided
2	tablespoons butter
1	large onion, minced
1	clove garlic, minced
1	(10-ounce) package frozen chopped spinach, defrosted and well drained
1/4-1/2	teaspoon salt
	Freshly ground pepper to taste
1	teaspoon ground mustard
3	eggs
1 1/2	cups shredded Swiss or Gruyère cheese
2/3	cup chicken broth
1/2	cup whipping cream

Heat oven to 450°. Bake pie shell for 5 minutes. Remove from oven and sprinkle with 2 tablespoons Parmesan cheese.

Sauté onion and garlic in butter. Combine with spinach, salt, pepper and mustard. Cool. Beat eggs and add to spinach mixture along with Swiss cheese, chicken broth and cream. Mix well. Pour into pie shell. Sprinkle with remaining Parmesan cheese. Bake at 450° for 10 minutes then at 350° for 20 to 25 minutes or until tester comes out clean.

Serves 6 to 8.

May be prepared ahead, covered and frozen for later use.

Grandpa's Pancakes

1 1/2	cups cake flour
1	tablespoon baking powder
2	tablespoons sugar
1	teaspoon soda
1	teaspoon salt
3	eggs
1 1/2	cups sour cream
1 1/2	cups buttermilk
1/4	cup vegetable oil

Sift flour, baking powder, sugar, soda, and salt several times. Set aside.

Beat eggs thoroughly. Add sour cream and buttermilk to eggs and mix until entirely smooth. Add flour mixture. Blend until smooth, then beat well. Add vegetable oil. Batter should be thin. Chopped nuts, blueberries, sliced apples or other fruit may be added, if desired. Ladle onto hot griddle and cook briefly until lightly browned on both sides.

Serves 6 to 8.

A breakfast treat for four generations in this contributor's family.

Baked Swiss Fondue

1/8	teaspoon dried minced garlic
1	teaspoon ground mustard, divided
2/3	cup butter, softened and divided
1	long French baguette loaf
3	tablespoons chopped onion
1/3	cup all-purpose flour
3 1/2	cups half-and-half or whole milk
2	teaspoons seasoned salt
1	teaspoon paprika
1	cup dry white wine
3	egg yolks, well beaten
3	cups (3/4 pound) shredded Swiss cheese

Heat oven to 350°. Blend garlic and 1/2 teaspoon mustard with 1/3 cup of butter. Cut bread into 1/4-inch slices and spread with butter mixture. Line bottom of a 13x9-inch baking dish with one-half of bread, buttered side down.

Sauté onion in remaining butter until tender. Blend in flour; cook and stir until smooth. Gradually add half-and-half and remaining 1/2 teaspoon mustard, seasoned salt and paprika. Cook to boiling and stir until thickened. Remove from heat. Add wine and egg yolks and blend. Return to heat just until heated through.

In a casserole place shredded cheese over bread. Add cream sauce and top with layer of bread, buttered side up. Press bread into sauce. Cover and refrigerate overnight.

Bake for 50 minutes or until cheese bubbles and bread is golden.

Serves 8.

Serve with a zippy salsa or add one (4-ounce) can chopped green chili peppers if you like more spice.

Zucchini, Leek and Chèvre Tart in Wild Rice Crust

Crust:

1   egg

¹/₃   cup freshly grated Parmesan cheese, preferably Parmigiano-Reggiano

2   tablespoons freshly squeezed lemon juice

3   tablespoons unsalted butter, melted

2¹/₂   cups cooked wild rice (1 cup uncooked)

Salt and freshly ground black pepper to taste

Filling:

2   cups finely chopped or coarsely shredded zucchini or other summer squash

1   teaspoon salt

2   cups thinly sliced leeks, including some of green tops

¹/₂   cup (1 stick) unsalted butter

4   eggs or 1 cup egg substitute

1¹/₂   cups whipping cream

1   teaspoon Dijon mustard

1   cup crumbled chèvre cheese

1   tablespoon chopped fresh marjoram or savory or 1 teaspoon crumbled dried marjoram

Salt and freshly ground black pepper to taste

Heat oven to 350˚. Beat egg, cheese, lemon juice and melted butter together in bowl. Stir in cooked rice and season to taste with salt and pepper. Transfer to a 9-inch pie or quiche pan. Press rice with your fingertips to cover bottom and sides evenly. Bake until set and crisp about 15 minutes. Remove from oven and cool to room temperature. You may cover and refrigerate overnight. Return to room temperature before filling.

Place squash in colander set over bowl or in sink. Generously sprinkle with salt and mix with your fingertips to distribute salt. Let stand for 30 minutes. Gather squash in your hand and gently squeeze to release any additional surface moisture. Reserve.

Sauté leeks in ¹/₂ cup butter over medium heat until tender or about 5 minutes. Add drained squash and sauté 5 minutes longer. Reserve.

Combine eggs, cream, mustard, cheese, marjoram, salt and pepper to taste in large bowl. Whisk to blend well. Stir in leek and squash mixture. Pour into rice shell. Bake until filling is set and top is golden about 30 to 35 minutes. Serve hot or at room temperature.

Serves 8 as side dish or 6 as main course.

Asparagus Frittata

2	small potatoes cut into ¹/₂-inch cubes
10-12	fresh asparagus spears, tough ends removed and cut into 2-inch pieces
3	teaspoons vegetable oil, divided
1	small onion, thinly sliced
1	clove garlic, finely chopped
¹/₂	teaspoon salt
¹/₂	teaspoon freshly ground pepper
1	teaspoon fresh rosemary or ¹/₂ teaspoon dried rosemary
1	tomato, cored, seeded, chopped and divided
4	large eggs
4	large egg whites
¹/₄	cup grated Gruyère cheese

Fresh chives for garnish

Place potatoes in steamer basket over boiling water. Cover and cook 4 minutes. Add asparagus and cook until vegetables are just tender about 3 minutes. Transfer potatoes and asparagus to bowl to cool.

Heat broiler.

Warm 2 teaspoons oil in large oven proof, nonstick skillet over medium heat. Add onion, garlic, rosemary and half of chopped tomato. Cook and stir until onions are limp about 8 minutes. Add mixture to potatoes and asparagus. Season with salt and pepper. Set aside. Wipe skillet and brush with remaining oil. Return skillet to low heat.

In medium bowl lightly whisk eggs, egg whites and Gruyère cheese. Add vegetables to egg mixture. Pour into skillet and stir gently to distribute vegetables. Cook over low heat until underside is golden color about 5 to 8 minutes.

Heat broiler. Place skillet under broiler. Broil until frittata top is puffed and golden brown about 1 to 2 minutes. Loosen frittata and slide onto platter. Garnish with chives and remaining tomatoes.

Serves 4.

Crab Souffle Roll

Souffle Roll:

1/4	**cup butter**
1/2	**cup all-purpose flour**
2	**cups milk**
4	**egg yolks, lightly beaten**
1/2	**teaspoon salt**
1/8	**teaspoon cayenne or black pepper**
2	**teaspoons chives, snipped**
4	**egg whites**
1/4	**teaspoon cream of tarter**
1/3	**cup freshly grated Parmesan cheese**

Filling:

4	**green onions, chopped**
2	**tablespoons butter**
2	**(12-ounce) packages frozen crabmeat, thawed and drained**
1	**(3-ounce) package cream cheese, softened**
1/3	**cup half-and-half**
2	**tablespoons parsley**

Salt and pepper to taste

Heat oven to 350°. Grease 15x10-inch jellyroll pan and line with waxed paper. Grease paper and lightly flour. Melt butter in large saucepan. Stir in flour and heat until bubbly. Remove from heat and stir in milk. Heat until boiling for one minute. Remove from heat. Add small amount of hot milk mixture to lightly beaten egg yolks and whisk vigorously. Gradually add egg mixture to the hot milk and stir to keep yolks from cooking. Stir in salt and pepper and chives. Cover with waxed paper.

In medium electric mixer bowl beat egg whites with cream of tarter until stiff. Stir 1/4 of whites into yolk mixture. Then gently fold egg yolk mixture and Parmesan cheese into remaining egg whites. Pour into jellyroll pan. Bake 45 minutes. Immediately loosen souffle from pan and invert onto a cloth covered rack.

In large skillet, sauté onions in butter until soft. Add rest of filling ingredients. Blend well. When souffle is finished baking, spread immediately with filling mixture. Roll up. Cut and serve while hot.

Serves 8.

Begun in 1994, **By Your Side** is a League of Catholic Women sponsored project that links League members with students from the College of St. Catherine, Minneapolis campus, in a supportive mentoring program. By Your Side participants meet together at least twice a year and students and LCW volunteers stay connected through telephone calls, letters and personal visits.

Traditions with Grandparents...

Each year we host a party for our children and grand-children the Sunday before Halloween. Children and adults must come in costume. The little ones can't wait to see grandma and grandpa in their silly get-ups and it gives us a chance to see our grandchildren in their Halloween finery.

When each grandchild reaches the age of seven, I ask them to plan an outing just for the two of us,whatever they would like to do, within reason! It gives us a chance to do something fun together and to get to know each other a little better. We continue this custom until they graduate from high school.

Lately I have tried this method of staying in touch with my distant grandchildren. I send each of them a book and buy the same one for myself. Then I call them and we read the book together over the phone. I have a friend who sends a book to her young grandchildren along with a tape of her reading the story.

Vegetables

Candied Sweet Potatoes with Glazed Peaches

1	cup dried peaches or apricots
2	cups boiling water
6	sweet potatoes, cooked and sliced
$\frac{1}{2}$	cup brown sugar, divided
5	tablespoons sugar
$\frac{1}{2}$	cup orange juice
$\frac{1}{4}$	cup honey
$\frac{1}{4}$	cup fine bread crumbs

Heat oven to 350°. Wash fruit and cover with boiling water. Let stand overnight. Drain.

In greased casserole arrange layer of sliced sweet potatoes. Sprinkle with 6 tablespoons brown sugar and dot with 4 tablespoons butter. Cover with half the fruit. Repeat layers.

Mix orange juice with honey. Pour over fruit and sweet potatoes. Combine breadcrumbs with remaining 2 tablespoons brown sugar and 1 tablespoon butter. Sprinkle on top. Cover and bake for 30 to 40 minutes. Remove cover last 15 minutes.

Serves 8 to 10.

Tomato Ruff

1	cup chopped tomato
2	cups chopped celery
1	cup chopped red onion
1	cup chopped green pepper

Dressing:

$\frac{1}{2}$	cup sugar
$\frac{1}{4}$	cup salad oil
$\frac{1}{2}$	cup white wine vinegar
$\frac{1}{2}$	teaspoon salt
1	teaspoon dried basil

Mix first 4 vegetable ingredients in shallow bowl or plastic container. Combine next 5 dressing ingredients. Pour dressing over vegetable mixture and refrigerate 3 to 24 hours.

Serves 4 to 6.

May be served as a side dish, salad or salsa.

Dijon Potato Gratin

6	large russet potatoes
1/4	cup (1/2 stick) butter
1	large yellow onion, thinly sliced

Sea or coarse salt to taste

Freshly ground black pepper to taste

4	tablespoons chopped fresh chervil or 4 teaspoons dried
1/2	cup chopped fresh parsley
2	cups crème fraiche
4	heaping tablespoons Dijon mustard
1/4	cup fresh lemon juice
6	ounces freshly grated Gruyère or Emmenthaler cheese

Heat oven to 400°. Place potatoes in large pot and cover with water. Bring to boil over medium-high heat. Cook until barely tender when pierced in center with small knife. Drain and let stand until cool enough to handle. Remove skins. Slice potatoes into 1/3-inch-thick rounds.

While potatoes cool melt butter in a small skillet over medium heat. Add onion and sauté, stirring frequently until light golden brown, about 15 minutes. Remove from heat.

Butter shallow 12-inch gratin dish. Set aside.

Gently combine sliced potatoes and onion in large mixing bowl. Season with salt, pepper, chervil and parsley. In small bowl, whisk together crème fraiche, mustard and lemon juice until smooth. Gently but thoroughly combine with potato/onion mixture. Turn into prepared gratin dish and arrange evenly. Sprinkle grated cheese over top of potatoes.

Bake gratin in oven until bubbly and lightly browned on top about 30 minutes. Let cool slightly and serve.

Serves 8 to 10.

Leftovers, if any, seem to taste even better when reheated the following day.

St Joseph Hall, established by the League of Catholic Women in 1912, served the needs of unwed, divorced or abandoned mothers and their infant children. In 1921, this mission was taken over by the Catholic Infant Home in St. Paul. League members also attended juvenile court sessions as advocates for mothers and children.

Chèvre Potatoes

5   **ounces creamy goat cheese or chèvre**

1¼ **cups warm chicken broth**

4   **large baking potatoes, peeled and sliced ¼-inch thick just before using**

Salt and freshly ground pepper to taste

1   **clove garlic, split**

Heat oven to 425°. Beat cheese and broth together. Toss in large bowl with potato slices. Add salt and pepper to taste. Mixture should be well combined.

Rub 12-inch gratin dish with cut sides of garlic. Leave garlic in dish if desired. Spread potato mixture in dish. Cover tightly with foil. Bake 30 to 40 minutes or until potatoes are very tender and sauce is thick and creamy. Stir contents of dish thoroughly after 15 minutes. Return to oven and bake additional 15 minutes.

Serves 8.

A modern update of the traditional potatoes au gratin-- excellent!

Oven-Roasted Vegetables with Garlic

6   **parsnips, peeled, halved crosswise and lengthwise**

6   **carrots, halved crosswise and lengthwise**

6   **shallots, peeled and halved**

2   **medium-size red onions, peeled and each cut into 8 wedges**

1   **large head garlic, separated into cloves and peeled**

3   **tablespoons chopped fresh rosemary or 1 tablespoon dried**

3   **tablespoons chopped fresh thyme or 1 tablespoon dried**

2   **tablespoons olive oil**

2   **tablespoons butter, melted**

Salt and freshly ground pepper to taste

Heat oven to 400°. Mix first 7 ingredients in large roasting pan. Drizzle with oil and butter. Toss to coat. Roast vegetables until golden and tender about 1 hour and 20 minutes, stirring occasionally. Season with salt and pepper. Transfer vegetables to platter and serve.

Serves 8.

Glazed Whipped Squash

5	pounds winter squash, cut in large pieces
2	tablespoons butter or margarine
2	tablespoons brown sugar
$1/3$	cup golden raisins
$3/4$	teaspoon salt
$1/4$	teaspoon ground nutmeg
$1/8$	teaspoon pepper

Topping:

1	tablespoon butter or margarine
1	tablespoon brown sugar
1	tablespoon light corn syrup
2	tablespoons chopped pecans

Heat oven to 400˚. Place squash, cut side down on baking pan. Bake 65 to 75 minutes. Scoop pulp into mixing bowl.

With an electric mixer blend squash, 2 tablespoons butter and 2 tablespoons brown sugar. Cook mixture uncovered in large saucepan over medium heat, stirring occasionally, 5 to 10 minutes. Stir in raisins, salt, nutmeg, and pepper. Cook additional 5 minutes, stirring frequently. Place in serving dish.

In small saucepan heat first 3 topping ingredients until dissolved. Stir in pecans. Drizzle over squash.

Serves 12.

Squash may also be baked in covered casserole in 350˚ oven. A welcome Thanksgiving dinner addition.

Horseradish Mashed Potatoes

6	medium russet potatoes, peeled and cut into 8 pieces
9	tablespoons or more warm milk
$4^{1}/_{2}$	tablespoons butter
3	tablespoons prepared horseradish

Salt and freshly ground pepper to taste

Cook potatoes in large pot of boiling salted water until very tender, about 20 minutes. Drain. Return potatoes to same pot. Add milk, butter and horseradish. Using electric mixer, beat potatoes until creamy. Season with salt and pepper to taste.

May be prepared two hours ahead. Cover and let stand at room temperature. Reheat in 350˚ oven about 15 minutes.

Serves 6 to 8.

To make garlic mashed potatoes, substitute 1 to 2 tablespoons roasted, crushed garlic for horseradish.

Parsley New Potatoes

18	medium new potatoes, with skins
1/2	cup (1 stick) butter
1/2	cup freshly shredded Parmesan cheese
1/4	cup chopped fresh chives or green onions
1/4	cup chopped fresh parsley

Salt and freshly ground pepper to taste

Heat oven to 350°. Quarter potatoes and steam until tender, filling water only to legs of steamer. Drain. Add remaining ingredients and toss. Place in casserole. Refrigerate. When ready to serve bring to room temperature. Bake covered 1/2 hour. For crispier potatoes, remove cover after ten minutes.

Serves 8.

Pan-fry the leftovers for another meal.

Tomatoes Niçoise

10	medium tomatoes
1/2	teaspoon salt
2	cups fresh bread crumbs
1	clove garlic, pressed
1/2	cup minced parsley

White pepper to taste

1 1/2	tablespoons chopped fresh basil or 1 teaspoon dried
1 1/2	tablespoons chopped fresh oregano or 1 teaspoon dried
1/2	teaspoon salt

Heat oven to 350°. Remove top 1/4-inch from tomatoes. Carefully remove seeds, leaving sectional walls intact. Sprinkle with salt and turn upside down on paper towels to drain.

Combine bread crumbs, garlic, parsley, white pepper, basil, oregano and salt. Moisten with olive oil. Spoon filling into tomato cases, packing rather firmly. Cover and refrigerate until baking time.

Place tomatoes on baking sheet. Bake about 25 minutes. This dish is best made ahead and refrigerated. Bring to room temperature before serving.

Serves 10.

Fresh bread crumbs are easy to make and superior to packaged variety. Remove crusts from bottom of 1 pound loaf white, whole wheat or rye bread. Cut slices in half. Place in food processor and make into medium to fine crumbs. A blender also works well. Add 4 half slices one at a time. Blend on medium speed to make crumbs. Remove crumbs to bowl. Repeat until all crumbs are made.

Baked Cabbage

1	medium green cabbage, shredded or 1 (16-ounce) package shredded cabbage
1	tablespoon all-purpose flour
1	tablespoon sugar
1	teaspoon salt
1	teaspoon ground mustard
$1/8$	teaspoon coarse freshly ground pepper
1	cup cream or half-and-half
3-4	strips raw bacon, chopped
$1/4$	teaspoon paprika

Heat oven to 350°. Shred cabbage. Place shredded cabbage in greased $1\frac{1}{2}$ quart baking dish. Mix flour, sugar, salt, pepper and mustard together. Toss thoroughly with cabbage. Pour cream over all. Cut raw bacon into small pieces. Arrange on top of cabbage. Sprinkle with paprika. Bake uncovered 45 minutes or until all cream is absorbed and bacon bits are nicely browned.

Serves 4 to 6.

Delicious served with beef brisket.

Vegetable Corn Casserole

2	eggs, slightly beaten
$1\frac{1}{4}$	cups milk
$2\frac{1}{2}$	cups fresh corn kernels
2	tomatoes, chopped
1	green pepper, chopped
1	red pepper, chopped
$1/2$	cup sliced black olives
$1/2$	cup yellow corn meal
1	teaspoon salt
$1/4$	teaspoon pepper
$1/4$	teaspoon paprika
$1/4$	teaspoon chili powder
$1/2$	cup (1 stick) butter or margarine, melted

Heat oven to 350°. Combine all ingredients except butter. Mix thoroughly. Pour into oiled 2-quart baking dish. Pour melted butter over top. Bake uncovered for about 1 hour or until set.

Serves 8 to 10.

Asparagus in French Aigrelette Sauce

1	large pasteurized egg yolk
2	tablespoons Dijon mustard
1½	tablespoons fresh lemon juice
⅓	cup peanut oil
¼	cup vegetable oil
¼	cup olive oil
2	tablespoons white Burgundy wine
1	tablespoon white wine vinegar
2	tablespoons chicken broth
½	cup assorted minced fresh herbs, (i.e. parsley, chives, tarragon, dill, basil, cilantro)

Sea or coarse salt to taste

Freshly ground black pepper to taste

2	pounds medium asparagus trimmed and bottom of stalks peeled

In medium bowl, whisk together egg yolk, mustard and lemon juice. Slowly whisk in peanut, vegetable and olive oils to form thick emulsion. Whisk in wine, vinegar and broth. Season with fresh herbs, salt and pepper. Refrigerate sauce if not using within an hour. Return sauce to room temperature before using.

Place asparagus spears in wide saucepan and add water just to cover. Bring water to boil and cook asparagus uncovered until tender-crisp, 3 to 4 minutes. Drain well. Immediately lightly coat with Aigrelette sauce. Save remaining sauce for another time. Cover and refrigerate. It will keep covered and refrigerated for 3 to 4 days with yolk added and for 1 week without it. Serve hot.

Serves 6 to 8.

This sauce is also delicious with warm or cold sliced salmon.

Glazed Brussels Sprouts with Pine Nuts

1½	pound Brussels sprouts
¼	cup (½ stick) unsalted butter
½	cup pine nuts

Salt and freshly ground pepper to taste

1	tablespoon orange juice

Heat oven to 350°. Remove outer leaves from Brussels sprouts. Cut small cross in stem ends. Steam Brussels sprouts over well-salted water until tender, 8 to 10 minutes. Drain and rinse under cold water. Cover and refrigerate. This portion of recipe may be prepared a day ahead.

Shortly before serving, melt butter in large skillet. Add pine nuts and toast lightly over moderate heat until golden, 3 to 4 minutes. Add Brussels sprouts and orange juice. Toss gently until warmed through. Season with salt and pepper to taste.

Serves 8.

Mushrooms with Garlic and Onions

1/2	cup olive or vegetable oil
1	green pepper, diced
1	large clove garlic, minced
2	onions, chopped
1	pound fresh mushrooms, sliced
1/4	teaspoon dried oregano
1/2	teaspoon pepper

Salt to taste

Heat oil in large saucepan. Add green pepper, garlic and onion. Sauté gently. Add mushrooms, salt, pepper and oregano. Simmer slowly uncovered on low heat, stirring occasionally, for 15 minutes. May be served hot or cold.

Serves 6 to 8.

These mushrooms make a perfect accompaniment to beef tenderloin.

Time Crunch Mashed Potatoes

1	(18-ounce) package prepared mashed potatoes found in dairy case (i.e. Island Valley)
1	(5-ounce) round of herbed Boursin cheese
2	tablespoons butter

Warm potatoes in microwave. Stir in Boursin cheese. Top with pats of butter.

Serves 3 to 4.

Just the thing to prepare on those extra-busy days or when unexpected company arrives. Easy and delicious.

Beets with Horseradish

2	pounds fresh beets
1/2	cup onion, chopped
2	tablespoons butter
1	tablespoon prepared horseradish, not horseradish sauce
1	tablespoon maple syrup or more to taste

Salt and pepper to taste

Cover beets in water and boil 30 to 40 minutes or until beets can be pierced with fork. Drain and cool in cold water. Snip off skins. Cut beets into small pieces. Beets may be cooked and cut up well in advance.

In large skillet sauté onion in butter until tender. Add horseradish and maple syrup. Stir in beets, salt and pepper. Mix thoroughly and heat through.

Serves 6 to 8.

Pikanter Potkahl (Sweet and Sour Cabbage)

¼   cup (½ stick) unsalted butter

1   pound red cabbage, shredded

½   cup chicken broth

½   cup cider vinegar

⅓   cup white or brown sugar

Roux:

1   tablespoon butter, softened

1   tablespoon flour

Heat oven to 325°. Melt butter in 2-quart casserole over low heat. Add cabbage and toss. Add remaining ingredients except for roux. Mix together and bring to boiling. Cover and cook over low heat until cabbage wilts. Cover and cook in oven 1 hour.

To make roux mash flour into butter in small skillet. Cook slowly over low heat until slightly browned. When cabbage is cooked remove casserole from oven and place on stove. Stir in roux. Simmer over low heat until flour cannot be tasted.

Serves 4 to 6.

Perfect with pork. Most guests give it a "ten."

Carrot Ring

1½   cups (3 sticks) butter

¾   cup packed brown sugar

4   eggs, separated

3   cups (about 1 pound) finely grated raw carrots

2   tablespoons cold water

2   tablespoons lemon juice

2   cups all-purpose flour

1   teaspoon baking soda

2   teaspoons baking powder

1   teaspoon salt

¼   cup fine dry bread crumbs

Heat oven to 350°. Cream butter and brown sugar in large bowl. Add egg yolks and beat until thick. Add carrots, water, lemon juice, flour, baking soda, baking powder and salt. Mix thoroughly. Beat egg whites until stiff peaks form. Gently fold egg whites into carrot mixture.

Oil 3-quart ring mold generously. Dust with fine breadcrumbs. Turn mixture into prepared mold. Bake 1 hour or until tester comes out clean. Remove from oven and cool 3 minutes. Run dinner knife around inner and outer edges of ring mold. Turn onto heated platter. Fill center with cooked green peas or beans.

Serves 10.

Carrot ring may be prepared the day before and refrigerated. Bake just before serving. Combines well with Stuffed Lamb in Entrees Section.

Sweet Carrots and Green Grapes

1/2	**cup (1 stick) butter**
4	**cups baby carrots**
1	**cup small seedless green grapes**
1	**tablespoon honey**
1	**tablespoon lemon juice**

Salt to taste

4	**mint leaves, chopped**

Melt butter in large skillet. Add carrots and turn until coated. Cover and cook until almost tender. Add grapes, honey, lemon juice and salt to taste. Heat through. Just before serving sprinkle with chopped mint leaves.

Serves 8.

Carrots may be cooked until tender-crisp and refrigerated. Mix with other ingredients just a few minutes before serving. May also be cooked in microwave oven.

Green Beans with Shallots

2	**pounds fresh green beans or haricots**
3-4	**tablespoons butter**
1/4	**cup minced shallots**
1/2	**cup coarsely chopped walnuts**
1/2	**teaspoon salt**
1/4	**teaspoon ground pepper**

In large container steam beans over hot water until tender-crisp about 6 minutes. Transfer to ice water to stop cooking process. Drain and pat dry. Refrigerate beans for up to 1 day if desired.

Just before serving melt butter in skillet over high heat. Add shallots and nuts. Sauté 1 minute. Add beans, salt and pepper. Toss until heated through. Serve immediately.

Serves 8.

Orange-Glazed Onions with Toasted Pecans

1/4	**cup coarsely chopped pecans**
3	**tablespoons butter or margarine**
3	**large onions, peeled and thinly sliced**
1	**tablespoon brown sugar**
3	**tablespoons orange juice concentrate**
1 1/2	**tablespoons lemon juice**
1/4	**teaspoon salt**

Toast pecans into small skillet over medium heat. Set aside.

In large heavy skillet melt butter over medium heat. Add onions and sauté 20 minutes until very soft. Stir in brown sugar, orange juice concentrate, lemon juice and salt. Cook 5 minutes.

Stir in the pecans. Serve immediately.

Serves 6.

Delicious with pork, lamb, beef or chicken.

Ritzy Corn Pie

1³/₄   cups crushed Ritz crackers

¹/₂   cup (1 stick) butter or margarine, melted and divided

¹/₄   cup chopped onion

¹/₂   cup green pepper, finely diced

1   (15-ounce) can cream-style corn

¹/₄   cup all-purpose flour

2   eggs, beaten

¹/₄   cup milk or cream

¹/₂   teaspoon salt

¹/₄   teaspoon curry powder

5-8   slices bacon, cooked and crumbled

Heat oven to 350˚. Combine crushed Ritz crackers with ¹/₃ of melted butter. Press crumbs into 9-inch quiche dish. Cook onions and green pepper in remaining butter until tender. Add corn and flour. Cook, stirring until thick. Combine eggs, milk, salt and curry powder. Stir rapidly into corn mixture. Add bacon. Pour into quiche pan. Bake 30 minutes or until golden. Serve immediately.

Serves 4 to 6.

Makes an attractive, tasty buffet dish with ham or pork.

Sweet Kraut with Caraway Seed

2   pounds fresh or frozen sauerkraut, not canned

¹/₃   cup sugar

1¹/₂   tablespoons all-purpose flour

¹/₄   teaspoon white pepper

1   teaspoon chicken base, available at supermarkets

2   teaspoons caraway seed

1¹/₄   cup chicken broth

Place sauerkraut in colander and rinse under cold water. Let drain. Mix sugar, flour, white pepper and chicken base together. Place sauerkraut, flour mixture, caraway seed and chicken broth in heavy pot and mix gently. Bring to slow boil over medium heat. Stir frequently. Simmer for 15 minutes.

Sauerkraut should be made at least 2 to 3 hours in advance to allow flavors to fuse. Reheat and serve.

Serves 4.

Excellent with sausage, bratwurst or German pot roast.

During World War II, the League of Catholic Women was a leader in founding Red Cross and Defense Support groups, campaigning for and purchasing Liberty bonds and entertaining soldiers with dances and dinners.

Lemon Roasted Potatoes

1	pound medium red new potatoes
1/4	cup olive oil
2	tablespoons lemon juice, freshly squeezed
1	tablespoon fresh oregano, minced
2	teaspoons freshly grated lemon zest
1/2	teaspoon salt
1/4	teaspoon pepper
6	small bay leaves

Heat oven to 375°. Quarter potatoes and place in 13x9-inch baking dish in single layer. In small bowl blend remaining ingredients except bay leaves. Pour over potatoes. Distribute bay leaves evenly among potatoes. Roast 45 minutes or until tender, turning occasionally with spatula. Discard bay leaves. Serve hot.

Serves 4.

Lemon and herbs give these potatoes a flavor boost.

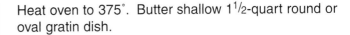

Cauliflower Gratin

1	medium head cauliflower
1	cup mascarpone cheese
	Sea or coarse salt to taste
	White pepper to taste
	Pinch of freshly ground nutmeg
	Pinch of ground cayenne pepper
4	ounces Gruyère cheese

Heat oven to 375°. Butter shallow 1 1/2-quart round or oval gratin dish.

Trim cauliflower and break into small florettes. Steam over boiling water until slightly cooked, about 3 to 5 minutes. Remove from heat immediately. Season mascarpone with salt, pepper, nutmeg and cayenne. Place seasoned mascarpone in large bowl. Add cauliflower and mix it gently but thoroughly. Transfer mixture to prepared baking dish.

Grate Gruyère as finely as possible. Sprinkle cheese evenly over top of cauliflower. Bake until bubbling and golden brown on top, 40 to 45 minutes. Serve at once.

Serves 6 to 8.

May substitute broccoli for cauliflower or combine the two for an attractive look. This stands alone as a memorable vegetarian meal for 2 or 3. If serving as a side dish, make portions small. It is delicious, but rich.

Accordion Potatoes

6   **medium baking potatoes**

Oil for preparing baking pan

4   **tablespoons ($^1/_2$ stick) butter, melted and divided**

$1^1/_4$ **teaspoons salt**

$^1/_8$ **teaspoon pepper**

2   **tablespoons freshly grated Parmesan cheese**

1   **teaspoon paprika**

Heat oven to 375°. Peel potatoes and place in water to keep from darkening. One by one remove potatoes from water. Turn in horizontal position and slice at $^1/_2$-inch intervals $^3/_4$ of the way through each potato leaving the bottom intact. Return potatoes to the water until all are sliced. Drain potatoes and pat dry.

Oil 13x9-inch baking dish. Arrange potatoes sliced side up in dish. Brush with half the melted butter and sprinkle with salt and pepper. Bake in middle rack 30 to 45 minutes depending upon size of potatoes. Add remaining butter. Sprinkle with Parmesan cheese and paprika. Roast another 15 to 20 minutes basting occasionally with butter from the pan. Finished potatoes should be golden brown and opened up like an accordion fan.

Serves 6.

Glazed Vegetables

2   **tablespoons olive oil**

1   **red bell pepper, cut into $^1/_4$-inch wide strips**

1   **yellow bell pepper, cut into $^1/_4$-inch wide strips**

1   **small onion, thinly sliced**

2   **zucchini, trimmed and cut crosswise into $^1/_2$-inch thick rounds**

2   **yellow summer squash, trimmed and cut crosswise into $^1/_2$-inch round**

2   **tablespoons balsamic or tarragon vinegar**

Heat oil in heavy large nonstick skillet over medium-high heat. Add peppers and onion. Sauté until beginning to soften about 4 minutes. Add zucchini and squash. Sauté until tender about 8 minutes. Add vinegar and boil until liquid is reduced to thickened glaze that coats vegetables, about 2 minutes. Season to taste with salt and pepper.

Serves 4.

Vichy French Carrots

2   tablespoons unsalted butter

1½   pounds baby carrots, trimmed, peeled, and sliced lengthwise in half

3   tablespoons minced fresh dill, chives, chervil or tarragon

Sea or coarse salt to taste

Freshly ground black pepper to taste

Melt butter in medium skillet with 2 to 3-inch sides over medium-low heat. Add carrots and cover pan with tight fitting lid. Cook carrots over medium-low heat, shaking pan from time to time. Carrots should be steaming slowly in their own moisture but should not brown. Cook until carrots are tender-crisp, about 15 to 20 minutes. Remove lid and increase heat until all of liquid has evaporated.

Add herb of your choice to carrots and toss to coat evenly. Season to taste with salt and pepper. Serve at once.

Serves 6.

Marmalade Carrots

2   pounds carrots, cut in julienne strips

¼   cup plus 2 tablespoons orange juice

¼   cup maple syrup

2   tablespoons orange marmalade

Steam carrots just until tender. Drain and set aside.

Combine orange juice, maple syrup and marmalade in saucepan. Bring mixture to boil, stirring constantly. Add carrots and stir to coat. Reduce heat. Simmer 3 minutes.

Serves 8.

Martha Stewart Asparagus

1   pound fresh asparagus

2   tablespoons balsamic vinegar or to taste

Cracked pepper to taste

Heat oven to 500°. Wash asparagus and snap off tough bottoms. Arrange in single layer in 13x9-inch pan. Sprinkle with balsamic vinegar and cracked pepper to taste. Roast for 10 to 12 minutes.

Serve 4 to 6.

Never knew Martha could make something so easy!

Snow Peas with Orange

1   **teaspoon vegetable oil**

1   **teaspoon garlic, finely chopped**

Grated zest of 1 orange

3   **cups snow peas, stems and strings removed**

2   **tablespoons orange juice**

Salt and freshly ground black pepper to taste

Heat oil in medium skillet over medium heat. Add garlic and orange zest. Cook, stirring, about 30 seconds or until golden. Add snow peas and orange juice. Cover and cook until peas are tender, 2 to 3 minutes. Uncover pan and cook until juices thicken slightly about 1 minute. Season with salt and pepper.

Serves 4.

Asparagus and Tomatoes with Herb Vinaigrette

1   **pound fresh asparagus**

$1/3$ **cup olive oil**

$1/4$ **cup red wine vinegar**

1   **tablespoon chopped fresh chives**

2   **teaspoons dried oregano, crushed**

$1/4$ **teaspoon salt**

$1/4$ **teaspoon pepper**

4-6   **plum tomatoes, sliced**

Chopped fresh chives for garnish

Snap off tough ends of asparagus. Cook in boiling water to cover 2 minutes or until crisp-tender. Drain. Plunge into ice water to stop cooking process. Drain. Cover and chill 3 hours.

Whisk together olive oil and next five ingredients. Arrange asparagus and sliced tomatoes in a bowl or on a plate. Drizzle with fresh herb vinegarette. Garnish with fresh chives. Serve cold.

Serves 4.

In 1949-50, the League's **Margaret Barry Settlement House** was chosen as the site of a demonstration project involving young children in a cooperative work project called "Yardville". It was intended to be a workground rather than a playground. McCall's magazine did a cover story on Yardville and President Truman stopped by to see it when he visited the Twin Cities in 1950.

Ragout of Wild Mushrooms

1¼	**pounds fresh wild mushrooms or a combination of wild and cultivated mushrooms**
1	**large yellow onion**
1	**large red onion**
1	**tablespoon olive oil, divided**
1	**tablespoon plus 1 teaspoon butter, divided**
3	**cloves garlic, chopped**

Salt and pepper to taste

1	**cup dry red wine, divided**
1	**bay leaf**
½	**teaspoon dried thyme**
2	**stalks celery, thinly sliced**

Pinch of cayenne

1	**tablespoon all-purpose flour**
2	**cups heated vegetable or chicken broth**
2	**tablespoons chopped parsley**

Clean mushrooms and cut into large pieces. Cut yellow and red onion in thin wedges. Heat 1 teaspoon olive oil and 2 teaspoons butter in large nonstick skillet. Sauté onion until soft but not brown. Add garlic. Saute until soft. Season with salt and pepper. Add ½ cup wine, bay leaf, thyme and sliced celery. Simmer gently until wine evaporates.

In separate large skillet heat 2 teaspoons olive oil with 2 teaspoons butter. Sauté mushrooms. Sprinkle with salt, pepper to taste and pinch of cayenne. Cook until excess liquid evaporates and mushrooms begin to color. Add remaining wine. Lower heat and allow wine to reduce by one-half. Add onion mixture to mushrooms.

After removing onions from first skillet melt 1 tablespoon butter in same skillet. Stir flour into butter over medium heat until mixture browns. Whisk in hot broth and continue whisking until sauce thickens. Add to mushroom mixture. Stir in parsley. Simmer together 10 minutes. Serve over beef or pork.

Makes 4 cups.

This ragout is delicious served over polenta or pasta.

Sautéed Portabello Mushrooms

1	**(8-ounce) package portabellos, cut into pieces**
2	**tablespoons onion, minced**
2	**tablespoons butter**
¼	**teaspoon garlic powder**
1	**tablespoon soy sauce**

Sauté mushrooms and minced onion in butter for 5 minutes. Add garlic powder and soy sauce until mixed. Serve warm as side dish or on toast.

Serves 2 to 4.

Baby Onions with Spinach and Parmesan Cheese

1 pound frozen small white baby onions

2 tablespoons butter

1 tablespoon minced garlic

8 ounces fresh spinach, washed, drained and stems removed

1/2 cup freshly grated Parmesan cheese, divided

1/4 cup whipping cream

Salt and pepper to taste

3 tablespoon dry bread crumbs

Heat oven 375°. Cook onions according to package directions. Cool and drain. Melt 2 tablespoons butter in medium saucepan. Add garlic. Cook over medium-high heat 2 minutes. Add spinach. Cook 5 more minutes. Add 1/4 cup grated Parmesan, cream, salt and pepper. Add onions. Place in a 1-quart baking dish. Top with remaining cheese and bread crumbs. Dot with butter. Bake 20 minutes or until bubbly and browned.

Serves 6.

Vidalia Onion Side Dish

1 extra-large vidalia onion, sliced and separated into rings

1/2 pint fresh mushrooms, sliced

2 tablespoons butter

1 egg beaten

1 cup heavy cream

3/4 teaspoon salt

1/2 teaspoon freshly ground pepper

1/2-1 cup shredded sharp Cheddar cheese

1/2 teaspoon paprika

Heat oven to 350°. Place sliced onions in 8-inch square baking dish. In medium skillet sauté mushrooms in butter for 3 minutes. Combine egg, cream, salt and pepper in small bowl. Pour over onions and mushrooms. Sprinkle with cheese and paprika. Bake 25 minutes until lightly browned and bubbly.

Serves 6.

Creamy Spinach Casserole

4	pounds fresh spinach or 5 (10-ounce) packages frozen, thawed
1	cup chopped onion
2	cloves garlic, minced
1/4	cup butter
1	cup whipping cream
1	cup milk
1/2	cup grated Parmesan cheese
1/2	cup plain bread crumbs
1	teaspoon dried marjoram
1	teaspoon salt
1	teaspoon freshly ground pepper
1/4	cup grated sharp Cheddar cheese

Heat oven 350°. Trim fresh spinach. Steam over boiling water until just wilted. Press excess moisture from spinach or thaw and drain frozen spinach very well. Do not cook. Set aside.

Combine spinach with other ingredients except Cheddar cheese. Spoon into buttered casserole. Sprinkle top with Cheddar cheese. Casserole may be refrigerated for several hours before baking.

Bake for 30 minutes until brown and bubbly.

Serves 8 to 10.

This make-ahead dish is perfect for buffets. Especially nice with ham.

Potato Galettes

4	small Yukon Gold potatoes, peeled and cut into 1/8-inch-thick slices
2	teaspoons olive oil

Salt and freshly black pepper to taste

Heat oven to 400°. Lightly coat 15x10-inch baking sheet with vegetable spray. To assemble galette overlap potato slices in a ring about 4 inches in diameter. Arrange second, slightly smaller ring on top of the first. Form 3 additional galettes in the same manner. Brush galette with oil and season with salt and pepper. Bake 25 to 30 minutes or until potatoes are tender and golden. Using wide metal spatula, invert galettes onto individual plates.

Serves 4.

Traditions & Prayers with Our Family...

When our children turn thirteen years old, we invite them to a restaurant dinner and present them with a simple ring to mark their passage from childhood to an age of greater responsibility and freedom. They seem to enjoy the individual attention and the recognition of their more adult status in the family.

On the occasion of their First Communion, we gave each of our children a silver goblet with his/her name and the Communion date. We are doing the same for our grandchildren. At special dinners everyone drinks from his or her silver cup. It reminds us of the communion we share at each family meal.

Bless Our Meal

Lord, bless our meal
And as you satisfy
The needs of each of us,
Make us mindful of the needs of others.

       Mount St. Mary's Abbey

Prayer Before Meals

To all else you have given us,
O Lord,
we ask for but one thing more:
give us grateful hearts.

       George Herbert

Family Table Prayer

Our Father,
we are grateful for this family who, hand in hand, form one unbroken circle.
Help us to do Thy will as caring individuals and as a loving family.

       Christian Retreat Center

Pastas,
Grains &
Vegetarian

Couscous with Sugar Snap Peas and Four Onions

1-3	tablespoons unsalted butter
1	cup thinly sliced leeks, whites plus 1 inch green parts
½	cup thinly sliced shallots
½	cup chopped sweet onion, Vidalia preferred
8	ounces sugar snap peas or snow pea pods
¼	teaspoon salt
¼	teaspoon ground cayenne pepper
1	(14-ounce) can low-fat chicken broth
1	cup couscous, uncooked
2	tablespoons chopped fresh chives

Melt desired amount butter in large heavy skillet over medium heat. Add leeks, shallots and onion. Cook 2 minutes. Reduce heat to medium low. Continue cooking 13 to 15 minutes or until mixture is golden brown. Add peas, salt and cayenne pepper. Cook 2 additional minutes. Add broth. Bring to boiling. Stir in couscous. Cover. Remove from heat. Let stand 5 minutes or until liquid is absorbed. Transfer to serving bowl. Sprinkle with chives.

Serves 6 to 8.

Hummus

1	(15-ounce) can chick peas (garbanzo beans)
½	cup olive oil
6	tablespoons sesame seed paste (Tahini)
5	tablespoons fresh lemon juice
1	medium clove garlic, mashed
½	teaspoon salt
Additional 3 tablespoons olive oil	
3	tablespoons sesame seed, lightly toasted
2	tablespoons chopped fresh parsley

Combine first 6 ingredients in food processor or blender. Blend until smooth and transfer to chilled serving dish. Drizzle with olive oil. Sprinkle with sesame seed and parsley.

Makes 2 cups.

Nice as a vegetable side dish on a hot day or an appetizer served with pita bread wedges.

Nutted Wild Rice

1	cup golden raisins
$\frac{1}{2}$	cup dry sherry
1	cup wild rice, uncooked
$4\frac{2}{3}$	cups boiling chicken broth, divided
6	tablespoons unsalted butter, divided
1	cup brown rice
1	cup slivered almonds
$\frac{1}{2}$	cup chopped fresh parsley
$\frac{1}{4}$-$\frac{1}{2}$	teaspoon salt

Freshly ground black pepper to taste

In small saucepan heat raisins and sherry to boiling. Reduce heat. Simmer 5 minutes. Set aside.

Place wild rice, 2 cups boiling broth and 2 tablespoons butter in top of double boiler over simmering water. Cook covered 1 hour.

Place brown rice, remaining $2\frac{2}{3}$ cups boiling broth and 2 tablespoons butter in medium saucepan. Bring to boil. Reduce heat to low. Simmer about 50 minutes until all water is absorbed. In small skillet sauté almonds in remaining 2 tablespoons butter over low heat until lightly toasted. Combine wild rice, brown rice, raisins with sherry, almonds and parsley. Season with salt and pepper. Serve immediately.

Serves 8 to 10.

Barbecued Beans

1	(15-ounce) can kidney beans
1	(15-ounce) can butter beans
1	(28-ounce) can B & M baked beans
$\frac{1}{2}$	pound bacon, fried crisp and crumbled
1	medium onion, chopped
$\frac{1}{2}$	pound lean ground beef
$\frac{1}{2}$	cup ketchup
$\frac{1}{2}$	cup chili sauce
$\frac{1}{2}$	cup brown sugar
2	tablespoons lemon juice
$\frac{1}{8}$	teaspoon Tabasco sauce or to taste
2	tablespoons molasses

Heat oven to 275˚. Drain kidney and butter beans well. Combine with baked beans in large casserole. Add crisply fried bacon broken into small pieces. In large skillet, sauté onion with ground beef. Add to bean mixture. Combine ketchup, chili sauce, brown sugar, lemon juice, Tabasco sauce and molasses. Stir into bean mixture. Bake covered 2 hours. May be prepared and refrigerated 24 hours before baking.

Serves 10 to 12.

These beans are a staple at this contributor's annual winter skating party and family reunions. Over 125 relatives and three generations have enjoyed this dish.

Creamy Greens Quinoa

³/₄	**cup quinoa**
1¹/₂	**cups chicken stock heated**
2	**tablespoons unsalted butter, divided**
1	**small head romaine or any lettuce of choice torn into bite-size pieces**
1	**tablespoon all-purpose flour**
¹/₄	**cup milk**
¹/₄	**cup whipping cream**
	Pinch of cayenne
¹/₈	**teaspoon ground nutmeg**
¹/₂	**teaspoon sugar**
¹/₄	**teaspoon salt**
¹/₈	**teaspoon pepper**

Rinse quinoa under cold water. Drain. Combine quinoa and chicken stock in heavy medium saucepan. Heat to boiling. Reduce heat and cook covered until all liquid has been absorbed and quinoa looks transparent, about 15 minutes. Lightly mix in 1 tablespoon butter.

In large saucepan cook greens in boiling salted water 2 minutes. Drain. Transfer to food processor and process until smooth.

In separate medium saucepan melt remaining tablespoon butter over low heat. Add flour. Cook 2 minutes, stirring constantly. Slowly add milk and cream whisking until thick, about 2 minutes. Add cayenne, nutmeg and sugar. Stir in greens and cook 1 minute longer.

Combine cooked quinoa with greens mixture. Season with salt and pepper and serve.

Serves 4.

Quinoa is a grain similar to couscous found in health food stores and many supermarkets.

Cheese Quartet Rigatoni

1	**pound rigatoni**
8	**ounces Gruyère cheese, shredded**
8	**ounces mozzarella cheese, shredded**
8	**ounces Gorgonzola cheese, grated**
8	**ounces Parmesan cheese, grated**
1²/₃	**cups cream**
¹/₄	**cup (¹/₂ stick) butter**
	Freshly ground pepper to taste

Cook pasta according to package directions. Drain.

Place cheeses in large heavy saucepan over low heat. Slowing stir in cream and butter as cheese begins to melt. Stir constantly to blend. When cheeses are melted, add pasta and toss. Season with pepper and serve.

Serves 4.

Add a variety of lightly steamed vegetables for a Pasta Primavera.

Layered Broccoli Wild Rice Casserole

1	**cup uncooked wild rice**
2	**tablespoons butter**
2	**tablespoons finely chopped onion**
2	**tablespoons all-purpose flour**
1/2	**teaspoon salt**
1	**cup milk**
1/2	**cup sour cream**
6	**broccoli stalks, cut in half, length-wise, cutting through the floweret**
1	**cup shredded Cheddar cheese, about 1/4 pound**
6	**slices bacon, fried, drained and broken into small pieces**

Heat oven to 350°. Prepare rice according to package directions. Melt butter in medium saucepan. Sauté onion in butter, stirring until onion begins to soften slightly. Sprinkle in flour and salt. Stir and cook over low heat until mixture is smooth. Slowly add milk. Stir until sauce thickens slightly. Fold in sour cream. Set aside.

Steam or microwave broccoli until just tender. Drain well. Layer half the cooked wild rice in bottom of lightly greased shallow 11x7-inch casserole. Place broccoli, cut-side down, on top of rice, flowerets facing sides of casserole. Spoon remaining rice down the center of broccoli stalks. Sprinkle with shredded cheese.

Pour sauce over center of rice and sprinkle bacon over both cheese and rice. If preparing ahead cover casserole and refrigerate. Bake covered about 20 minutes. Uncover and bake another 10 minutes or until cheese bubbles.

Serves 6 to 8.

Asparagus may be substituted for broccoli.

Savory Rice

8	**ounces fresh mushrooms, sliced**
1/2	**cup (1 stick) butter or margarine, divided**
1	**cup regular white rice, not Minute Rice, uncooked**
1	**(10³/4 ounce) can beef consommé**
1	**(10³/4 ounce) can onion soup**

Heat oven to 350°. In large skillet sauté mushrooms in 1/4 cup butter or margarine. Combine rice, consommé, onion soup and remaining butter or margarine. Add mushrooms. Pour into 2-quart casserole. Bake covered 1 hour or until liquid is completely absorbed.

Serves 6.

No one will ever guess that the delicious flavor of this dish comes from adding a can of soup.

Broccoli Rice Strata with Cashews

1½   cups uncooked brown rice

2   tablespoons vegetable oil

1   large onion, chopped

2   large cloves garlic, minced

½   teaspoon dried dill weed

1   teaspoon dried thyme

1   teaspoon dried oregano

½   bunch parsley, minced

½   pound mushrooms, sliced

1   green bell pepper, thinly sliced

2   pounds broccoli, cut into flowerets and tough ends discarded

½   cup unsalted cashews

½   pound Gruyère cheese, shredded

¼   cup freshly grated Parmesan cheese

1   pint sour cream, room temperature

Heat oven to 350˚. Cook brown rice according to package directions. In large skillet heat oil and sauté onion and garlic with dill, thyme and oregano. When vegetables are tender, add parsley, mushrooms and green pepper. Continue cooking 2 minutes. Stir in broccoli. Sauté until broccoli is tender crisp. Add nuts and remove from heat.

Spread rice over bottom of lightly greased 13x9-inch baking dish. Cover with vegetable mixture. Sprinkle with both cheeses and cover with sour cream. Cover and refrigerate if made ahead. Bake 20 minutes, 30 minutes if refrigerated, or until mixture is bubbling and cheese is melted.

Serves 8.

¾ cup white rice plus ¾ cup wild rice may be substituted for brown rice.

1 (10 ¾-ounce) can cream of chicken soup, diluted with ½ can of water may be substituted for sour cream.

Roasted Tomato Sauce

4   pounds fresh vine-ripened tomatoes

4   cloves garlic, peeled and sliced

Approximately 1 cup olive oil

Salt and pepper to taste

12   fresh basil leaves

1   tablespoon balsamic vinegar

Heat oven to 350˚. Peel tomatoes. Place in 13x9-inch pan. With sharp knife, make a deep "x" on each tomato. Place garlic slices in and around tomatoes. Pour olive oil into pan about ½-inch deep. Season tomatoes with salt and pepper. Sprinkle with basil leaves. Bake 30 to 40 minutes. Remove from oven and sprinkle vinegar over top. Crush tomatoes with fork to make a chunky sauce. Serve over pasta or polenta.

Makes about 1 quart.

Gorgonzola Spaghettini with Lemon and Prosciutto

$^1/_4$	cup lemon zest, cut in long thick strips
2	large cloves garlic, minced
2	large shallots, minced
4	tablespoons unsalted or salted butter
2	tablespoons olive oil
6	ounces thinly sliced prosciutto
2-3	ounces Gorgonzola cheese
1	teaspoon coarsely ground black pepper
$^3/_4$	pound spaghettini pasta

Freshly grated Parmesan cheese to taste

Blanch lemon zest strips in small saucepan of boiling water for 1 minute. Drain and set aside.

Sauté garlic and shallots in butter and olive oil in medium skillet until softened, stirring constantly. Increase heat to medium-high. Add prosciutto and lemon zest. Cook about 3 minutes until prosciutto is lightly browned. Stir in Gorgonzola. Add black pepper. Sauce may be made ahead and reheated.

Cook spaghettini according to package directions. Drain. Toss pasta and prosciutto together. Serve with freshly grated Parmesan cheese. May be served hot or at room temperature.

Serves 4 to 6.

To vary, add $^1/_4$ to $^1/_2$ cup of cream instead of Gorgonzola or replace Gorgonzola with 3 ounces goat cheese. May also prepare with no cheese or cream.

Gourmet Grits

4	cups whole or skim milk
$^1/_2$	cup (1 stick) butter, cut into small pieces
1	cup Quaker Quik Grits
1	teaspoon salt

Pepper to taste

4	ounces Gruyère cheese, grated
4	ounces Parmesan cheese, freshly grated
$^1/_3$	cup butter, melted

In large heavy saucepan bring milk to boiling. Add butter and grits. Cook over medium heat until thick. Remove from heat. Add salt and pepper. Beat 5 minutes with electric mixer. Pour into lightly greased 9x9-inch square or round pan. Refrigerate up to 24 hours.

Heat oven to 350°. Sprinkle two cheeses over top of grits. Pour $^1/_3$ cup melted butter over cheese. Bake 30 to 35 minutes. If desired, place under broiler briefly to brown before serving. Cut into small squares or wedges. These grits are rich!

Serves 6 to 8.

A nice substitute for potatoes especially with pork or ham.

Lemon Rice with Leeks

1	tablespoon slivered sun-dried tomatoes packed in oil
2	cups shredded leeks, about 4 medium leeks
$\frac{1}{2}$	teaspoon sugar
$\frac{1}{8}$	teaspoon ground cinnamon
$\frac{1}{2}$	teaspoon salt

Freshly ground pepper to taste

1	cup Arborio rice
$1\frac{1}{2}$	teaspoons freshly grated lemon zest
$3\frac{1}{4}$	cups low-fat chicken broth
1	cup chopped fresh parsley

Drain tomatoes, reserving 1 teaspoon oil. In large skillet heat reserved oil over medium heat. Add leeks and sugar. Sauté 6 to 8 minutes until leeks begin to soften. Add sun-dried tomatoes, cinnamon, salt, pepper and rice. Cook and stir 2 minutes. Stir in lemon zest, chicken broth and parsley. Cover and simmer 10 minutes. Remove skillet from heat and uncover. Quickly place piece of cheesecloth or clean dishtowel over skillet and replace lid. Let rice stand in warm place for 15 to 20 minutes. When all liquid is absorbed rice is ready to serve.

Serves 4.

Lemon Risotto with Parmesan Cheese

$\frac{1}{2}$	cup (1 stick) butter, divided
1	medium onion
1	cup dry white wine
1	cup Arborio rice
1	teaspoon salt
$\frac{1}{4}$	teaspoon freshly ground pepper
3	tablespoons fresh lemon juice
4-5	cups chicken broth, divided
1	cup freshly grated Parmesan cheese

Melt 5 tablespoons butter in large saucepan over medium heat. Add chopped onion and cook until transparent. Add wine. Cook over high heat until wine is evaporated. Add rice and season with salt and pepper. Add lemon juice and 2 cups chicken broth. Cook and stir until almost all liquid has evaporated. Gradually add remaining broth. Reduce heat and continue to cook, stirring frequently, 20 to 25 minutes. Add remaining butter and Parmesan cheese to taste. Serve immediately.

Serves 6.

Although regular long-grained white rice may be used, risotto is best made with short-grained Italian Arborio rice. The key to success with Arborio is stirring the rice continuously as the liquid is absorbed. One-quarter teaspoon saffron softened in 1 tablespoon hot (not boiling) water is a flavorful substitute for the lemon juice in this recipe.

Calico Rice

1 cup regular long grain white rice, not Minute Rice

$\frac{1}{2}$ cup ($\frac{1}{4}$ stick) butter

3 cups boiling chicken broth

Pepper to taste

6 tablespoons minced parsley

6 tablespoons minced onion

6 tablespoons minced celery

6 tablespoons minced green onions

6 tablespoons silvered almonds, toasted

Heat oven to 350°. In medium skillet sauté rice in butter 5 minutes. Remove rice to 2-quart casserole. Add boiling broth and pepper. Cover and bake 45 minutes. Stir in vegetables and bake 10 minutes longer or until all liquid is absorbed. Sprinkle with toasted almonds before serving.

Serves 6.

Boiling broth before adding is essential.

Heartland Pasta

1-1$\frac{1}{2}$ pounds fettuccine, cooked according to package directions

3 tablespoons olive oil

1 tablespoon chopped garlic

1 large onion, chopped

1 tablespoon chopped fresh rosemary or 1 teaspoon dried

1 pound fresh spinach, torn

6 tablespoons crisply cooked crumbled bacon

$\frac{1}{4}$ cup white wine, optional

$\frac{1}{4}$ teaspoon salt

$\frac{1}{4}$ teaspoon pepper

Red pepper flakes to taste

Pecorino Romano or Parmesan cheese to taste

While pasta is cooking, pour olive oil into large skillet. Add garlic, onion and rosemary. Sauté until onion is tender. Add spinach and cook until limp. Add crumbled bacon. Remove mixture. Deglaze pan with white wine. Return mixture to pan. Add salt, pepper and red pepper flakes. Toss with cooked fettuccini. Sprinkle Pecorino Romano or Parmesan cheese on top and serve.

Serves 6 to 8.

Vegetarian Lasagna

Pesto:

3   **cups fresh basil leaves, stems removed**

3-4   **cloves garlic**

$1/4$-$1/2$ teaspoon salt

$3/4$ **cup freshly grated Parmesan cheese**

$1/2$ **cup pine nuts or walnuts**

$1/2$ **cup olive oil**

$1/2$ **cup chopped fresh parsley**

$1/4$ **cup ($1/2$ stick) butter, softened, optional**

Coarsely ground black pepper to taste

Filling:

1   **pound or 1 (16-ounce bag) fresh spinach**

1   **cup minced onion**

5   **tablespoons olive oil, divided**

4   **cups ricotta cheese**

1   **cup pesto**

$1/4$ **cup sunflower seeds, toasted**

$1/2$ **cup grated Parmesan cheese, divided**

$1/2$ **teaspoon salt**

$1/4$ **teaspoon pepper**

20-24 spinach lasagna noodles

1   **pound mozzarella cheese, thinly sliced**

Purée all pesto ingredients in blender to form uniform paste. May be stored in tightly covered container until needed.

Clean and chop spinach. Set aside. In large heavy skillet, sauté onion in 2 tablespoons olive oil 6 to 8 minutes until soft. Stir fresh spinach into hot onion. Transfer to large bowl. Add ricotta, pesto, sunflower seeds, half the Parmesan cheese, salt and pepper. Mix thoroughly.

To assemble place layer of uncooked noodles in bottom of oiled 13x9-inch pan. Spread $1/3$ filling over noodles. Place $1/3$ mozzarella slices over filling. Layer noodles, filling and cheese two more times. Top with final layer of noodles and remaining Parmesan cheese. May be covered and refrigerated for several hours if preparing ahead.

Heat oven to 350˚. Drizzle top of lasagna with remaining 2 tablespoons olive oil. Cover with foil and bake 35 to 40 minutes.

Serves 8.

Fresh lasagna noodles are preferred since they require no pre-cooking. If using dry noodles, cook according to package directions.

Chilled Pasta Primavera with Basil Cream

Pasta:

1	**pound fettuccini, broken up and cooked according to package directions**
1	**tablespoon sherry**
1/4	**cup white wine vinegar**
1/3	**cup olive oil**

Salt and pepper to taste

Vegetables:

16	**small asparagus spears, cut into 1 1/2-inch lengths**
2	**cups broccoli flowerets**
2	**cups frozen tiny peas, uncooked**
6	**green onions, cut into 1-inch pieces**
1	**pint cherry tomatoes, halved**
1	**pound fresh spinach for garnish**
2	**pounds cooked shrimp, optional**

Basil Cream:

1/3	**cup white wine vinegar**
2	**tablespoons Dijon mustard**
1/2	**cup chopped fresh basil**
1-2	**cloves garlic**
1/3	**cup olive oil**
1	**cup sour cream**
1/2	**cup whipping cream**
3	**tablespoons chopped fresh parsley**

Drain pasta. Place in large bowl. Add sherry, vinegar and oil. Season to taste with salt and pepper. Cover and refrigerate.

In separate batches steam asparagus, broccoli and peas. Be careful not to overcook. Cool. Store in plastic bags or tightly sealed containers and refrigerate. Wash and refrigerate other vegetables.

Combine vinegar, mustard, basil and garlic in blender or processor. Mix until smooth. With machine running, drizzle in oil. Add sour cream, whipping cream and parsley. Mix until smooth. Season with salt and pepper. Chill.

To serve arrange spinach around outer edge of platter. Toss pasta with vegetables. Add shrimp if desired. Arrange pasta in center of spinach. Serve with basil cream on side or tossed with the pasta.

Serves 8.

This is a beautiful cold buffet side dish or entree. It may be prepared the day ahead and assembled just before serving.

Prawns and Pasta

8-10 ounces dry linguini

2 **tablespoons olive oil**

1/2 **cup olive oil, divided**

16 **prawns or large shrimp, peeled and deveined**

4 **large mushrooms, sliced**

1 1/2 **cloves garlic, minced, divided**

2 **plum tomatoes, quartered, seeded and cut into julienne strips**

2 **green onions, trimmed and sliced**

1/4 **cup white wine**

Juice of 1 lemon

Salt and pepper to taste

2 **tablespoons freshly grated Parmesan cheese**

In large pot cook pasta according to package directions. Drain and cool in cold water. When cool, drain and toss with 1/8 cup olive oil. Set aside. Pasta may be prepared up to 1 day ahead and kept in refrigerator.

In heated skillet sauté shrimp in 1/8 cup olive oil. Cook shrimp about 2 minutes until pink. Add mushrooms and 2/3 of minced garlic. Cook just 30 seconds. Do not burn or brown. Add tomatoes, green onions, wine, lemon juice, salt and pepper

In another large skillet sauté cooked linguini in 1/4 cup olive oil. Season with remaining garlic, salt and pepper.

To assemble place pasta in center of two plates or bowls. Arrange 8 shrimp around base of pasta. Top pasta with mushrooms, tomato and green onions. Sprinkle with fresh grated Parmesan.

Serves 2.

This dish is a favorite at the Lake Elmo Inn according to Owner/Chef John Schiltz who contributed this recipe.

Specialita Della Cabina (Pasta with Giovanni's Sauce)

1/4 **pound bulk hot Italian sausage**

2 **cloves garlic**

1/4 **cup olive oil**

3 **slices thick ham, diced**

1/2 **cup dry red wine**

1 **teaspoon dried basil or 1 tablespoon shredded fresh basil leaves**

4 **large tomatoes, peeled and crushed or 1 (30-ounce) can tomatoes**

Salt and pepper to taste

Cook sausage in large skillet chopping meat into small bits. Set aside. Sauté 2 whole cloves garlic in olive oil. Add ham and precooked sausage. Sauté about 3 minutes. Sprinkle with 1/2 cup red wine and cook down until most of liquid is evaporated. Season to taste with basil, salt and pepper. Add fresh or canned tomatoes. Cook about 10 minutes. Wonderful over 1 pound of your favorite pasta.

Serves 4.

Many thanks to Father John Forliti, Pastor of St. Olaf Catholic Church, for this recipe, a reflection of his Italian heritage.

Pasta with Bacon, Spinach and Cheese

8	slices bacon
1	cup chopped onion
$1/2$	medium red bell pepper, cut in julienne strips
$1/2$	medium green bell pepper, cut in julienne strips
12	ounces rigatoni pasta
$1^1/_3$	cups freshly grated Parmesan cheese
$1^1/_3$	cups freshly grated Fontina cheese
6	tablespoons butter, cut into pieces, warmed to room temperature
8	cups chopped fresh spinach, stems removed
3	tablespoons brandy
$1/2$	cup chopped toasted walnuts

Salt and pepper to taste

Cook bacon in large skillet until crisp. Remove to paper towels. When cool, break into pieces. Drain all but 3 tablespoons bacon fat from skillet. Add onions and bell peppers. Sauté until tender. Remove skillet from heat. Cook rigatoni in large pot of salted water according to package directions. Drain. Return pasta to pot. Add cheeses and butter stirring until melted. Add spinach and brandy. Cook over medium heat about 3 minutes. Add sautéed vegetables and bacon bits to pasta. Season with salt and pepper. Transfer pasta to large bowl. Sprinkle with toasted walnuts and serve.

Serves 4.

In 1980 the Advisory Board of the League assumed responsibility for starting an **Endowment Fund** to ensure the perpetuity of the League of Catholic Women and its mission. Peter Lupori was commissioned to design a plaque acknowledging benefactors from 1911 through 1979 and major donors to the Endowment Fund thereafter. The earnings from this fund have helped support League out-reach programs for twenty years. The plaque can be seen at the LCW Downtown Center.

Ziti and Portabellos

2	tablespoons unsalted butter, divided
3	tablespoons olive oil, divided
6	medium onions, chopped
$\frac{1}{2}$	teaspoon salt
1	teaspoon sugar
2	pounds portabello mushrooms
$\frac{1}{4}$	teaspoon coarsely ground pepper
6	tablespoons chopped flat leaf parsley
$1\frac{1}{2}$	pounds ziti
8	ounces goat cheese, crumbled
3	tablespoons freshly grated Parmesan cheese

Melt butter and 1 tablespoon olive oil in large skillet. Add onions, salt and sugar. Cook about 20 to 30 minutes over medium heat, stirring frequently, until onions are browned. Season with $\frac{1}{2}$ teaspoon salt and sugar. Transfer onion mixture to bowl. Onions may be prepared up to 3 hours ahead.

Stem and halve mushrooms and slice cross-wise into $\frac{1}{4}$-inch slices. Melt second tablespoon butter. Add second tablespoon olive oil, $\frac{1}{2}$ teaspoon salt and mushrooms. Cook over medium heat about 8 minutes, stirring occasionally, until tender and brown. Add pepper, reserved onions and parsley. Season with additional salt and pepper to taste.

Cook ziti al dente in large pot according to package directions. Reserve 1 cup pasta water before draining ziti. In large bowl, toss ziti with reserved pasta water, mushroom onion mixture, goat cheese and Parmesan. Add third tablespoon olive oil and toss once more.

Serves 8.

Fettuccine with Tomato Basil Cream

$\frac{1}{2}$	cup half-and-half
$\frac{1}{2}$	cup chicken broth
$\frac{1}{4}$	cup olive oil
$\frac{1}{2}$	pound (about 2 large) tomatoes, seeded and chopped
$\frac{1}{3}$	cup shredded fresh basil leaves
8	ounces fettuccine
4	tablespoons freshly grated Parmesan cheese

In large skillet, combine half-and-half, chicken broth and olive oil. Bring liquid to boiling. Reduce heat. Simmer 5 minutes. Add tomatoes and basil. Continue to simmer 1 minute more.

While sauce is simmering, cook pasta al dente according to package directions. Drain well. Place in skillet with tomato sauce. Add Parmesan cheese and toss to coat well.

Serves 6.

Land O'Lakes nonfat half-and-half is a good substitute for regular half-and-half. It does not break down in cooking.

Ravioli with Roasted Red Pepper Cream

1	**(24-ounce) package frozen cheese ravioli**
1	**(7-ounce) jar roasted sweet red peppers, drained**
$^1/_2$	**cup dry white wine**
1	**cup whipping cream**
$^3/_4$	**cup freshly grated Parmesan cheese**

Bring $2^1/_2$ quarts unsalted water to boiling in large saucepan. Add ravioli and cook about 5 minutes until tender. Drain well. Set aside.

Drain and rinse red peppers. Remove seeds. Blot with paper towels to remove excess moisture. Cut peppers into small pieces. Place in medium saucepan. Add wine and cook over medium-high heat just to boiling. Reduce heat and simmer 5 minutes until only about 2 tablespoons liquid remain. Watch carefully, liquid evaporates quickly. Add cream. Bring to boiling. Reduce heat. Simmer 3 to 5 minutes until slightly thickened, stirring frequently. Remove from heat. Add Parmesan cheese. Cook and stir about 2 minutes until Parmesan is melted.

Divide ravioli among 4 shallow pasta bowls or soup bowls. Top each serving with $^1/_2$ cup sauce and serve.

Serves 4.

To make a thick delicious sauce for chicken or fish, simmer cream a little longer until reduced by half.

In 1998, the League of Catholic Women opened a "clothing store" called **First Impression** in its Downtown Center. The clothes are brand new and free. The sales assistants, pressers and fitters are League volunteers. After the client makes an appointment, First Impression provides a complete wardrobe, personal attention and a bit of confidence to the low-income woman who is preparing to enter/re-enter the job market. This project cooperates with over 20 area back-to-work programs.

Sun-Dried Tomato Pasta

$1/2$ cup chopped sun dried tomatoes

1   (12-ounce) can evaporated skimmed milk

$1^1/2$ cups low-fat cottage cheese

2   cloves garlic, quartered

$1/2$ teaspoon salt

$1/2$ teaspoon freshly ground pepper

$1/8$ teaspoon red pepper flakes

$3/4$ cup freshly grated Parmesan cheese

2   tablespoons extra virgin olive oil

$3/4$ cup chopped fresh basil

1   pound pasta noodles, cook's choice

In small bowl soak tomatoes in hot water for 10 minutes. Drain. Combine milk, cottage cheese, garlic, salt, pepper, red pepper flakes and Parmesan cheese in blender or food processor. Process until smooth. With blender on low speed add oil until well blended. Pour sauce into heavy medium saucepan and warm over low heat. Do not boil.

Cook pasta according to package directions. Drain and place in bowl. Pour sauce over pasta. Add drained tomatoes and basil. Toss to mix well. Serve immediately.

Serves 6.

This contributor's recipe file has become a history of friendships made in other times and other places. Many favorites like this one were passed along by treasured friends and are rich in memories.

Sun-dried tomatoes, bacon, and many herbs can be cut more easily with a scissors than a knife.

White Beans with Sage and Olive Oil

1   pound dried Great Northern beans

6   cups cold water

$1/4$ cup extra virgin olive oil

$1^1/2$ tablespoons chopped fresh sage

1   large clove garlic, minced

Additional olive oil

Place beans in large sauce pan. Add enough cold water to cover by 3 inches and let soak overnight.

Drain beans and return to pan. Add 6 cups cold water, $1/4$ cup oil, chopped sage and garlic. Bring to boil. Reduce heat to medium-low. Cover partially; simmer until beans are just tender, stirring occasionally, about 45 minutes. Season with salt and pepper. To serve transfer beans to bowl using slotted spoon. Top with a little olive oil if desired.

Serves 6.

Can be made 1 day ahead. Cool. Cover and keep chilled. Rewarm when ready to serve.

Lite Turkey and Artichoke Fettuccine

8   **ounces dried fettuccine noodles**

1   **(9-ounce) package frozen artichoke hearts or 1½ cups lightly cooked broccoli flowerets**

1   **pound turkey breast tenderloins or boneless skinless chicken breasts, all visible fat removed**

Vegetable spray

½   **teaspoon minced fresh garlic**

1   **tablespoon all-purpose flour**

1   **(12-ounce) can evaporated skim milk**

¼   **teaspoon salt**

¼   **teaspoon crushed, dried marjoram or basil**

⅛   **teaspoon black pepper**

⅛   **teaspoon ground nutmeg**

½   **cup shredded or grated Parmesan cheese**

In large saucepan cook fettuccine according to package directions omitting oil and salt. Add artichokes to boiling fettuccine water during last 5 minutes of cooking. Drain. Halve any large artichoke hearts.

Rinse turkey and pat dry. Cut into small pieces. Spray large skillet with vegetable oil. Place over medium-high heat. Add turkey pieces and garlic to hot skillet. Cook 3 minutes or until turkey is tender and no longer pink. Stir in flour. Add remaining ingredients except Parmesan cheese. Cook 1 minute more stirring constantly. Add turkey mixture to saucepan with drained fettuccine and artichokes. Add Parmesan cheese. Toss until well combined.

Serves 4.

Since the fall of 1993, the League of Catholic Women has been providing **scholarships for women attending the College of St. Catherine,** Minneapolis campus. The League also provides resources for a special fund assisting single mothers enrolled in the college's **Access and Success** program. These funds help provide for these students in emergency situations.

Low-Fat Lasagna

1	**pound ground turkey breast**
1	**large onion, diced**
1	**clove garlic, diced, optional**
2	**(14$\frac{1}{2}$-ounce) cans Italian stewed tomatoes**
1	**(6-ounce) can Italian tomato paste**
1	**teaspoon dried basil**
3	**tablespoons dried parsley flakes, divided**
2$\frac{3}{4}$	**cups (18 ounces) nonfat cottage cheese**
$\frac{1}{2}$	**cup (4 ounces) freshly grated Parmesan cheese**
1	**teaspoon dried oregano**
8	**ounces uncooked lasagna noodles**
8	**ounces mozzarella cheese, sliced**

In medium skillet brown ground turkey. Add onion and garlic and sauté. Combine stewed tomatoes, tomato paste, basil and 2 tablespoons parsley flakes in large bowl. Combine tomato mixture with meat mixture.

In separate small bowl combine cottage cheese and Parmesan. Add 1 tablespoon parsley flakes and oregano.

In bottom of 13x9-inch pan spread $\frac{1}{2}$ of meat/tomato sauce. Add layer of lasagna noodles. Spread all of the cottage cheese mixture on top of noodles. Layer with remaining lasagna noodles and sauce. Top with Mozzarella cheese slices. Serve with green salad and crusty Italian bread.

Serves 6 to 8.

Basic Polenta

2$\frac{1}{2}$	**cups milk**
$\frac{3}{4}$	**cup cornmeal**

Slowly bring milk to boiling in heavy medium saucepan. Gradually add meal. Whisk together over medium-low heat about 5 minutes until polenta is smooth and thick.

Using bowl scraper pour mixture into lightly buttered 9 or 10-inch pie plate. Cool on wire rack, then refrigerate 1 hour.

To serve cut polenta into wedges and either dust with Parmesan and broil until browned or sauté lightly in butter.

Serves 6.

Serve with tomato or wild mushroom sauce found in Complements section.

Portabello and Vegetable Sandwich

1   medium eggplant, peeled and sliced crosswise into $1/2$-inch slices

1   teaspoon salt

2   medium zucchini

4-6 tablespoons olive oil

2   teaspoons minced fresh garlic

1   medium red onion, peeled and sliced crosswise into $1/2$-inch slices

1   (6-ounce) package sliced portabello mushrooms

6   crusty sandwich rolls or focaccia bread slices, halved

6   large slices bottled roasted sweet red peppers

6   slices Swiss or Havarti cheese

Heat oven to 450°. Sprinkle eggplant with salt and let stand 20 minutes. Cut each zucchini in half crosswise and each half into 3 lengthwise slices. Combine olive oil and minced garlic in small bowl. Brush oil mixture onto two 10x15-inch jelly roll pans. Arrange in single layer in pans, brush with oil mixture and sprinkle lightly with salt. Roast 20 to 25 minutes. Heat broiler. Broil rolls until light brown. Arrange layers of each vegetable on roll bottoms. Top with roasted peppers and cheese. Broil until cheese is slightly melted. Serve immediately.

Serves 6.

White Beans in Tomato Sauce with Sage and Pancetta

1   cup chopped onion

$3/4$ cup chopped peeled carrot

$3/4$ cup chopped celery

2   ounces thinly sliced pancetta or 2 bacon slices, chopped

3   cloves garlic, minced

$3/4$ teaspoon dried rubbed sage

2   (15-ounce) cans cannellini (white kidney beans), rinsed and drained

1   ($14 1/2$-ounce) can diced tomatoes in juice

$1/2$ cup canned low-salt chicken broth

Combine onion, carrot, celery, pancetta and garlic in heavy, large saucepan. Cover and cook over medium-high heat until vegetables are tender, stirring occasionally, about 10 minutes. Add sage; stir 15 seconds. Stir in cannellini, tomatoes with juice and broth. Simmer covered until flavors blend, about 7 minutes. Season with salt and pepper. Transfer to bowl.

Serves 6.

Mexican Veggie Stew

$^1/_4$ **cup olive oil**

4   **cloves garlic, minced**

2   **large onions, diced**

1   **teaspoon ground cumin**

1   **(28-ounce) can tomatoes with juice, chopped**

5   **($10^3/_4$-ounce) cans vegetable broth**

Salt and pepper to taste

2   **medium carrots, thinly sliced**

2   **medium zucchini, cut lengthwise into sixths, then inch-long pieces**

2   **cups dry kidney beans, soaked in water according to directions or 1 (15-ounce) can kidney beans drained and rinsed**

2   **cups fresh or frozen corn kernels**

1   **cup freshly grated Cheddar cheese**

1   **cup taco chips, broken into small pieces**

Warm olive oil over medium heat in large heavy pot. Sauté garlic, onion and cumin for 10 minutes, stirring often. Add tomatoes with juice, vegetable broth, salt and pepper. Bring to boil. Add carrots. Cook 15 minutes. Add zucchini. Cook 5 to 10 minutes or until zucchini is tender but not mushy. Add kidney beans and corn. Cook 2 minutes. Remove 2 cups of stew and puree in food processor. Return to pot. Taste and adjust seasoning.

Ladle into bowls. Top with the grated cheese and taco chips.

Serves 8.

A good choice for the vegetarians in your family. This dish is even better if cooked and refrigerated overnight.

Many soups and stews taste better if they are made a day or two ahead and refrigerated. This gives the flavors time to blend.

Roasted Vegetable Sandwich

1	zucchini, sliced in $\frac{1}{8}$-inch thick strips
1	yellow squash, sliced in $\frac{1}{8}$-inch thick strips
1	small eggplant, sliced in $\frac{1}{8}$-inch strips
1	red bell pepper, cored and seeded and cut into julienne strips
1	medium yellow onion, peeled and sliced into thin rings

Salt and cracked black pepper to taste

2	cloves garlic, chopped
$\frac{1}{4}$	cup olive oil
1	teaspoon fresh thyme, snipped
6	focaccia or semolina buns
6	ounces Boursin or Rondelé cheese

Juice from 2 lemons

3	tomatoes, sliced
1	bunch fresh arugula

Heat oven to 450°. In large mixing bowl combine zucchini, squash, eggplant, bell pepper, onion, salt and pepper to taste, garlic, oil and thyme. Arrange vegetables in a thin layer on baking sheet. Bake 20 to 30 minutes or until tender. Set aside to cool completely. Split buns. Spread cheese on bottom halves. Cover with vegetables. Squeeze lemon juice over vegetables. Add tomato slices. Season with salt and pepper. Top with arugula leaves and other half of buns.

Serves 6.

Roast vegetables in larger pieces for ease of eating. Baby field greens work as well as arugula.

To mark its 80th anniversary in 1991, the League of Catholic Women commissioned local needlepoint designer, Joanne Mahoney, and New England artist, Mary McGee, to design a large (approximately 5 x 6 foot) **Heritage Needlepoint.** Twenty-one LCW members worked for months to complete this visual record of the League's history of service and friendship. This unique and artfully crafted textile is on view at the LCW Downtown Center

Mealtime Prayers with Children

A Child's Prayer

Bless us, Father, while we eat.
Keep us healthy, wise and sweet.
Make us loving, kind and good
That we may love Thee as we should.

A Simple Prayer

Thank you for the world so sweet,
Thank you for the food we eat.
Thank you for the birds that sing,
Thank you, God, for everything.

A Circle Prayer

Join hands around the table. Beginning with the
youngest child, let each member of the circle state what
he or she is most grateful for that day. "Dear God, thank
you for this food and for_____." Another time you
might express thanks for a special person or family
member, or something in nature; the list is endless.

Table Prayers

Table Prayer for Peace

Faithful God,
let this table be a sign of tomorrow's hope
already here,
when, with all the peoples of the world
who hunger for justice and peace,
we shall come together singing Your name
as our very own.

The Benedictine Grange

A Table Prayer of Thanksgiving

For each new morning with its light,
For rest and shelter of the night.
For health and food, for love and friends,
For everything Thy goodness sends.

Ralph Waldo Emerson

Meat
& Poultry

Roasted Chicken with Apple Thyme Honey Sauce

2	**whole frying chickens**

Salt and pepper to taste

15	**large sprigs fresh thyme, divided**
3	**tablespoons olive oil**
$1/2$	**cup (1stick) butter**
1	**apple, cored, peeled and sliced**
$1/4$	**cup lemon juice**
$1/4$	**cup honey**

Heat oven to 375°. Season chickens with salt and pepper inside and out. Place $1/2$ of thyme sprigs in each chicken cavity. Remove leaves from remaining thyme, mince and set aside. Rub chickens with olive oil. Place in roasting pan breast side up. Roast chickens 1 hour, basting occasionally with pan juices until juices run clear.

Melt butter in heavy skillet. Add apple slices and sauté for about 3 minutes. Add lemon juice, honey and minced thyme. Stir for 1 to 2 minutes. Remove from heat and taste for final seasoning. Transfer chicken to platter. Let rest 10 minutes. Carve chickens. Drizzle with sauce.

Serves 6.

We are grateful to Lucia Watson, owner/chef of Lucia's Restaurant in Minneapolis, for contributing this original recipe.

Pistachio Chicken with Cream

4	**boneless skinless chicken breasts, pounded thin**
3	**tablespoons all-purpose flour**
1	**teaspoon garlic salt**
1	**teaspoon lemon-pepper**
2	**tablespoons olive oil**
1	**tablespoon butter**
$1/2$	**cup Marsala wine**
1	**$1/4$-inch-thick slice honey baked ham, diced**
1	**(8-ounce) package fresh mushrooms, cleaned, thinly sliced**
$1/2$	**cup shelled pistachios, cut in half**
1	**cup whipping cream**
1	**tablespoon chopped parsley**
3	**cup cooked rice, white or wild**

Heat oven to 225°. Mix flour with garlic salt and lemon pepper in shallow bowl. Dredge chicken breasts in seasoned flour. In large skillet sauté breasts in olive oil and butter on both sides until lightly browned. Transfer breasts to shallow baking dish. Cover with foil and keep warm in oven.

Add $1/2$ cup Marsala wine to skillet and scrape browned bits to incorporate them over low heat. Add diced ham, sliced mushrooms, pistachios and whipping cream. Cook until sauce is thickened stirring frequently. Add chopped parsley.

Place $1/2$ cup of cooked rice on each plate. Arrange breasts on top and pour sauce over each serving.

Serves 4.

Serve with cooked baby carrots sautéed in 1 tablespoon maple syrup and 1 tablespoon butter. To reduce fat, substitute $1/2$ cup low-fat chicken broth and $1/2$ cup half-and-half for 1 cup whipping cream.

Chicken Breasts Veronique

4	boneless skinless chicken breasts, halved

Lemon pepper to taste

Garlic salt to taste

1	teaspoon butter
1	teaspoon olive oil
1	teaspoon orange marmalade
1/4	teaspoon tarragon
4	green onions, chopped
1/2	cup white wine
1	cup halved green and red seedless grapes
1/3	cup chicken broth
2	teaspoons all-purpose flour or Wondra flour if available

Sprinkle breasts with lemon pepper and garlic salt on both sides. Heat butter and oil in large skillet over medium heat. Sauté chicken breasts until lightly browned. Add marmalade, tarragon, onions and white wine. Cover. Reduce heat. Simmer 15 minutes. Add grapes. Cover and simmer 15 minutes more. Remove chicken and grapes to heated platter. Mix flour with chicken broth. Add to juices in pan. Cook until thickened. Pour sauce over chicken and serve.

Serves 4.

Orange rice makes a tasty accompaniment. Simply substitute orange juice for the water when cooking rice and add toasted almonds.

California Turkey Sauté

4	boneless skinless turkey cutlets or tenderloins
1	tablespoon vegetable oil
2	ounces dry vermouth
3	ripe tomatoes, peeled, seeded and diced
3	green onions, sliced
1	cup sliced fresh mushrooms
2	cloves fresh garlic, minced
1/8	teaspoon ground black pepper
1/4	cup chopped fresh basil

Heat oven to 300°. Place turkey cutlets between 2 pieces of wax paper. Lightly pound with mallet to tenderize and flatten to 1/4-inch-thick. Add oil to large hot skillet. Sauté turkey cutlets 4 minutes on each side or until cooked through. Do not over cook.

Remove turkey to warm platter. Deglaze pan with vermouth. Reduce by half. Add tomatoes, green onions, mushroom, garlic and pepper. Simmer 5 minutes. Add basil. Stir 1 minute.

Pour sauce over turkey. Bake 10 minutes. Serve over rice or pasta if desired.

Serves 4.

This recipe was contributed by Gary Bedoworth, Director of Food Services at North Memorial Hospital.

Chicken or Turkey Pot Pie with Biscuit Crust

Filling:

3   **cups homemade chicken stock or reduced-sodium canned broth, divided**

2½   **cups diced cooked chicken or turkey breast**

3   **carrots, diced**

2   **medium potatoes, peeled and diced**

2   **stalks celery, diced**

1   **cup chopped onion**

¼   **cup (½ stick) butter**

4   **tablespoons unbleached all-purpose flour**

½   **cup whole milk**

½   **teaspoon dried thyme**

¼   **teaspoon ground nutmeg**

¼   **cup peas, fresh or frozen**

¼   **cup corn kernels, fresh or frozen**

Salt and freshly ground pepper to taste

Crust:

1½   **cups unbleached all-purpose flour**

½   **teaspoon baking powder**

½   **teaspoon baking soda**

¾   **teaspoon salt**

¼   **cup (½ stick) butter**

⅓   **cup grated sharp Cheddar cheese**

1   **egg**

½   **cup buttermilk**

Egg Wash

Heat oven to 425°. Simmer diced chicken, carrots, potatoes, celery and 1 cup chicken broth in large kettle until vegetables are tender. Drain and reserve broth. Set vegetables aside.

Melt butter in large skillet and sauté chopped onion until tender. Slowly stir in flour. Cook and stir for 5 minutes. Stir in milk and 2 cups reserved chicken stock. Bring to boiling. Add thyme and nutmeg. Cook and stir until thickened. Add peas and corn. Taste to adjust seasonings. Add diced chicken, cooked carrots, potatoes and celery. Stir to combine. Turn mixture into 2-quart-casserole dish or deep pie tin. Set aside.

Sift together flour, baking powder, baking soda and salt in large bowl. Cut in butter until dough resembles coarse meal. Toss in grated cheese. In separate bowl, whisk egg with buttermilk. Add to flour mixture. Gently stir to make soft dough. Turn dough out onto lightly floured board. Pat into large round. Cut dough into 2½-inch circles. Arrange biscuits on top of chicken filling. Brush with egg wash.

Place in oven and bake 20 to 25 minutes or until crust is golden brown.

Serves 6 to 8.

To make a shiny crust brush top with egg wash made with 1 egg yolk combined with 1 tablespoon milk.

Making a pot pie is a good way to use leftover chicken or turkey. To make individual pies place chicken filling in single-serving ramekins and top with 1 circle of dough. Shorten cooking time to 15 minutes.

Coq au Vin

1	whole chicken, quartered

Salt and pepper to taste

1	cup all-purpose flour
3	tablespoons vegetable or olive oil
2	strips bacon, chopped
3	stalks celery, coarsely chopped
2	carrots, chopped
1	cup quartered mushrooms
1	large onion, chopped
2	cloves garlic, chopped
2	cups red wine
3	quarts veal or chicken stock
2	tablespoons Herbs de Provence

Heat oven to 300˚. Season chicken with salt and pepper. Dredge in flour. Heat oil in large skillet. Brown chicken. Remove chicken from skillet and set aside. Add bacon and coarsely chopped vegetables, including garlic. Sauté until tender. Add wine, stock and herbs. Simmer for 15 minutes. Place browned chicken in large roasting pan. Cover with vegetable stock mixture. If stock does not cover chicken add more stock or water. Cover roasting pan.

Bake in oven 2 to 3 hours or until chicken is extremely tender. Test by pushing a paring knife to the bone. If it gives very little resistance, it is done. Remove chicken and set aside. Place roasting pan with vegetable stock mixture over medium heat. Simmer until mixture begins to thicken. Add chicken again and simmer for an additional 10 minutes. Serve chicken and ladle sauce over top.

Serves 4.

Owner Michael Morse sent in this popular recipe which is served at his Café Un Deux Trois just down the block from the League.

Honey-Baked Chicken

$\frac{1}{2}$	cup (1 stick) butter, melted
$\frac{1}{2}$	cup honey
$\frac{1}{4}$	cup Dijon mustard
1	teaspoon salt
1	teaspoon ground curry
8	boneless skinless half-chicken breasts

In a small bowl mix first 5 ingredients together early in the day so flavors will blend. Refrigerate. Bring to room temperature before pouring over chicken.

Heat oven to 325˚. Place chicken in 15x9$\frac{1}{2}$-inch shallow baking dish. Cover with sauce and bake uncovered 30 minutes. Turn chicken over and bake an additional 30 minutes basting every 10 minutes.

Serves 6 to 8.

This dish is especially good with any of the couscous recipes found in Pasta, Grains and Vegetarian section.

Tri-Color Chicken Enchiladas

12	**(6-inch) corn tortillas**
1	**cup vegetable oil**
4	**cups shredded fresh Monterey Jack or Colby cheese**
2	**cups shredded cooked chicken**
1	**cup chopped onion**
$1^{1}/_{2}$	**cups sour cream**
$^{1}/_{4}$	**cup cold water**
1	**(12-ounce) jar salsa**
1	**(8-ounce) can tomatillo sauce or salsa verde**

Heat oven to 350°. In small skillet heat oil until hot over medium-high heat. Dip tortillas, one at a time, into hot oil for 30 seconds or until softened. Drain on paper towels. Place tortillas on clean surface. Sprinkle with cheese, chicken and onion. Roll loosely and place in lightly greased 13x9-inch baking pan. Repeat with remaining tortillas.

In medium bowl mix sour cream with $^{1}/_{4}$ cup water or more to thin to desired consistency for pouring. Pour sour cream down center of tortillas in baking dish. Pour red salsa over left side of tortillas and green tomatillo sauce over right side. Bake 20 to 30 minutes until hot and bubbly.

Serves 6.

Gracias to Roberto Flores, owner of La Cucaracha restaurant, for sharing this house specialty which he always serves on Cinco de Mayo, Mexican Independence Day. Red, white and green are the colors of the Mexican flag.

King Ranch Chicken

4	**whole chicken breasts**
1	**cup chicken stock or broth**
2	**cans ($10^{3}/_{4}$-ounce) low-fat cream of mushroom soup**
2	**cans (10-ounce) chopped tomatoes with chilies, i.e. Rotel**
2	**cups low-fat sour cream**
12	**(10-inch) corn tortillas torn into pieces or 12 taco shells**
2	**onions, finely chopped**
1	**bell pepper, finely chopped**
3	**cups grated cheese, Monterey Jack, sharp Cheddar or cook's choice, divided**

Heat oven to 350°. In large saucepan poach chicken in broth. Remove chicken from pan, skin and cut into small pieces. Combine soup, chopped tomatoes and sour cream in large bowl. Grease 13x9-inch casserole. Layer ingredients three times in following order: tortillas or tacos, chicken, soup mixture, onions, peppers and cheese. Reserve $^{3}/_{4}$ cup cheese for topping. Bake 45 minutes.

Serves 8 to 10.

Chicken Piccata

8	boneless skinless half-chicken breasts, pounded to ½-inch thickness
½	cup all-purpose flour mixed with salt and pepper for dredging
2	tablespoons olive oil or clarified butter for sautéing
1	tablespoon minced shallots
2	tablespoons capers
2	tablespoons chopped parsley
¼	cup dry white wine
¼	cup lemon juice

Salt and pepper to taste

3	tablespoons unsalted butter

Dredge chicken in flour. In large skillet sauté chicken in 1½ tablespoons butter or oil 2 to 3 minutes each side over moderate heat. Juices should run clear. Do not overcook. Remove to serving platter and keep warm. Reduce heat. Add remaining butter or oil.

Sauté shallots briefly being careful not to brown or burn. Add capers, parsley, white wine, lemon juice, salt and pepper. This dish will not require a lot of salt because capers are salty. Reduce liquid until almost evaporated. Remove from heat and swirl in unsalted butter. Taste sauce for seasoning. Pour over chicken breasts and serve immediately. This recipe works equally well with veal scaloppini.

Serves 4.

Chef Richard Thomas of The Creamery Restaurant in Downsville, WI, contributed this often requested entree.

Grand Slam Chicken

4	boneless skinless chicken breasts
½	cup mayonnaise
½	cup sour cream
2	tablespoons chutney, Mango or cook's choice
1	teaspoon ground curry

Juice of 1 lemon

Pepper to taste

Heat oven to 450°. Place chicken in shallow 9-inch baking dish. Combine all remaining ingredients and pour over chicken. Bake uncovered 12 to 15 minutes. May also be baked covered 45 to 60 minutes at 350°.

May be made ahead and refrigerated. Pour sauce over chicken just before baking.

Serves 4.

This recipe has been a favorite with this contributor's bridge club since 1962.

Grilled Turkey Breast

1	**whole turkey breast**
2	**cups white wine, Chablis or Sauterne**
1	**cup soy sauce**
1	**cup vegetable oil**
½	**teaspoon garlic powder**
½	**teaspoon MSG (i.e. Accent)**

Combine wine, soy sauce, vegetable oil, garlic powder and Accent in medium bowl. Place turkey breast and marinade in heavy sealed plastic bag. Marinate breast at least 2 and up to 24 hours, turning bag occasionally.

Prepare grill. Place breast in foil pan. Cover loosely with foil. Baste occasionally with marinade. Cook 1½ to 2 hours or until meat thermometer registers 170°. Uncover during last 15 minutes. Turkey may also be roasted in 350° oven.

Serves 6 to 8.

Roast Pheasant with Lemon and Cream

1	**cup all-purpose flour**
½	**teaspoon paprika**
½	**teaspoon salt**
2	**pheasants, cleaned and cut up**
2	**tablespoons vegetable oil or shortening for browning**
2	**tablespoons chopped onion**
1	**lemon, sliced thinly, seeds removed**
1	**cup chicken stock or broth**
1	**cup cream**

Heat oven to 350°. In shallow dish combine flour, paprika and salt. Dredge pheasant pieces in flour mixture and brown in oil or shortening in large skillet. Transfer pheasant to roaster. Add chopped onion, lemon slices and enough stock or broth to cover pheasant pieces.

Bake covered 1 to 1½ hours until tender. Add cream. Return to oven uncovered another 15 minutes.

Serves 4 to 6.

In 1981-83, the League of Catholic Women donated start-up costs and volunteer assistance for **Ascension House** in north Minneapolis. Here women who are victims of domestic abuse can find a safe haven.

Pheasant With Mushrooms

3	pheasants, prepared for cooking and split
$3/4$	cup ($1^1/2$ sticks) butter
3	cups sliced mushrooms
1	cup dry white wine
3	tablespoons lemon juice
$3/4$	cup chopped green onions
1	teaspoon salt

Freshly ground black pepper to taste

In large skillet sauté each pheasant in butter 10 minutes on each side until lightly browned. Remove pheasants. Sauté mushrooms in same skillet until golden brown. Remove mushrooms. Return pheasants to skillet. Spoon mushrooms over pheasants. Add wine, lemon juice, onions, salt and pepper. Cover and simmer 1 to $1^1/2$ hours or until tender.

May deglaze pan with a bit of white wine. Add $1/2$ cup of chicken broth to deglazed pan if a little sauce is desired.

Serves 6.

Ducks with Sauerkraut

4	wild ducks, prepared for cooking

Salt and pepper to taste

2	Granny Smith apples, halved
2	oranges, halved
12	slices good quality bacon, diced
2-4	fresh or frozen chicken giblets, diced
1	large onion, chopped
4	cloves garlic, chopped
1	package (32-ounce) refrigerated sauerkraut
1	(28-ounce) can tomatoes
10-15	juniper berries, crushed
1	teaspoon caraway seed
$1/4$	cup sugar
$1^1/2$	cups dark beer or ale

Heat oven to 350°. Rinse ducks inside and out. Pat dry. Salt and pepper inside and out. Place $1/2$ unpeeled apple and $1/2$ unpeeled orange inside each duck. In large skillet, sauté bacon, chicken giblets and onion. Add garlic, sauerkraut, tomatoes, juniper berries, caraway seed, sugar and beer. Stir well. Simmer about 15 minutes.

Place ducks on rack in roasting pan. Roast in oven 30 minutes until lightly browned. Remove from oven and spread sauerkraut mixture over ducks. Reduce oven temperature to 325°. Cover and bake about $2^1/2$ hours more.

Serves 4 to 6.

Good accompanied by Horseradish Mashed Potatoes found in the Vegetables section.

Honey Wild Duck

3	**ducks, prepared for cooking**
1	**teaspoon dried basil**
1	**teaspoon ground ginger**
1	**teaspoon salt**
2	**oranges, cut in half**
2	**cups water**
1	**cup honey**
1	**cup (2 sticks) butter**
1	**teaspoon lemon juice**
$1/2$	**cup undiluted orange juice concentrate**

Sauce:

6	**tablespoons currant jelly**
2	**tablespoons sugar**
2	**tablespoons grated orange rind**
2	**tablespoons orange juice**
2	**tablespoons red wine**
2	**tablespoons lemon juice**
$1/4$	**teaspoon salt**
$1/4$	**teaspoon pepper**

Heat oven to 350˚. Mix together basil, ginger and salt in small bowl. Sprinkle mixture inside and outside ducks. Place $1/2$ unpeeled orange in each duck. Lay ducks breast side up in roasting pan. Add 2 cups water.

In small saucepan mix together honey, butter, lemon juice and orange juice concentrate. Simmer until syrupy. Pour $1/2$ over ducks. Save remainder for basting.

Cover roaster and bake $1/2$ hour. Reduce heat to 300˚ and turn ducks so breasts are down. Roast $2^1/2$ hours basting frequently. When ducks are tender turn breast side up and brown for an additional 10 to 15 minutes.

Blend first 3 sauce ingredients in a blender or food processor for 5 minutes. Add last 5 ingredients, mix well and serve at room temperature with duck.

Serves 6.

This recipe was developed to serve hunters on a wild game farm.

At the request of Catholic Charities, the League of Catholic Women opened a **Boys Group Home** in 1969. The operating procedure followed that of the Girls Group Home, Hennepin County Social Services providing per diem funding, Catholic Charities providing staffing and the LCW purchasing the property and providing management and volunteer services.

Braised Lamb Shanks with Caramelized Onions and Shallots

4	tablespoons olive oil, divided
1	pound onions, sliced
5	large shallots, sliced, about 1 cup
2	tablespoons chopped fresh rosemary or 2 teaspoons dried

Salt and pepper to taste

6	($^3/_4$ to 1 pound) lamb shanks
3	tablespoons all-purpose flour or enough to coat lamb shanks
2$^1/_2$	cups dry red wine, divided
2$^1/_2$	cups canned beef broth
1$^1/_2$	tablespoons tomato paste
2	bay leaves

Heat 2 tablespoons olive oil in large heavy Dutch oven over medium-high heat. Add sliced onions and shallots. Sauté about 20 to 25 minutes until brown. Mix in rosemary. Remove from heat.

Sprinkle lamb shanks with salt and pepper. Coat with flour. Heat remaining 2 tablespoons olive oil in large heavy skillet over high heat. Working in batches add lamb shanks to skillet and cook about 10 minutes until brown on both sides. Using tongs transfer lamb shanks to platter. Add 1 cup red wine to skillet. Bring to boiling, scraping up browned bits. Pour into Dutch oven along with onion mixture. Add remaining 1$^1/_2$ cups red wine, beef broth, tomato paste and bay leaves. Bring to boiling, stirring until tomato paste dissolves. Add lamb shanks turning to coat with liquid. Bring mixture to boiling again. Reduce heat. Cover and simmer about 1$^1/_2$ hours until lamb is almost tender turning lamb shanks occasionally. May be prepared 1 day ahead. Cover and refrigerate.

Uncover Dutch oven. Boil shanks and liquid about 30 minutes until liquid is reduced to sauce consistency. Stir and turn shanks occasionally. Season with salt and pepper. Sprinkle with additional fresh rosemary and serve. Good served with mashed potatoes or noodles.

Serves 6.

Grilled Hoisin-Marinated Butterflied Leg of Lamb

1/3	cup hoisin sauce
3	tablespoons rice vinegar, not seasoned variety
2	tablespoons soy sauce
2	tablespoons minced garlic
1/4	cup minced scallions
1	tablespoon honey
1/2	teaspoon salt
1	(7-pound) whole leg of lamb, trimmed, boned and butterflied or 5 pounds boneless

Scallion brushes for garnish

In small bowl whisk together hoisin sauce, vinegar, soy sauce, garlic, minced scallions, honey and salt.

Trim as much fat as possible from lamb. Place lamb in shallow dish large enough to hold lamb flat. Spread marinade over lamb. Cover and refrigerate 4 to 24 hours.

Bring lamb to room temperature. Prepare grill. Place lamb on oiled rack set 5 or 6 inches over glowing coals. Grill 12 to 15 minutes on each side or until meat thermometer registers 140° for medium-rare meat. Lamb may also be broiled under preheated broiler about 4 inches from heat for approximately the same time. Transfer lamb to cutting board and let stand 20 minutes before carving.

Holding sharp knife at a 45° angle cut lamb across grain into thin slices. Garnish with scallion brushes.

Serves 4 to 6.

Nice served with eggplant, brushed with olive oil and grilled.

To make scallion brushes, trim roots and green parts from scallions, leaving about 2 1/2 inch stalks. Make 1/2 inch lengthwise cuts at both ends of stalks and spread fringed ends gently. Put scallions in a bowl of ice cold water. Dry and use as a garnish.

In 1986, the League of Catholic Women commissioned Michael Joncas to compose a hymn in honor of its 75th Anniversary. "No Greater Love" had its first performance at the LCW Anniversary Mass at St. Olaf Catholic Church. It is now sung in many parishes nationwide.

Rack of Lamb

2¼ **pounds rack of lamb, prepared for roasting by butcher**

¼ **cup chopped fresh parsley, divided**

1 **tablespoon snipped fresh rosemary or ½ teaspoon dried crushed rosemary**

1 **teaspoon salt**

4 **tablespoons (½ stick) butter, melted**

2 **cloves garlic, minced**

1 **tablespoon Dijon mustard**

½ **cup toasted bread crumbs**

Heat oven to 475°. Place rack of lamb in shallow roasting pan. Combine 1 tablespoon chopped parsley, rosemary and salt in small bowl. Rub mixture on all surfaces of lamb. In a separate bowl, combine remaining parsley, melted butter, garlic, Dijon mustard and bread crumbs. Press crumb mixture onto all sides of lamb.

Roast rack 12 to 14 minutes at 475°. Reduce heat to 400° and roast about 15 minutes more or until meat thermometer registers 135° for rare or 150° for medium.

Serves 4.

Marinated Flank Steak

1 **(1 to 3-pound) flank steak**

Marinade:

½ **cup soy sauce**

½ **cup water**

2 **tablespoons lemon juice**

1 **tablespoon brown sugar**

¼ **teaspoon Tabasco sauce**

1 **clove garlic, crushed**

¼ **teaspoon freshly ground pepper**

Place flank steak in heavy plastic bag. Shake marinade ingredients together in tightly covered container. Pour marinade over steak. Seal bag tightly and refrigerate. Marinate 24 hours, turning bag occasionally. Prepare grill. Grill steak to desired doneness, about 8 minutes per side for medium-rare. Slice on the diagonal into thin strips.

Serves 4 to 6.

Stuffed Leg of Lamb with Currant Jelly Sauce

1	**(6 to 8 pound) leg of lamb, boned leaving 3 inches of shank bone**
1	**teaspoon salt, divided**
1	**teaspoon pepper, divided**
1/4	**pound uncooked veal**
1/4	**pound cooked ham**
1/4	**pound dry bread crumbs**
1/4	**pound fresh mushrooms, finely chopped**
1	**egg**
1	**small clove garlic, crushed**
1	**tablespoon Worcestershire sauce**
1	**tablespoon orange marmalade with rind**
1	**teaspoon dried oregano**

Sauce:

1/2	**cup dry sherry**
1/2	**cup currant jelly**
1/2	**cup ketchup**
1/2	**teaspoon marjoram**

Heat oven to 325°. Wipe lamb with damp paper towel. Season with 1/2 teaspoon salt and pepper. In large bowl, combine veal, ham, crumbs, mushrooms, egg, garlic, Worcestershire sauce, marmalade, remaining salt, pepper and oregano. Mix well. Pack into cavity left by removal of the leg bone. Close opening securely with skewers.

Place lamb fat side up on rack in roasting pan. Roast about 30 minutes per pound until desired doneness.

Combine sauce ingredients in small saucepan. Stir over medium heat until jelly melts and mixture is combined. Use some as a marinade to brush lamb during last hour of cooking. Remove lamb. Combine remaining sauce with juices from roasting pan, stirring until sauce thickens. Serve with lamb.

Serves 10 to 12.

During its 90 year history, the LCW has opened its Downtown Center to many service organizations such as the Sisters of the Good Shepherd, who used the League rooms to counsel former residents. The Center has also played host to dances for adults with mental disabilities and many other organizations. The Little Brothers of the Poor continue to use the LCW as a venue for their special holiday dinners three times a year.

Sautéed Veal Slices with Leeks and Cream

8	veal scallopini slices, about 1¼ pounds
3	tablespoons all-purpose flour
2	tablespoons butter or margarine

1-2 medium leeks, cleaned and white parts only cut into julienne strips

½	cup white wine
⅔	cup cream or gourmet nonfat half-and-half

Salt and pepper to taste

1	pint red raspberries

Pound veal to ⅓-inch thickness. Dredge slices in flour. In medium skillet cook veal in melted butter over medium heat about 6 minutes or until browned and cooked through, turning once. Transfer veal to platter and keep warm.

Add trimmed leeks to skillet. Cook 30 seconds over medium heat. Add wine. Cook about 1 minute over high heat to reduce by half. Add cream slowly using a whisk so it will not curdle. Add salt and pepper. Simmer 5 minutes. Return veal slices to pan for 5 minutes to warm. Spoon sauce over veal slices. Garnish with 8 to 10 raspberries on each veal slice.

Serves 4.

Veal with Brie and Basil

6	veal scaloppini slices, about 1½ pound total
⅓	cup all-purpose flour
1	teaspoon salt
3	tablespoons butter
6	ounces Brie, rind removed
6	large leaves fresh basil, more if small
½	cup water, white wine or chicken broth
¼	teaspoon paprika

Heat oven to 400°. Pound veal to ⅓-inch thick. Mix flour with 1 teaspoon salt in shallow dish. Coat veal with flour mixture. May cover and refrigerate for up to 4 hours at this point. Melt 3 tablespoons butter in large skillet. Cook veal pieces no more than 1 to 2 minutes per side over medium-high heat. Add more butter as needed. Remove from skillet and transfer to ovenproof pan. Place 1 or 2 fresh basil leaves on each veal slice. Top with 6 thin slices of Brie or enough to completely cover veal. Sprinkle with paprika. Bake 5 minutes or until Brie starts to melt.

Do not to overcook veal when cooking or meat will become tough.

Serves 6.

Chicken breasts, pounded thin, make an excellent substitute for veal.

Osso Buco

6	meaty pieces veal hind-shank
$1/4$	cup all-purpose flour seasoned with salt and pepper
$1/4$	cup olive oil, divided
$1/4$	cup ($1/2$ stick) unsalted butter, divided
1	large onion, finely chopped
1	stalk celery, chopped
2	carrots, thinly sliced
6	garlic cloves, minced
1	cup dry white wine
2	cups chicken broth
1	(28-ounce) can Italian pear tomatoes, drained and chopped
$1/2$	teaspoon dried marjoram
$1/2$	teaspoon dried basil
$1/2$	teaspoon dried oregano
$1/4$	cup finely chopped parsley
1	tablespoon finely chopped lemon peel
1	teaspoon finely chopped orange peel
1	clove garlic, minced

Salt and pepper to taste

Heat oven to 325°. Dredge veal shanks in seasoned flour. In heavy skillet brown shanks in oil and butter on all sides over medium-high heat. Use $1/2$ oil and butter for first 3 shanks, remainder for last 3 shanks. Drain shanks on paper towels. In same pan sauté onion, celery, carrots and garlic until golden brown, about 10 minutes.

Transfer vegetables to large roasting pan. Top with veal shanks. Add white wine, chicken broth, tomatoes and the 3 spices. Cover and slowly simmer in oven $1^1/4$ to $1^1/2$ hours or until veal is fork tender.

Recipe may be prepared to this point, refrigerated up to 24 hours and reheated gently before continuing.

When shanks are cooked remove from broth. Place in shallow roasting pan. Increase oven temperature to 450°. Bake in oven for 5 to 10 minutes to finish.

Bring broth to a boil over high heat. Skim fat and thick foam from center as liquid boils. Reduce by half. Remove from heat. Stir in parsley, lemon, orange peel and garlic. Add salt and pepper to taste. Serve gravy over shanks.

Serves 6.

Veal Forestier

1½ **pounds thin (¼-inch) veal steak or cutlets**

1 **clove garlic, cut in half**

3 **tablespoons flour for dredging**

½ **cup (1 stick) butter**

½ **pound mushrooms, thinly sliced**

Salt and pepper to taste

⅓ **cup dry vermouth**

1 **teaspoon fresh lemon juice**

Snipped parsley for garnish

Cut thin veal into 2-inch strips. Rub both sides of veal with cut garlic clove. Sprinkle with flour. In large skillet sauté several pieces at a time in hot butter until golden brown on both sides. Heap sliced mushrooms on top of veal pieces in the skillet. Sprinkle with salt, pepper and vermouth.

Cook covered over low-heat about 15 minutes until veal is fork tender. Do not overcook. Check once or twice to see that veal remains moist, adding one tablespoon or so water if needed. Uncover. Sprinkle with lemon juice and parsley and serve. Excellent served with wild rice.

Serves 4 to 6.

Chinese Lamb With Walnuts

8 **lamb or pork chops**

1 **tablespoon all-purpose flour**

4 **tablespoons oil, divided**

2 **large onions, sliced**

1 **large clove garlic, chopped**

1½ **cups pineapple juice**

¼ **cup tomato puree**

3 **tablespoons vinegar**

2 **tablespoons soy sauce**

Coarsely ground pepper to taste

1½ **teaspoons brown sugar**

½ **teaspoon curry powder**

4 **thin strips lemon peel**

½-¾ **cup chopped walnuts**

Heat oven to 350°. Dredge chops with flour and brown in 2 tablespoons oil. Place chops in 3-quart casserole. Sauté onion and garlic in remaining 2 tablespoons oil until golden. Add all other ingredients except walnuts. Simmer 5 minutes. Pour over chops in casserole. Add walnuts. Cover and bake approximately 50 minutes to 1 hour.

Serves 4.

Monterey Casserole

2   pounds lean ground beef

1   onion, chopped

1   (1.25-ounce) package taco seasoning mix

1   cup water

1   cup bottled taco sauce, divided

10   (8-inch) flour tortillas

2   (10-ounce) packages frozen, chopped spinach, cooked, drained and divided

3   cups shredded Monterey Jack cheese, divided

1$\frac{1}{2}$-2 cups diced cooked ham

1   cup sour cream

Heat oven to 375°. In large skillet brown beef with onion. Stir in taco seasoning mix and water. Combine well. Cover and simmer about 10 minutes. In bottom of 3-quart greased casserole container layer 5 tortillas which have been brushed with taco sauce. Stir half of spinach into beef mixture. Spoon over tortillas. Sprinkle with half the shredded cheese. Top with remaining tortillas. Pour remaining taco sauce over tortillas. Sprinkle diced ham on top. Spread sour cream over ham. Scatter remaining spinach over sour cream. Top with remaining cheese.

Bake covered 25 minutes. Uncover and bake another 25 minutes.

Serves 8 to 10.

Buffet Barbecued Beef

1   (3 to 4 pound) chuck roast

1   medium onion, sliced

1   teaspoon celery salt

$\frac{1}{2}$ teaspoon hot pepper sauce

1   teaspoon Worcestershire sauce

$\frac{1}{2}$ teaspoon garlic juice or $\frac{1}{4}$ teaspoon garlic powder

1   tablespoon chili powder

1   cup water

1   (14-ounce) bottle ketchup

$\frac{1}{3}$ cup brown sugar

Heat oven to 250°. Place beef in roaster. Combine remaining ingredients and pour over meat. Bake covered 6 hours. Remove from oven. Pull meat into pieces, do not shred. Stir. Serve on buns.

Serves 16.

Cornish Pasties

4	refrigerated ready made pie crusts
3	medium potatoes, sliced $1/4$-inch-thick and quartered
3	medium carrots, thinly sliced
1	large rutabaga, thinly sliced and quartered
2	large yellow onions, coarsely chopped
2	cups frozen peas, thawed, drained and rinsed under running hot water
3	cups sirloin or top round steak, cut into $1/2$-inch cubes
2	teaspoons dried sage leaves
2	teaspoons bouquet garni
5	tablespoons tomato paste
1	egg yolk lightly beaten with 2 tablespoons water

Heat oven to 450°. Lay pie crusts on flat surface. Combine potatoes, carrots, rutabaga, onions, peas, beef, herbs and tomato paste in large bowl. Toss gently to mix. Fill $1/2$ of each crust with $1/4$ beef mixture. Moisten edge of $1/2$ crust with egg wash. Fold over pie crust and crimp edge using fork tines to insure that mixture does not leak out while baking.

Place on lightly greased baking sheet. Lightly brush top of each pasty with egg wash. Bake 15 minutes. Reduce oven temperature to 350°. Bake another 45 minutes until golden brown. Serve immediately.

Serves 4.

This contributor's grandmother used to prepare a simplified version of pasties as a lunch for her grandfather who worked in the mines. They emigrated from County Cork and eventually ended up on the Iron Range. Pasties were prepared early in the morning, wrapped in newspapers and placed in the miners' lunch pails to be eaten on the job. Contemporary palates prefer a little more spice which this recipe provides.

Paul & Dick Wrazidlo, owners of Olde World Meats in Duluth, a place famous for its pasties, suggest making your own piecrust, substituting cream cheese for shortening. That is their secret to success!

In 1989, Minnesota Governor, Rudy Perpich, declared August 16 " **League of Catholic Women Day.**" During that year WCCO also honored a LCW volunteer with a "Good Neighbor Award " and President Bush sent commendations to eight League members for doing outstanding community service through LCW projects.

Tenderloin Deluxe

2	pounds beef tenderloin
4	tablespoons butter or margarine, softened and divided
1/4	cup chopped green onion
2	tablespoons soy sauce
1	teaspoon Dijon mustard
1/8	teaspoon freshly ground pepper
3/4	cup dry sherry

Heat oven to 400°. Rub tenderloin with 2 tablespoons softened butter or margarine. Place on rack in shallow baking pan. Bake uncovered 20 minutes.

In small saucepan cook green onions in remaining 2 tablespoons butter or margarine until tender. Add soy sauce, mustard, and pepper. Stir in sherry. Heat just to boiling. Pour over tenderloin. Bake 20 to 25 minutes more for rare to medium-rare beef. Baste frequently with sauce. Pass remaining wine sauce.

Serves 4 to 6.

Excellent as a main course or in cocktail buns for a buffet. Contributor recommends using a meat thermometer to assure desired doneness.

Italian Meat Balls

1	pound lean ground beef
1	cup fine dry bread crumbs or crushed saltines
1/4	cup grated Parmesan cheese, fresh or packaged
1/4	cup grated Romano cheese, fresh or packaged
1	tablespoon fresh minced parsley or 1 teaspoon dried
1/4	teaspoon garlic powder or 1 clove garlic, minced
1/2	cup whole or low-fat milk
2	eggs or Egg Beaters, beaten
1 1/2	teaspoons salt
1/8	teaspoon pepper
1	tablespoon olive oil
2	cups marinara sauce, homemade or bottled

Mix all ingredients together in large bowl. Shape into 1-inch balls. In large skillet brown meatballs on all sides in oil. Add to marinara sauce. Heat 20 minutes Serve over pasta.

Serves 6 to 8.

May be prepared in advance. Place uncooked meat balls on cookie sheet and freeze. When frozen remove and place in freezer bag for future use.

Hawaiian Beef

2	pounds boneless chuck, cut into $\frac{1}{2}$-inch cubes
2	tablespoons olive oil
2	cups beef broth
2	ounces good quality sherry
1	cup ketchup
$\frac{1}{2}$	cup brown sugar, packed
1	bay leaf
1	tablespoon Worcestershire sauce
$\frac{1}{4}$	cup sliced fresh mushrooms
1	clove garlic, minced
2	tablespoons wine vinegar
$\frac{1}{4}$	cup raisins
1	onion, chopped
1	teaspoon curry powder
1	tablespoon cornstarch, optional

Toppings:

3	slices bacon, cooked crisp and crumbled
1	small can (3.25-ounce) Macadamia nuts, chopped
3	green onions, chopped
$\frac{1}{2}$	cup shredded coconut

Heat oven to 400˚. Place beef and oil in roaster. Braise beef in oven 30 minutes. Remove from oven and drain. Add beef broth and sherry. Reduce oven temperature to 325˚. Simmer beef uncovered in oven 1 hour. Add ketchup, brown sugar, bay leaf, Worcestershire sauce, mushrooms, garlic, vinegar, raisins, onion and curry powder. Simmer another 30 minutes or until very tender. Thicken with 1 tablespoon cornstarch or more to desired thickness or continue to cook until beef mixture thickens on its own. Add beef and mix well.

Serve over brown or white rice if desired. Top 6 servings with a portion of each of the topping condiments or let guests help themselves to their choice of toppings.

Serves 6.

From 1922 until 1937, the League of Catholic Women operated a **Tea Room**, later converted into a **Lunchroom**, where working women could meet one another, socialize and enjoy an inexpensive meal.

Sloppy Josés

³/₄	pound lean ground beef
¹/₂	(15-ounce) can refried beans
¹/₂	cup salsa
1	(4¹/₂-ounce) can diced green chili peppers
1	small onion, chopped
¹/₄	cup beer
1	clove garlic, minced
¹/₂	teaspoon ground chili powder
6	hamburger buns, split and toasted

In large skillet brown beef, breaking meat into small pieces as it cooks. Drain fat. Stir in refried beans, salsa, chili peppers, chopped onion, beer, garlic and chili powder. Bring mixture to boil. Reduce heat. Simmer uncovered 10 to 15 minutes or until mixture reaches desired consistency. Spoon mixture into toasted buns and serve warm.

Serves 6.

Try this updated version of a "meal in a bun" popular in the 1960's. Sloppy Joes were often served to the young adults who gathered at the League for Chi Rho Club.

Hawaiian Bar-B-Q Ribs

2	pounds thick-cut beef or pork country ribs
1	lemon, halved
1	medium onion, chopped
¹/₂	cup ketchup
1	(20-ounce) can pineapple tidbits
1¹/₂	tablespoons Worcestershire sauce
¹/₂	teaspoon salt
¹/₂	cup water

Heat oven to 425°. Season ribs with salt and place in 13x9-inch baking pan. Arrange lemon slices over ribs. Roast 30 minutes. Combine remaining ingredients. Pour over ribs. Reduce heat to 350°. Bake 2 more hours, basting every 15 to 30 minutes.

Serves 4.

Pork Tenderloin Stroganoff

2	**tablespoons olive oil**
1	**tablespoon lemon juice**
$^1/_4$	**teaspoon lemon pepper**
1	**clove garlic, minced**
$1^1/_2$	**pounds pork tenderloin, cut into small pieces**
$^1/_4$	**cup ($^1/_2$ stick) butter**
1	**onion, finely chopped**
$^1/_2$	**pound mushrooms, sliced**
3	**tablespoons dry sherry**
$^1/_2$	**cup half-and-half**

Combine olive oil, lemon juice, lemon pepper and garlic in large bowl. Stir in pork pieces. Marinate 30 minutes.

Melt butter in electric or large heavy skillet. Sauté onion about 5 minutes until tender. Add mushroom slices and sauté until done. Remove vegetables from skillet. Add more butter if needed to sauté pork. Do not drain pork before cooking, the marinade gives the dish extra flavor. When pork is thoroughly cooked, remove from skillet and keep warm. Add sherry to skillet stirring constantly. Add half-and-half, pork and vegetables. Heat gently until sauce has thickened. Serve with white or wild rice or noodles if desired.

Serves 6.

Curried Cider-Braised Pork Chops

$1^1/_2$	**tablespoons butter**
4	**thin boneless pork chops or 2 thick bone-in pork chops**
Salt and pepper to taste	
2	**cups chopped onions**
1	**large stalk celery, chopped**
1	**bay leaf**
1	**tablespoon curry powder**
$1^1/_2$	**cups apple cider**

Melt butter in large skillet over medium heat. Sprinkle pork with salt and pepper. Add pork to skillet. Sauté about 3 minutes per side until browned.

Using tongs transfer pork to plate. Add onions, celery and bay leaf to skillet. Sauté about 6 minutes until onions are golden. Stir in curry powder. Add cider. Boil about 6 minutes until sauce is slightly reduced. Return pork and any accumulated juices to skillet. Simmer about 3 minutes for boneless chops and about 5 minutes for thick bone-in chops until just cooked through. Season with salt and pepper if desired.

Serves 2.

Nice served with noodles tossed with butter and chives.

Festive Pork Chops

6   thick pork chops, excess fat removed

1   tablespoon olive oil

1/2   cup water

1   very large red onion, cut into large pieces

3   stalks celery, cut into large pieces

2   large green bell peppers, cut into large pieces

2   cloves garlic, minced

1   cup tomato soup

1/2   cup sweet vermouth

Salt and pepper to taste

In large heavy skillet with high sides brown pork chops on both sides in olive oil. Add water, onions, celery, peppers and garlic. Cover pan. Simmer slowly for 1 hour. Add tomato soup. Cover and simmer meat and vegetables 20 minutes. Add sweet vermouth. Cover and simmer about 20 minutes. Chops may also be baked covered in 300˚ oven. When meat can be cut away from the bone with a fork, pork chops are ready to serve.

Serves 4 to 6.

This recipe, with its slightly southern flavoring, comes from Archbishop Harry Flynn, currently presiding over the diocese of St. Paul-Minneapolis, but formerly Bishop of Lafayette, Louisiana. He adds this comment, "The secret to this recipe is to simmer very, very slowly. If you are familiar with Cahchere Seasoning, add a couple of shakes."

Chinese Barbecued Pork

2   whole pork tenderloins, 1 1/2 pounds each

2   tablespoons light soy sauce

2   tablespoons hoisin sauce

1   tablespoon sherry

1   tablespoon black bean sauce

1 1/2 teaspoons minced fresh gingerroot

1 1/2 teaspoons packed brown sugar

1   clove garlic, minced

1/2   teaspoon sesame oil

1/8   teaspoon five spice powder

Trim fat from tenderloins. Tuck thin ends under and tie. Place in shallow 13x9-inch glass baking dish. Whisk together remaining ingredients for marinade. Pour marinade over tenderloins turning to coat. Cover and refrigerate 2 to 24 hours turning occasionally. Let stand 30 minutes at room temperature before cooking.

Heat oven to 375˚. Place tenderloins on rack in roasting pan reserve marinade. Pour 1 cup water into pan. Bake 30 to 35 minutes basting generously four times. Meat thermometer should register 160˚ and meat should still have a hint of pink. Remove to cutting board and tent with foil. Let rest for 10 minutes. Cut diagonally into thin slices.

Serves 6.

Equally delicious served with Chinese noodles and pea pods or on buns as a more casual meal.

Honey-Gingered Pork Tenderloin

2	whole pork tenderloins, ³/₄ pound each
¹/₄	cup honey
¹/₄	cup soy sauce
2	tablespoons packed brown sugar
1	tablespoon plus 1 teaspoon fresh minced gingerroot
1	tablespoon minced garlic
1	tablespoon ketchup
¹/₄	teaspoon onion powder
¹/₄	teaspoon ground cayenne pepper
¹/₄	teaspoon ground cinnamon

Parsley sprigs for garnish

Pat pork dry and arrange in shallow dish. In medium bowl whisk together all remaining ingredients. Pour marinade over pork. Turn pork to coat well. Refrigerate pork covered for 8 to 24 hours, turning once or twice.

Prepare grill. Remove pork from marinade reserve marinade. Arrange on lightly oiled rack set 5 to 6 inches over glowing coals.

Grill pork about 10 minutes basting with reserved marinade and turning every 3 minutes. Discard marinade. Continue to cook pork 10 minutes more, turning every 3 minutes or until meat thermometer, diagonally inserted 2 inches into center of tenderloin, registers 155˚. Let pork stand 5 minutes before slicing thinly. Garnish with parsley sprigs.

Serves 4.

Fresh gingerroot may be wrapped and kept in freezer for further use.

Pork Cutlets with Maple, Mustard and Sage Sauce

4	boneless pork loin chops or cutlets
3	teaspoons minced fresh sage or 1 teaspoon dried, divided

Salt and pepper to taste

1	tablespoon butter or margarine
¹/₂	cup canned reduced-sodium chicken broth
1	tablespoon pure maple syrup
1	tablespoon coarse-grained mustard

Place pork between sheets of wax paper and pound to ¹/₃-inch thickness. Sprinkle with 1¹/₂ teaspoons sage, salt and generous amount of pepper. Melt butter or margarine in large heavy skillet over medium-high heat. Add pork. Cook about 1¹/₂ minutes per side until browned and cooked through. Transfer pork to plate leaving drippings in skillet. Add broth, maple syrup, mustard and remaining 1¹/₂ teaspoons sage to skillet. Boil about 3 minutes until syrupy. Scrape up browned bits. Reduce heat to low. Return pork and any accumulated juices to skillet. Cook 1 minute or until just heated through. Serve pork with sauce.

Serves 2 to 4.

Jambalaya

1	cup sliced onions
2	cloves garlic, minced
3/4	cup diced green pepper
3	tablespoons butter or margarine
1	(28-ounce) can tomatoes, coarsely chopped
1/2	cup dry white wine
1	teaspoon salt
1/4	teaspoon Tabasco sauce
1/2	teaspoon dried thyme
1/4	teaspoon dried basil
1/4	teaspoon ground marjoram
1/2	teaspoon paprika
2	cups diced ham or shrimp
1	cup long grained white rice, not Minute Rice
1	cup chopped fresh parsley for garnish

In large skillet sauté onion, garlic and green pepper in butter or margarine until onion is tender and lightly golden. Add tomatoes, wine, salt, Tabasco, herbs and ham or shrimp. Mix well and bring to boiling. May be prepared a day in advance to this point.

Gradually stir rice into prepared mixture in skillet. Cover. Reduce heat and simmer 25 minutes. Pour into serving bowl. Sprinkle lavishly with chopped fresh parsley. Jambalaya may also be poured into ovenproof casserole and baked $1^{1}/_{2}$ hours at 350°.

Serves 6 to 8.

This Jambalaya is a favorite with guests attending the League's special Tuesday Club luncheons for senior citizens.

For one and a half years, following a fire which burned St. Olaf Catholic Church to the ground in 1953, the League of Catholic Women's Downtown Center served as an office for pastor Rev. Leonard Cowley, who later became Bishop Cowley. The League also was used as a site for weekly Masses and confessions.

Grilled Pork Tenderloin

1	(1½ pound) whole pork tenderloin
¾	cup vegetable oil
¼	cup dry white wine or apple juice
4	cloves garlic, minced

Mustard Sauce:

¾	cup dry white wine
3	tablespoons minced shallots
1	cup whipping cream
3	tablespoons Dijon mustard
½	teaspoon Worcestershire sauce

Salt and pepper to taste

Combine oil, wine and garlic in small dish. Place pork and marinade in heavy sealed plastic bag. Refrigerate overnight. Drain pork.

Prepare grill. Grill pork 25 minutes or until meat thermometer registers 155˚. If grill is not available, cook tenderloin in 2 tablespoons oil in large skillet. Turn and brown 10 to 15 minutes.

To prepare sauce bring wine and shallots to a boil in small saucepan. Cook until reduced to about 2 tablespoons. Add cream and bring to boil. Simmer 2 minutes until slightly thickened. Strain through a sieve. Whisk in mustard, Worcestershire, salt and pepper. Cut pork in diagonal slices and serve with mustard sauce.

Serves 4 to 6.

This contributor, a busy mother with young children, has found this pork a wonderfully easy dinner for company, especially since her husband does the grilling!

Hot Ham Buns

¼	cup (½ stick) butter, softened
1-2	tablespoons horseradish
2	tablespoons prepared mustard
2	teaspoons poppy seed
2	tablespoons finely chopped onion
4	hamburger buns
4	thin slices ham
4	slices Swiss cheese

Combine butter, horseradish, mustard, poppy seed and onion in small bowl. Blend well. Spread butter mixture evenly over split bun halves. Place 1 slice ham and 1 cheese slice between bun halves. Wrap each bun securely in foil. May be prepared up to this point and either refrigerated or frozen until ready to use.

Heat oven to 350˚. Wrap buns in foil and bake for 20 minutes.

Serves 4.

Cold Peppery Tenderloin with Creamy Herb Sauce

2 pounds beef tenderloin, at room temperature, trimmed and tied

1 tablespoon coarsely ground black pepper

¾ teaspoon salt

2 tablespoons vegetable oil

Sauce:

1 pasteurized egg yolk

2 tablespoon whipping cream

2 tablespoon white wine vinegar

1 tablespoon Worcestershire sauce

2 teaspoons Dijon mustard

½ cup olive oil

2 teaspoons minced fresh tarragon or ¾ teaspoon dried

1 tablespoon capers, drained

2 tablespoons minced scallions

2 tablespoons minced fresh parsley

Salt to taste

Heat oven to 500°. Pat tenderloin dry and coat all sides with pepper and salt. In ovenproof skillet just large enough to hold meat, heat oil over high heat until hot but not smoking. Place tenderloin in skillet and brown on all sides. Roast tenderloin in oven 15 to 20 minutes or until meat thermometer registers 130°. Do not overcook; check at 10 minutes. Let cool to room temperature. May cover and refrigerate for several hours if desired.

To prepare sauce blend egg yolk, cream, vinegar, Worcestershire sauce and mustard in blender or food processor. While machine is running add oil slowly until the mixture is emulsified. Transfer mixture to small bowl. Stir in tarragon, capers, scallions, parsley and salt.

Slice meat cross-wise into ⅓-inch slices. Arrange slices on platter and spoon sauce over meat.

Serves 4.

Filet of Beef with Gorgonzola Sauce

4	beef filets, 5 to 6 ounces each

Salt and pepper to taste

1	package (about 3½ ounces) enoki mushrooms
3	tablespoons butter, divided
2	tablespoons vegetable oil
1	tablespoon finely chopped shallots
¼	cup port wine
½	cup fresh or canned beef broth
2	tablespoons grated or crumbled Gorgonzola cheese

Season filets with salt and pepper.

Cut off tough ends of mushroom stems. Melt 1 tablespoon butter in small skillet. Add mushrooms. Cook 1 minute or less until heated through. Remove from heat. Set aside.

Heat oil in heavy skillet large enough to hold the filets in 1 layer. Cook filets 3 minutes on one side. Turn the pieces and cook 2 minutes on the other side. Transfer filets to warm platter. Drain off fat from skillet. Add 1 tablespoon butter and shallots to skillet. Cook and stir for 1 minute. Add wine and broth. Stir to incorporate brown particles from bottom and sides of pan. Add cheese. Cook, stirring briskly, until cheese is melted and sauce is reduced to about ½ cup. Line small saucepan with a sieve. Pour sauce into sieve. Press around with rubber spatula to extract as much liquid as possible. Remove sieve. Bring sauce to a simmer. Stir in remaining 1 tablespoon butter.

Spoon sauce over filets and garnish each serving with an equal portion of mushrooms.

Serves 4.

A good quality Gorgonzola cheese (Brocciold di Manzo) is the secret to proper melting.

1993 found the League of Catholic Women answering the call to provide support and R & R for women whose lives are affected directly or indirectly by AIDS. The **AIDS Ministry** plans activities to nourish the bodies and spirits of their clients - picnic lunches, a cruise on the Jonathan Paddleford, a day at a spa or a quiet retreat. Volunteers and participants get together several times a year.

Duxbury Pork Chops

6	cups cubed white bread
6	(1-inch thick) pork chops or 6 large boneless skinless chicken breasts
1	large onion, chopped
1	cup sliced celery
6	tablespoons butter
1	teaspoon bouillon, beef or chicken
1	cup water
$1/2$	cup cranberry-orange relish
$1/2$	cup sliced fresh mushrooms, optional
$1/2$	teaspoon salt
$1/2$	teaspoon dried sage
$1/2$	teaspoon dried thyme
$1/4$	teaspoon pepper

Heat oven to 350°. Place bread cubes in shallow pan. Toast in oven 20 minutes or until golden brown. In medium skillet sauté onion and celery very lightly in butter. Stir in bouillon, water, relish, mushrooms and seasonings. Heat to boiling. Pour over bread cubes and toss. Spoon into lightly greased 13x9-inch pan or casserole. Arrange chops or chicken breasts on top and cover. Bake $1^{1}/_{2}$ hours or until meat is tender.

Serves 6.

For crispier texture, do not sauté onion and celery. Instead add to bread cubes along with melted butter and other ingredients.

In 1916, the Twin City Rapid Transit Company sent 200 tokens per month to "those good women from the League of Catholic Women who travel so many miles by streetcar to accomplish their good works."

Cumin Pork Roast with Wild Mushrooms

1 (3½-pound) center-cut pork loin

Salt and pepper to taste

4 teaspoons ground cumin, divided

3 tablespoons butter, divided

14 ounces oyster mushrooms, halved

½ cup plus 1 tablespoon chopped shallots, divided

2 cloves garlic, minced or to taste

1 tablespoon plus 1 teaspoon finely chopped jalapeno peppers with seeds, divided

2 tablespoons finely chopped fresh cilantro

2 tablespoons finely chopped fresh oregano

1 (14½-ounce) can reduced sodium chicken broth

2 tablespoons all-purpose flour

¼ cup dry sherry

Cilantro sprigs for garnish

Heat oven to 375°. Sprinkle pork with salt and pepper. Rub 3 teaspoons cumin over pork. Place in roasting pan. Roast pork about 50 minutes or until meat thermometer inserted into center registers 150°.

Melt 2 tablespoons butter in large skillet over medium heat. Add mushrooms, ½ cup shallots, garlic and 1 tablespoon jalapenos. Sauté about 15 minutes until mushrooms are tender and beginning to brown. Remove from heat. Add chopped cilantro, oregano and remaining 1 teaspoon cumin. Season with salt and pepper. Set aside.

Transfer pork to platter, tent with foil. Add broth to roasting pan. Scrape up browned bits. Transfer to heavy medium saucepan. In medium bowl gradually whisk flour into sherry. Whisk sherry mixture, remaining tablespoon butter, 1 tablespoon shallots and 1 teaspoon jalapenos into broth. Bring to boil, whisking until smooth. Stir in mushroom mixture and any accumulated juices from pork on platter. Boil until mixture thickens to sauce consistency stirring occasionally. Slice pork. Garnish with cilantro sprigs. Serve pork with sauce.

Serves 8.

A Thanksgiving Prayer

For food that nourishes the body,
For knowledge that nourishes the mind,
For love that nourishes the heart,
For beauty that nourishes the spirit,
Lord, we are grateful.
Lord, we give thanks.

Ruth Johnson

Harvest Table Blessing for League Fall Luncheon

Thank you, Lord, for the abundance of nature;
For the labor of those who plant, harvest and prepare;
For health and appetite to enjoy Thy bounty
And for all who gather around this table.
May this food and fellowship
Give us the strength we need
To carry out your work in the world. Amen.

A Table Blessing for a Wedding or Rehearsal Dinner

Guest at Cana, be our guest.
May our food and wine be blessed.
Join our toasts around the room.
Smile upon this bride and groom.

Come into the life they'll share.
Bless it by your presence there.
Make their home an image of
The new wine of Your gift of love.

Share their joy and celebration.
Accept their wedding invitation.
Stay close to them their whole life through
And bring them one day home to You. Amen.

Mary Ritten

A Breakfast Table Prayer

Father, we thank Thee for the night
And for the pleasant morning light,
For rest and food and loving care
And all that makes the day so fair.

Help us to do the things we should,
To be to others kind and good.
In all we do, in all we say,
To grow more loving every day.

Rebecca J. Weston

Fish & Seafood

Roasted Sea Bass Provencal

1/4	cup chopped oil packed sun-dried tomatoes
2	tablespoons reserved sun-dried tomato oil
2	tablespoons drained capers
1	tablespoon chopped fresh garlic
1	tablespoon minced fresh thyme or 1 1/2 teaspoons dried
1/2	cup dry white wine
1/2	cup bottled clam juice
4	sea bass fillets, 6 to 7 ounces each

Heat oven to 450°. Heat 2 tablespoons reserved oil in heavy large ovenproof skillet over medium high heat. Add tomatoes, capers, garlic and thyme. Stir 1 minute. Add wine and clam juice. Boil about 3 minutes until liquid is reduced almost to a glaze.

Sprinkle fish with salt and pepper. Add to skillet. Turn to coat with sauce. Place skillet in oven. Roast fish 15 minutes until just opaque in center. Transfer fish and sauce to platter or plates.

Serves 4.

Seafood Medley

1/2	green pepper, chopped
1/2	red pepper, chopped
1	cup chopped celery
1	(6 1/2-ounce) can crabmeat
1/2	pound fresh shrimp, cut into small pieces
1	cup mayonnaise
1	cup sliced mushrooms, fresh or canned
1/2	teaspoon salt
1/2	teaspoon Worcestershire sauce
2	tablespoons butter, melted
1	cup crushed saltine crackers

Heat oven to 350°. Combine all ingredients except butter and cracker crumbs in large bowl. Place in lightly greased 2-quart casserole. Mix cracker crumbs with melted butter. Sprinkle buttered crumbs on top of casserole. Cover and refrigerate up to 6 hours if desired. Remove cover from casserole. Bake 30 minutes or until browned and bubbly.

Serves 6.

This recipe comes from the kitchen of a first-generation League member who often served it to her family of twelve on meatless Fridays before Vatican II. She must have doubled or tripled it!

Salmon Rolls

1	**(8-ounce) salmon fillet**
1	**large dill pickle**
1-2	**tablespoons regular or low-fat mayonnaise**
1	**tablespoon tarragon vinegar**
$1/4$	**teaspoon ground cayenne pepper**

Salt and pepper to taste

6	**crisp French rolls, buttered**
1	**cup chopped lettuce or watercress**

Poach salmon in large deep skillet about 10 minutes until done. Chill. Place chilled salmon in blender with dill pickle and enough mayonnaise to mix into thick paste. Season with tarragon wine vinegar, cayenne and salt and pepper to taste. Cut tops from 6 crisp French rolls. Remove part of soft center and butter the remaining crust. Fill with salmon paste and cover with layer of chopped lettuce or watercress. Replace roll top.

Serves 6.

Delightful and unusual luncheon or picnic fare.

Salmon with Lime and Fresh Ginger

4	**medium carrots, cut in julienne strips**
4	**medium leeks, cut in julienne strips**
4	**stalks of celery, cut in julienne strips**
4	**(6-ounce) salmon fillets**
4	**(8x12-inch) pieces of parchment**
4	**tablespoons black olive puree or canned black olives pureed in blender until smooth**
$1/4$	**cup peeled, seeded and diced tomatoes**
4	**teaspoons grated fresh gingerroot**
4	**tablespoons chopped fresh basil**
4	**teaspoons lime juice**

Preheat oven to 400°. Blanch all vegetables together by dropping in boiling water. Remove when water returns to boiling. Place each salmon fillet in center of one piece of parchment. Spread 1 tablespoon olive puree over each. Top puree with some of vegetables, tomatoes, ginger, basil and lime juice.

Fold top long side of parchment over fish and pinch together with bottom long end to seal. Pick up each short end and tuck underneath. Bake approximately 15 minutes. Just before serving, make small slit in packet. Serve with dollop of plain yogurt.

Serves 6.

Baked Halibut with Paprika, Olives and Mushrooms

4	**(8-ounce) halibut fillets or other firm white fish, 1-inch thick**

Vegetable oil for spraying

4	**teaspoons fresh lemon juice**

Salt and pepper to taste

2	**tablespoons olive oil**
1	**onion, chopped**
$\frac{1}{2}$	**pound mushrooms, chopped**
1	**red bell pepper, chopped**
12	**pimiento stuffed green olives, chopped**

1-1$\frac{1}{2}$ teaspoons hot paprika

Heat oven to 375°. Spray 10-inch baking dish with vegetable oil. Place fillets in baking dish. Sprinkle lemon juice over fillets. Season with salt and pepper.

Heat oil in medium nonstick skillet over medium-high heat. Add onion, mushrooms and bell pepper. Sauté about 6 minutes until crisp tender. Add olives and paprika. Stir about 1 minute until fragrant. Season to taste with salt and pepper.

Spread vegetable mixture over fillets. Bake uncovered 20 minutes until fillets are cooked through.

Serves 4.

Coquilles Saint-Jacques a la Bretonne

12	**large sea scallops**
$\frac{1}{2}$	**cup (1 stick) butter, melted and divided**
1	**small clove garlic, crushed**
1	**small shallot, minced**
1	**tablespoon chopped fresh parsley**
$\frac{1}{4}$	**cup fine dried bread crumbs, homemade or packaged**

Salt and pepper to taste

1	**tablespoon lemon juice**
$\frac{1}{2}$	**teaspoon paprika**

Heat oven to 425°. Wash and pat dry scallops. Cut scallops in half. Spoon a little melted butter into bottom of 4 gratin dishes or ovenproof shell-shaped dishes. In small bowl, combine garlic, shallots, parsley, bread crumbs and seasonings to taste. Sprinkle a little of this mixture in each dish.

Divide scallops evenly between gratin dishes. Cover with remaining bread crumb mixture. Drizzle with rest of butter. Add a dash of lemon juice to each. Sprinkle with paprika. Place on baking sheet and bake 12 to 15 minutes until scallops turn white and top is slightly browned. Cool slightly before serving.

Serves 4.

Greenbrier Shrimp with Red Sauce

Red Sauce:

1/2	cup chili sauce
1/3	cup ketchup
2-3	tablespoons horseradish
2	tablespoons (1/4 cup) fresh lemon juice
2	teaspoons Worcestershire sauce
1/8	teaspoon Tabasco sauce
1/8	teaspoon salt

Shrimp:

2 1/2	pounds large (16 to 20 per pound) fresh raw shrimp, shelled or unshelled
1	tablespoon mild chili powder
1	teaspoon ground cumin
1	teaspoon sugar
1	teaspoon salt
1/2	teaspoon ground mustard
1/2	teaspoon dried thyme
1/2	teaspoon freshly ground pepper
1/2	teaspoon curry powder
1/4	teaspoon ground cayenne pepper
2	tablespoons extra virgin olive oil plus olive oil for cooking

To prepare red sauce combine all ingredients in bowl and chill for up to 2 days.

If shelled, peel shrimp leaving tail in tact. Devein and rinse. Pat shrimp dry with paper towels. Combine remaining ingredients in bowl and toss shrimp until coated. Cover and refrigerate 30 minutes or up to 6 hours.

Heat grill or heavy skillet. Brush pan or grill with olive oil. Cook shrimp 1 to 2 minutes per side until barely opaque. If cooking in skillet, cook only 10 or so shrimp at a time in single layer. Re-brush pan with oil before adding next batch.

Shrimp and sauce can be served either hot, room temperature or cold.

Serves 4 to 6 as main course or 10 to 12 as appetizer.

Serve hot with red beans and rice for a spicy southwest entree.

Sizzling Skewered Shrimp

1	onion, quartered
1½	cups white wine vinegar
1	cup ketchup
¼	cup apple juice
¼	cup packed brown sugar
¼	cup vegetable oil
2	tablespoons Dijon mustard
1½	tablespoons celery seed
1½	teaspoons Worcestershire sauce
2	teaspoons hot pepper sauce
2	garlic cloves, chopped
½	teaspoon ground cayenne pepper
½	teaspoon turmeric
3	pounds jumbo shrimp (10 to 16 per pound)

In blender or food processor purée onion with vinegar until smooth. Add ketchup, apple juice, brown sugar, oil, mustard, celery seed, Worcestershire, hot sauce, garlic, cayenne and turmeric. Blend well.

Transfer mixture to medium nonstick saucepan and bring to boiling. Reduce heat to medium. Simmer about 20 minutes, stirring frequently, until sauce is slightly thickened. Let cool. The sauce may be prepared up to 1 week ahead and refrigerated in tightly covered container.

Soak bamboo skewers in water at least 30 minutes to prevent burning. Prepare grill. Shell shrimp, leaving tails on. Split each shrimp lengthwise down back, cutting only about halfway through. Remove vein. Flatten to butterfly. Thread 2 shrimp lengthwise onto each bamboo skewer. Brush shrimp with sauce.

Cook shrimp 4 to 6 inches from coals brushing often with sauce and turning once until shrimp are opaque throughout, about 5 minutes. Serve warm or at room temperature using reserved sauce as a zesty dip.

Serves 8.

Scallop, Shrimp and Chicken Sauté

¹/₄ **cup (¹/₂ stick) unsalted butter**

1 **tablespoon olive oil**

1 **medium sweet onion, thinly sliced**

¹/₂ **medium sweet red pepper, seeded and cut into thin strips**

1 **hot banana pepper, seeded and cut into rounds**

1 **clove garlic, minced**

¹/₂ **boneless skinless chicken breast, cut into small pieces**

¹/₄ **cup all-purpose flour**

¹/₂ **pound cooked medium shrimp**

¹/₂ **pound bay scallops**

¹/₈ **teaspoon basil**

¹/₈ **teaspoon dried dill weed**

Freshly ground pepper to taste

¹/₂ **cup white wine or dry vermouth**

Juice of ¹/₂ lemon

Melt butter and oil in large skillet over medium heat. Add onion, peppers and garlic. Sauté 5 to 10 minutes until onion is transparent. Dredge chicken in flour and add to skillet. Cook chicken about 4 minutes, stirring occasionally, until chicken turns white. Add shrimp, scallops, basil, dill and onion/pepper mixture. Cook and stir about 5 minutes until scallops are firm and cooked. Add wine and lemon juice. Stir and cook 5 minutes longer or until liquid is reduced to a thin sauce.

Serves 4 to 6.

White rice flavored with a pinch of saffron makes a nice accompaniment.

Shrimp Parmesan

1 **pound jumbo shrimp (10 to 16 per pound), shelled or unshelled**

2 **tablespoons lemon juice**

¹/₂ **cup freshly grated Parmesan cheese**

1 **tablespoon fresh minced garlic**

Clean and devein shrimp. Sprinkle with lemon juice. Let stand 20 minutes. Heat broiler for 5 minutes or more. Roll shrimp in mixture of grated Parmesan cheese and garlic. Spread shrimp in single layer on foil lined baking sheet. Broil 5 inches from the heat 3 to 4 minutes on each side. Shrimp may also be sautéed lightly in butter.

Serves 2 to 3 as main course or 6 as appetizer.

These shrimp make a great topping for creamy linguine.

Paella Rapida

2	cups defatted homemade or low-fat, reduced-sodium canned chicken broth
½	teaspoon saffron threads, crushed, or ⅛ teaspoon of powdered saffron
3	teaspoons olive oil, divided
½	pound medium shrimp, peeled and deveined
½	pound boneless skinless chicken breasts, sliced into ½-inch thick strips

Salt and freshly ground black pepper to taste

1	medium onion, chopped
2	cloves garlic, finely chopped
1	(14½-ounce) can tomatoes, with juice
⅛	teaspoon red pepper flakes
1	cup Arborio or medium-grain white rice
1	cup frozen artichoke hearts, thawed
1	cup frozen peas, thawed
⅓	cup bottled roasted peppers, cut into strips
⅓	cup smoked mussels, not packed in oil

In small saucepan combine chicken stock and saffron. Bring to a simmer. Remove from heat and set aside.

Heat 1 teaspoon oil over high heat in large nonstick skillet. Add shrimp. Sauté 3 to 4 minutes until pink and curled. Remove from skillet. Season with salt and pepper. Set aside.

Add another 1 teaspoon oil to skillet. Add chicken and sauté 3 to 4 minutes until lightly browned on outside and opaque inside. Remove from skillet. Season with salt and pepper. Set aside.

Reduce heat to medium. Add remaining 1 teaspoon oil to skillet. Stir in onions and garlic. Sauté about 5 minutes until softened. Add 1 or 2 tablespoons water if they become too dry. Stir in tomatoes and red pepper flakes. Simmer 3 minutes, breaking up the tomatoes with a spoon. Add rice and stir to coat well. Stir in reserved chicken stock. Bring to a simmer. Cover and cook over low heat 20 minutes. Gently stir in artichokes, peas, red peppers, mussels, reserved shrimp and chicken into rice mixture. Cover and cook 5 to 10 minutes more, stirring occasionally, until the rice is tender. Season with salt and pepper. Serve immediately.

Serves 4.

In 1913, the League of Catholic Women gave its endorsement to a bill entitling women to a minimum wage and helped fund other community-based projects designed to improve employment opportunities for women at that time and again during the Great Depression in the 1930's.

Steamed Salmon with Vegetables

2½   cups small Brussel sprouts

2½   cups snow peas

2½   cups julienne-cut carrots

2½   cups julienne-cut shitake mushrooms

2½   cups julienne-cut leeks

12   (6-ounce) salmon fillets

2   tablespoons minced fresh gingerroot

3   tablespoons minced cilantro

2   tablespoons minced fresh garlic

¼   cup soy sauce

2½   tablespoons sesame oil

2½   cups chicken broth

1   cup dry white wine

10   green onions, chopped

Heat oven to 425°. Put first 5 vegetables in one or two rectangular baking dishes large enough for salmon to be placed in single layer. Lay salmon side by side on vegetables. In large bowl mix final 8 ingredients. Pour over salmon. Cover tightly with aluminum foil. Bake 20 minutes or a little more depending on thickness of fillets.

Serves 12.

Baked Cod Au Fromage

4   (7 to 8 ounce) cod fillets or any firm white fish, fresh or frozen

1   cup regular or low-fat mayonnaise

½   cup freshly grated Parmesan cheese

¼   cup chopped green onions

2   tablespoons lemon juice

1   teaspoon Worcestershire sauce

1   teaspoon Tabasco sauce

½   cup bread crumbs

1   tablespoon paprika

Heat oven to 375°. Place fillets on greased baking sheet. Combine mayonnaise, cheese, onions, lemon juice, Worcestershire sauce and Tabasco sauce. Top fillets with mayonnaise mixture. Sprinkle with bread crumbs and paprika. Bake 20 to 25 minutes or until fish can be flaked with fork.

Serves 4.

Spinach Stuffed Sole

1 (12-ounce) package Stouffer's Spinach Soufflé

6 sole or other white fish fillets

¹/₄ teaspoon freshly ground pepper

¹/₄-¹/₂ teaspoon ground nutmeg

1 (10³/₄-ounce) can low-fat cream of mushroom soup

1 tablespoon dry sherry

1¹/₂ cups freshly shredded Swiss or Parmesan cheese

Let frozen soufflé stand at room temperature 30 minutes.

Heat oven to 375°. Cut soufflé into 6 equal pieces. Rinse sole, pat dry with paper towel. Sprinkle with pepper and nutmeg. Place 1 portion of spinach soufflé on each fillet and wrap fillet around spinach. Place seam side down in buttered 9-inch square or round baking dish.

Stir together soup, sherry and additional pepper and nutmeg, if desired. Pour over fish roll-ups. Sprinkle with Swiss or Parmesan cheese. Bake uncovered 30 minutes.

Serves 6.

This method of preparing fish leave no "fishy" odor in the kitchen.

Basil-Baked Fish Fillets

¹/₂ cup white wine or water

1 tablespoon butter

1 cup basil leaves

4 thin fish fillets, such as tilapia, flounder, red snapper or trout

Juice of 1 lemon or ¹/₄ cup lemon juice from frozen concentrate

Salt and black pepper to taste

¹/₂ teaspoon onion powder

2 tablespoons plain fine dry bread crumbs

Paprika to taste, optional

Heat oven to 450°. Pour wine and butter into 2-cup glass measure and microwave on high until butter begins to melt, about 1 minute. Spread basil leaves over bottom of 13x9-inch glass baking dish. Place fish fillets over basil.

Remove wine mixture from microwave. Add lemon juice to the mixture. Stir with a fork or whisk to blend. Pour wine mixture over fish.

Season fillets with salt and pepper to taste. Sprinkle onion powder and bread crumbs evenly over fillets. Sprinkle with paprika to taste, if desired.

Cover dish with aluminum foil. Bake in lower third of oven 12 minutes. Uncover fish and continue to cook until fillets are opaque and flake easily with a fork, about 2 to 3 minutes more. Serve at once using basil leaves under fish if desired.

Serves 4.

Grilled Tuna with Lemon and Capers

3   **large cloves garlic, minced**

3   **tablespoons drained and chopped capers**

6   **tablespoons lemon juice**

1½   **tablespoons olive oil**

Freshly ground black pepper, to taste

1½   **pounds tuna steaks**

In a small bowl, mix garlic, capers, lemon juice, oil and pepper. This can be done a day ahead and refrigerated, well covered, overnight.

To serve, place tuna in a nonaluminum bowl and marinate with the mixture for 1 hour only.

Heat broiler, stovetop or outdoor grill. Grill tuna, spooning marinade over fish while it cooks. Follow the Canadian rule: measure tuna at its thickest point and cook 8 minutes to the inch for medium, less if you like rare tuna and more if you prefer it well done.

Serves 4.

North Shore Walleye

Nonstick spray coating

¼   **cup butter**

2-3   **large cloves garlic, finely chopped**

1-2   **tablespoons fresh lemon juice**

2½   **pounds boneless, skinless walleye fillets or other lean white-fleshed fish fillets**

Salt and freshly ground pepper to taste

¾   **cup grated Romano cheese**

1   **cup fine dry bread crumbs**

Diagonally cut chives or green onion tops, optional

Spray 15x10x1-inch baking pan with nonstick coating; set aside.

In a small saucepan melt butter and stir in garlic and lemon juice. Rinse fillets. Cut into 6 servings if necessary. Place fillets in a single layer in baking pan. Brush with garlic-lemon butter; season lightly with salt and pepper. Sprinkle fish with Romano cheese and cover with bread crumbs. Drizzle the fish with any remaining garlic-lemon butter. Fish may be prepared up to this point covered and refrigerated up to 1 hour.

Heat oven to 450°. Bake for 10 to 12 minutes or till fish flakes easily with a fork. Transfer fillets to warm serving plates. If you like sprinkle with chives or green onion tops.

Serves 6.

Around the World...

A Swedish Grace

In Jesus' name
To table we go.
God bless the food
We receive. To God
The honor, us the gain,
So we have food
In Jesus' name.

A Japanese Prayer

Creator of the world,
Help us to love one another.
Help us care for each other
As sister or brother,
That friendship may grow
From nation to nation.
Bring peace to the world,
O Lord of Creation.

Desserts

Glazed Peach Crepes

Crepes:

1½	**cups milk**
1	**cup all-purpose flour**
3	**eggs**
1	**tablespoon salad oil**
4	**teaspoons butter or margarine, divided in eight parts**

Filling:

2	**tablespoons butter or margarine**
6	**cups sliced peaches, fresh or partially thawed frozen peaches**
1	**teaspoon grated lemon zest**
1	**tablespoon lemon juice**
¼	**teaspoon ground nutmeg**
½	**cup sugar**
2	**tablespoons brandy**

Topping:

Whipped cream or Crème Fraiche*

Combine milk, flour, eggs and oil in food processor or electric mixer until smooth. Let batter rest 1 hour or cover and refrigerate overnight.

Heat 6 to 7-inch crepe pan until drop of water will sizzle in pan. Grease pan slightly with about ½ teaspoon butter. Stir batter and pour 2 to 3 tablespoons into center of crepe pan. Quickly tilt pan in all directions so batter flows evenly over entire flat surface. Cook until edges of crepe are slightly brown and surface looks dry, 30 to 40 seconds. Run small knife around edge to loosen. Lift crepes and flip over. Cook second side about 20 seconds. It will not look browned. Turn onto plate. Repeat process for remaining 7 crepes. Cool and stack between layers of paper towel or parchment paper. Repeat with remaining 7 crepes. Can be made ahead and refrigerated.

Melt 2 tablespoons butter in wide frying pan over medium heat. Add peaches, lemon zest, lemon juice and nutmeg. Cook gently over low heat, turning occasionally with wide spatula, until peaches begin to soften, about 7 minutes. Gradually sprinkle in sugar and cook, stirring constantly, 2 more minutes. Sprinkle with brandy and continue cooking until mixture thickens. Remove from heat and cool slightly.

Heat oven to 325°. Spoon 3 tablespoons filling down center of unbrowned side of each crepe. Roll to enclose filling. Place filled crepes, seam side down, in buttered baking dish. Cover with foil and bake 25 minutes until heated through. Serve 2 crepes per person. Top with spoonful of crème fraiche or whipped cream just before serving.

Serves 4.

*Crème fraiche, a favorite French topping, is available in many supermarkets.

Fresh Strawberries with Raspberry Puree and Pistachio Nuts

1   **(12-ounce) package frozen raspberries, thawed**

1½   **tablespoons sugar**

1   **tablespoon orange juice**

1½   **tablespoons lemon juice**

3   **pints fresh strawberries, halved**

2   **tablespoons powdered sugar**

3   **tablespoons Grand Marnier**

2   **teaspoons unsalted slivered pistachio nuts**

Drain raspberries and puree in blender. Stir in sugar, orange and lemon juices. Refrigerate. Layer strawberries in bowl. Sift powdered sugar over each layer. Add Grand Marnier and refrigerate. To serve, pour raspberry puree onto individual plates. Arrange strawberries on top of sauce. Sprinkle with nuts.

Serves 6.

The perfect dessert for a hot summer night.

Peach Kuchen

1¼   **cups all-purpose flour**

¼   **teaspoon salt**

½   **cup (1 stick) cold unsalted butter**

2   **tablespoons sour cream**

Filling:

3   **large egg yolks**

⅓   **cup sour cream**

1   **cup sugar**

¼   **cup all-purpose flour**

¼   **teaspoon salt**

1½   **pounds fresh peaches, thickly sliced**

Heat oven to 425°. In large bowl combine flour, salt and butter until crumbly. Add sour cream and blend until mixture forms a ball. Gather dough together and shape onto bottom and side of 9-inch springform pan. Bake 18 to 20 minutes or until lightly browned. Cool 15 minutes.

Heat oven to 350°. Make filling by combining eggs, sour cream, sugar, flour and salt in medium bowl. Pour ½ cup mixture over baked crust. Top with peaches. Pour remaining mixture evenly over peaches. Bake 50 to 60 minutes or until custard is set and top browned.

Serves 10.

How to Skin a Peach
To skin a peach easily, cut an "x" on bottom of each peach, carefully cutting just through the skin. Heat large pot of water to boiling, and drop in peaches. Cook 20 seconds to 1 minute, the riper they are, the less time they need. Remove peaches from water with a slotted spoon. Place them in sink filled with ice water. Pick them out and use a paring knife or your fingers to remove skins, which should slip right off, leaving picture-perfect peaches.

Strawberries Jubilee

2	pints fresh strawberries
3	tablespoons butter
1/4	cup sugar
2	tablespoons water
3	thin strips lemon zest
2	tablespoons orange-flavored liqueur (Grand Marnier)
2	tablespoons brandy
1	quart vanilla ice cream or frozen yogurt, divided

Wash strawberries and drain on toweling. Set aside. In chafing dish heat butter until bubbly. Add sugar, water, lemon zest and liqueur. Stir over high heat until sugar dissolves and mixture is syrupy, 2 to 3 minutes. Warm brandy. Ignite and pour over syrup. When flame dies stir in 1 scoop of ice cream until melted. Add berries. Poach 1 minute continually spooning sauce over berries. Spoon remaining ice cream into dessert dishes. Top with berries and sauce. Serve at once.

Serves 6.

Frozen Soufflé

2	pints vanilla ice cream
8	teaspoons Grand Marnier
6	macaroons, crumbled
1	cup whipping cream, whipped until stiff
3	tablespoons chopped toasted almonds
3	teaspoons powdered sugar

Sauce:

2	pints fresh strawberries or raspberries, stemmed and crushed
8	teaspoons Grand Marnier
2-4	tablespoons sugar

In large bowl soften ice cream, stir in Grand Marnier and macaroons. Fold in whipped cream. Pour into 5-cup ring or other shaped mold which has been lightly sprayed with vegetable oil. Sprinkle with toasted almonds and powdered sugar. Cover and freeze for up to 1 week.

Mix sauce ingredients together in medium bowl and spoon over individual soufflé servings.

Serves 8.

Also good with caramel or chocolate sauce, commercial or homemade.

Individual Summer Berry Puddings

2 slices stale potato bread, challah or other good-quality white bread

2 pints strawberries, rinsed, hulled and sliced

1 pint raspberries

1/2 pint blueberries

1/2 pint blackberries

1/4 cup sugar

2 tablespoons lemon juice

1/2 cup whipping cream, whipped until stiff

Leave bread on counter overnight to dry out.

Heat strawberries, raspberries, blueberries, blackberries and sugar in large nonreactive saucepan over medium heat about 5 minutes, stirring occasionally until berries begin to release their juices and sugar is dissolved. Turn off heat, add lemon juice and let cool to room temperature.

Spray 6 (6-ounce) ramekins with vegetable spray. With cookie cutter or sharp knife, cut 12 bread rounds sized to fit bottom of ramekins from center of bread slices. Place ramekins on rimmed cookie sheet. With slotted spoon, place about 1/4 cup of fruit in bottom of each ramekin. Lightly soak 6 bread rounds in juices left in saucepan and place on fruit in ramekins. Divide remaining fruit among ramekins, about 1/2 cup per ramekin. Lightly soak remaining bread rounds in fruit juice and place on top of fruit. Bread should sit above ramekin lip. Top with remaining juices and cover ramekins loosely with plastic wrap. Place baking sheet on top of plastic. Weight baking sheet with several heavy cans or books. Refrigerate at least 4 and up to 8 hours.

Remove weights, baking sheet and plastic from ramekins. Unmold on individual plates. Top with dollop of whipped cream.

Serves 6.

Glazed Oranges

1/4 cup sugar

1 tablespoon cornstarch

1 cup orange juice

Zest of 1 orange

1/4 cup brandy

4 navel oranges

Mint leaves for garnish

In heavy medium saucepan combine sugar and cornstarch over medium-low heat. Add orange juice, orange zest and brandy. Stir constantly until mixture begins to thicken. Remove from heat. Peel oranges, remove white pith and cut into 1/2-inch slices. Place orange slices in serving dish, pour sauce over and chill before serving. Garnish with mint.

Serves 4.

Crème Brulée Le Cirque

½   **cup packed light brown sugar**

4   **cups whipping cream**

1   **vanilla bean, split**

½   **cup plus 2 tablespoons granulated sugar**

6   **large egg yolks**

Spread brown sugar on small baking sheet. Place sheet uncovered in dry spot for at least 24 hours or until the sugar is quite dry. Push through fine sieve. Set aside.

Heat oven to 350°. In medium saucepan heat cream and vanilla bean over medium heat 3 minutes or until warm. Remove vanilla bean. In medium bowl whisk together granulated sugar and egg yolks. When well blended whisk in cream. Strain through fine sieve into bowl.

Divide cream mixture among 6 (8-ounce) shallow oval ramekins. Place in shallow roasting pan and add enough hot water to come halfway up sides of ramekins. Bake about 30 minutes or until set and a knife inserted in center comes out clean. The custards will still be soft. Do not overbake.

Transfer ramekins to wire racks to cool for at least 30 minutes. Heat broiler. Spoon brown sugar into fine sieve and sprinkle evenly over the tops of custards. Broil about 15 seconds to melt and burn the sugar topping. Watch carefully to prevent charring. Serve immediately.

Serves 6.

This is the ultimate crème brulée, the most classic of all French desserts. There are now many Americanized versions, but this is the one and only rich and delicious "burnt cream".

Tuesday Club, an outreach program for senior citizens living alone in the downtown area, began operating in 1974. On two Tuesdays a month women and men gather at the League of Catholic Women's Downtown Center for a home cooked meal provided by LCW volunteers, professional entertainment and social interaction. Birthdays are celebrated, bingo is played with gusto and friendships are made in an atmosphere of warm hospitality.

Rich Chocolate Mousse

16	ounces unsweetened chocolate
$1/2$	cup (1 stick) butter
4	pasteurized eggs, separated
Pinch of cream of tartar	
1	cup sugar, divided
3	cups whipping cream

Melt chocolate and butter in microwave in large bowl. Stir until smooth. Add egg yolks. In medium bowl whip egg whites with cream of tartar until they form soft peaks. Gradually add $1/2$ cup sugar. Beat until stiff. Fold whites into chocolate. In separate small bowl whip cream with remaining sugar. Fold into chocolate mixture.

Serve in demitasse cups or other small delicate serving dishes.

Serves 16 to 20.

Peaches and "Skyr"

4	firm ripe medium peaches
$1/4$	cup packed light brown sugar
$1/2$	cup well-chilled whipping cream
$1/2$	cup sour cream

Halve and pit peaches. Holding each half over bowl to catch any juices, slice peaches into bowl. Sprinkle brown sugar over peaches and toss to combine well. Let peaches stand at room temperature until juices are released, 20 to 30 minutes.

Just before serving beat whipping cream in small bowl just until it holds soft peaks. Stir in sour cream to make "skyr". With slotted spoon divide peaches among 4 bowls, reserving juices. Top peaches with "skyr" and drizzle with reserved juices.

Serves 4.

A simple delicious dessert when peaches are in season.

To find a good peach at the market, smell it! If it smells peachy, it is usually good.

Autumn Fruit Caramel Crisp

Filling:

2	**large tart red apples, peeled, cored, sliced**
2	**large Granny Smith apples, peeled, cored, sliced**
2	**pears, peeled, sliced**
1	**pound peaches, fresh or frozen, sliced**
1½	**cups toasted pecan halves, divided**
½	**cup sugar**
6	**tablespoons all-purpose flour**
2	**tablespoons freshly grated nutmeg**
1	**(12-ounce) jar good quality caramel sauce, divided**
6	**tablespoons unsalted butter, chilled, cut into pieces**

Crisp Topping:

1	**cup all-purpose flour**
1	**cup old-fashioned rolled oats**
⅔	**cup packed golden brown sugar**
½	**cup (1 stick) unsalted chilled butter, cut into pieces**
1	**quart vanilla ice cream**

Heat oven to 350˚. In large bowl combine apples, pears, peaches and 1 cup pecans. In small bowl combine sugar, flour and nutmeg; mix well. Toss with fruits to coat. Chop remaining ½ cup pecans and mix with ½ cup caramel sauce. Add to fruit mixture and toss to coat. Stir in butter pieces. Transfer to buttered 13x9-inch baking dish.

To make topping, mix flour, rolled oats and brown sugar in small bowl. Add butter. Using pastry blender, cut butter into flour mixture until it resembles coarse meal. Sprinkle topping over fruit. Bake uncovered until fruit is tender, about 1 to 1¼ hours. Cool slightly.

Heat remaining caramel sauce in small saucepan or microwave. Spoon warm crisp into serving bowls, top with ice cream and drizzle with remaining warmed caramel sauce.

Serves 8 to 10.

This recipe received rave notices from the Gourmet Dinner Group which contributed it.

During the depression year of 1933, the LCW donated funds to the Women's Occupational Bureau to furnish a house for unemployed women.

Happy Cranberries

1	pound fresh cranberries
2	cups sugar
4	tablespoons bourbon (i.e. Makers Mark or other good quality bourbon)

Additional $\frac{1}{2}$ cup sugar

Heat oven to 350˚. Spread cranberries in shallow pan. Cover with 2 cups granulated sugar and bake uncovered 1 hour. Remove from oven, sprinkle with bourbon and remaining sugar. Store in refrigerator up to 2 weeks.

Makes 2 cups.

Serve over ice cream, cake or almost anything. These cranberries will keep you happy to the bottom of the jar!

Sherry Wine Jelly Dessert

$2^3/_4$	cups boiling water
Juice and zest of 2 lemons	
2	envelopes unflavored gelatin (4 teaspoons), dissolved in $\frac{1}{4}$ cup cold water
1	cup sugar
1	cup dry sherry wine

Sauce:

2	pasteurized egg yolks
$\frac{1}{2}$	cup sifted powdered sugar
3	tablespoons rum
$\frac{1}{2}$	cup whipping cream

Add juice and finely grated lemon zest to boiling water in medium saucepan. Bring to boiling again. Stir in dissolved gelatin and sugar. When cool, add sherry. Pour entire mixture into oiled 5 to 6-cup ring or other shape mold. Chill until firm. Will keep up to 2 days in refrigerator.

Unmold on large plate and surround with fresh peach halves filled with blueberries or other seasonal fruits.

In a large electric mixer bowl beat egg yolks until thick and lemon colored. Add powdered sugar and rum. In separate small bowl beat whipping cream until stiff. Fold whipped cream into egg yolks. Serve sauce in attractive separate container or spoon over individual servings.

Serves 6.

This summer dessert is beautiful to look at as well as delightful to taste.

If recipe calls for uncooked eggs always use pasteurized eggs.

Oranges in Avocado Cream

1   **(3 ounce) package cream cheese, softened**

1/4   **cup lime juice**

1/2   **cup sugar**

1   **tablespoon Cointreau**

2   **medium avocados, pared and halved**

3   **oranges, peeled and sectioned**

1/2   **cup slivered pistachios or almonds**

In medium bowl combine cream cheese, lime juice, sugar and Cointreau until fluffy. Mash avocado and add to cream cheese mixture. Beat 3 minutes. Refrigerate.

Divide oranges among 6 clear fluted champagne or sherbet glasses. Top with avocado cream. Sprinkle with pistachios or almond slivers if desired.

Serves 6.

Jim Dodge's Blueberry-Lemon Cobbler

3   **cups fresh blueberries, rinsed and well drained or 3 cups frozen unsweetened blueberries**

3/4   **cup granulated sugar, divided**

2   **tablespoons grated fresh lemon zest**

1   **cup all-purpose flour**

1/4   **teaspoon salt**

1/4   **teaspoon baking powder**

1/2   **teaspoon baking soda**

3   **tablespoons butter**

1   **large egg**

1/2   **cup buttermilk**

1/4   **teaspoon vanilla**

1   **cup whipping cream, lightly whipped**

Heat oven to 375°. Toss berries with 1/2 cup of the sugar and lemon zest in 1-quart soufflé or other deep baking dish. Mix flour, remaining 1/4 cup sugar, salt, baking powder and soda in medium-size bowl. Cut in butter until particles resemble fine crumbs. In a separate bowl, beat egg, buttermilk and vanilla with a fork. Add to flour mixture stirring well. Drop by spoonfuls over berries.

Bake 35 minutes or until topping is golden brown. Remove to rack; cool slightly. Spoon warm dessert into shallow dessert bowls keeping crust on top. Pass whipped cream or serve with homemade ice cream.

Makes 5 servings.

Fresh Banana Éclair

Éclair:

³/₄	**cup water**
6	**tablespoons butter**
¹/₄	**teaspoon salt**
³/₄	**cup all-purpose flour**
3	**eggs**

Filling:

2	**cups whipping cream**
2	**tablespoons sugar**
2	**large ripe bananas**
¹/₄	**cup Crème de Cocoa liqueur**

Glaze:

1	**cup powdered sugar**
¹/₃	**cup cocoa**
1	**additional tablespoon butter, melted**
3-4	**tablespoons boiling water**

Heat oven to 400°. Bring water, butter and salt to boil in medium saucepan over medium heat. Add flour all at once stirring vigorously with spoon until dough forms ball and leaves sides of pan. Remove from heat. Beat in eggs one at a time until dough is stiff and glossy. Set aside ¹/₃ dough. On greased baking sheet form remaining ²/₃ dough into one oblong shape 2 inches wide. Spoon reserved dough in 6 little mounds atop oblong dough. Bake 30 minutes. With sharp knife make slits along sides of éclair and mounds to let steam escape. Return to oven and continue baking 10 minutes longer. Remove to rack. Slice off top and remove any soft dough inside. Cool.

In medium bowl whip cream to soft peaks. Gradually add sugar, whipping until stiff. Mash bananas and fold into whipped cream along with Crème de Cocoa. Fill éclair. Replace top.

Combine powdered sugar with cocoa, melted butter and vanilla in medium bowl. Stir in enough boiling water to make thin glaze. Pour glaze over éclair. Chill at least 1 hour.

Serves 6.

Father Robert Cassidy, Pastor of Our Lady of Grace Catholic Church, is well known for his excellent desserts. This is one of them. It has won the seal of approval from many archdiocesan priests who have sampled it.

In 1997, League of Catholic Women volunteers began tutoring students at Risen Christ, an inner-city elementary school. At present, in addition to supplying classroom tutors, the League's **Risen Christ Outreach** is providing funding for a part-time coordinator to ensure quality volunteer services at Risen Christ and to integrate parents into the educational setting.

Creamy Orange Ice Cream Pie

1	**pint orange sherbet**
1	**pint vanilla ice cream or frozen yogurt**
1	**(16-ounce) prepared chocolate or graham crumb crust**
1/2	**cup crushed chocolate wafers**
1	**cup chocolate syrup, optional**

Soften ice cream and sherbet slightly. Spoon half of sherbet into crust. Spread in even layer. Spoon ice cream over sherbet. Spread in even layer. Spoon remaining half of sherbet over the ice cream. Spread in even layer. Cover with plastic wrap and freeze.

When ready to serve sprinkle with cookie crumbs. If desired drizzle chocolate syrup on individual dessert plates before placing pie on plates.

Serves 6 to 8.

Lemon Macaroon Dessert

1	**quart lemon sherbet, softened**
1	**cup whipping cream**
1/4	**cup powdered sugar**
6	**almond macaroons, crushed**
1/4	**cup chopped pecans**

Oil 8-cup ring mold. Press sherbet in bottom of mold. Cover and freeze. In small bowl whip cream until it forms stiff peaks. Fold in sugar, macaroons and pecans. Spread mixture over sherbet. Cover with plastic wrap and freeze. Remove plastic wrap, unmold and serve.

Serves 12.

To unmold most frozen desserts run dinner knife around edges of mold. Place large platter over mold. Carefully turn mold and platter over. Lift mold gently. If contents are not released place warm cloth on upturned mold until it can be easily lifted.

Pumpkin Pie with Coconut Crust

¼	cup (½ stick) butter
2	cups Bakers Angel Flake Coconut
1	cup whipping cream
¾	teaspoon ground cinnamon
½	teaspoon ground nutmeg
¼	teaspoon ground ginger
¼	teaspoon cloves
⅔	cup milk
1	cup canned pumpkin
1	(3-ounce) package vanilla instant pudding

Melt butter and mix with coconut. Toast in oven until golden brown, about 10 to 15 minutes. Watch carefully. Press into buttered 9-inch pie plate. Cool. Reserve 1 tablespoon toasted coconut for garnish.

In large bowl whip cream. Blend in 4 spices. Add milk and pumpkin. Mix well. Add pudding. Blend only about 1 minute. Pour into crust. Chill at least 3 hours. Top with whipped cream and toasted coconut.

Serves 8.

A different take on the usual pumpkin pie which this contributor has made a family tradition.

Lemon Pie

4	eggs, separated, reserving whites for meringue
1	cup sugar
⅓	cup cornstarch
¼	teaspoon salt
1½	cups water
2	tablespoons butter
6	ounces lemonade concentrate
1	baked pie shell

Meringue:

4	egg whites
⅓	cup sugar
¼	teaspoon cream of tartar

Heat oven to 325°. In a large bowl beat egg yolks until thick. In medium saucepan, mix together egg yolks, sugar, cornstarch, salt, water and lemonade. While stirring bring to boil. Add butter and boil 1 minute. Cool to lukewarm. gradually add to egg yolk mixture. Mix well. Pour into baked pie shell.

In small bowl of electric mixer, beat egg whites until frothy. Slowly add sugar and cream of tartar until whites form stiff peaks. Cover lemon filling with meringue, carefully sealing edges. Bake pie 20 to 25 minutes until meringue is golden brown. Cool and cut into wedges.

Serves 6 to 8.

Auntie Betty's Famous Mince Pie and Fluffy Hard Sauce

3   **frozen or homemade 9-inch pie crusts**

2   **cups prepared mincemeat**

$1/2$ **cup orange marmalade**

1   **cup diced apples**

2   **tablespoons brandy**

$1/3$ **cup finely chopped walnuts**

Hard Sauce:

$1/2$ **cup (1 stick) butter softened**

$2/3$ **cup powdered sugar**

2   **tablespoons brandy, optional**

Heat oven to 425˚. If using frozen pie crusts, thaw. Combine mincemeat, marmalade, apples, brandy and walnuts. Sprinkle flour over all and mix well. Pour mixture into 2 pie shells. Cut remaining pie crust into strips to make latticework top.

Bake 35 to 40 minutes or until filling has bubbled around edges.

In medium bowl of electric mixer, beat $1/2$ cup butter until soft and fluffy. Gradually add $2/3$ cup powdered sugar, beating until thick and glossy. Add brandy if desired. Sauce may be kept at room temperature 1 to 2 days.

Cut warm or cool pie into wedges. Serve with hard sauce at room temperature.

Serves 8 to 12.

Rhuberry Pie

Pastry for one 2-crust 9-inch pie

3   **cups fresh strawberries, sliced**

3   **cups fresh rhubarb, chopped**

Grated zest of 1 orange

$1^1/2$ **cups sugar**

3   **tablespoons all-purpose flour**

3-4   **teaspoons tapioca**

3   **tablespoons butter, optional**

Heat oven to 425˚. Prepare bottom pie crust and place in deep pie plate. In large mixing bowl gently but thoroughly combine all filling ingredients except butter. Pour $1/2$ mixture into prepared pie shell. Dot with half of butter. Add rest of fruit and dot with remaining butter. Top with upper pie crust which has been slit for steam vents.

Bake 15 minutes. Reduce temperature to 375˚ and bake additional 30 to 40 minutes or until lightly browned on bottom and bubbling in center. Cool on rack. Serve warm with ice cream if desired.

Serves 8.

Hawaiian Wedding Cake

2	cups all-purpose flour
2	teaspoons baking soda
2	cups sugar
2	eggs beaten
1	(20-ounce) can crushed pineapple and juice
1	cup chopped nuts

Frosting:

1½	cups powdered sugar
½	cup (1 stick) butter, softened
1	(8-ounce) package cream cheese, softened
¼	teaspoon vanilla

Heat oven to 350°. Mix flour and soda together in large bowl. Add remaining ingredients and mix thoroughly by hand or mixer. Spread batter into lightly greased 13x9-inch baking pan. Bake 40 minutes or until tester comes out clean.

Mix all frosting ingredients in medium bowl until smooth. Spread on cool cake.

Serves 9 to 12.

This recipe comes from a contributor who has been a League member for over 70 years.

Lemon Cake

1	cup (2 sticks) butter
2	cups sugar
3	eggs
3	cups flour
1	teaspoon baking soda
¼	teaspoon salt
1	cup buttermilk
3	tablespoons fresh lemon juice

Grated zest of 1 lemon

Glaze:

¼	cup (½ stick) butter, softened
1½	cups powdered sugar
3	tablespoons lemon juice

Heat oven to 300°. In large bowl of electric mixer cream together butter and sugar. Beat in eggs one at a time. Mixture should be light. Mix together flour, soda and salt in separate bowl. Add buttermilk and flour alternately to mixture. Begin and end with flour. Add lemon juice and lemon zest. Bake 50 minutes in non-stick (10-inch) tube or bundt pan. Cool slightly before removing from pan and applying glaze.

Glaze: Beat all ingredients together in medium bowl. Pour slowly over cake. Decorate with tiny curls of lemon rind if desired.

Slice glazed cake into 1-inch slices and serve.

Serves 8 to 10.

To allow a glaze to permiate any cake more thoroughly, poke holes in cake with a toothpick before applying glaze.

Gateau Chocolate au Rhum

1	(18.5-ounce) package devils food cake mix
1/2	cup white Karo syrup
1/2	cup white rum
1/2	cup whipping cream
Grated chocolate for garnish	

Heat oven to 350°. Mix cake according to package directions. Pour into greased and floured 10-inch tube pan. Bake 35 to 45 minutes or until tester come out clean.

In small bowl combine syrup and rum until well blended. When cake has cooled about 15 minutes, slowly pour half rum mixture over top of cake while still in pan. When cake has cooled completely run dinner knife around all edges. Invert tube pan on serving platter and gently loosen cake. Pour remaining rum mixture over cake. Cover and refrigerate several hours.

Shortly before serving whip cream and spoon over top of cake. Sprinkle with grated chocolate.

Serves 12.

Christmas Carol Cake

1	cup oil
2	cups sugar
3	eggs
2	cups flour
2	teaspoons vanilla
1 1/2	teaspoons ground cinnamon
1	teaspoon baking soda
3	apples, diced
1	cup chopped walnuts
3/4	cup raisins

Glaze:

2/3	cup sugar
1/2	teaspoon baking soda
1/2	cup buttermilk
1/2	cup (1 stick) butter
1	tablespoon light corn syrup
1	teaspoon vanilla

Heat oven to 350°. Spray 12-cup bundt or tube pan with non-stick spray. In large bowl combine cake ingredients one ingredient at a time in order listed, blending well after each addition. Bake 70 minutes or until toothpick comes out clean. Cool 45 minutes. Invert on cake plate. Glaze when cool.

Combine all glaze ingredients, except vanilla, in small saucepan and bring to boiling. Cook 5 minutes stirring occasionally. Remove from heat and stir in vanilla. Pour slowly over cake using pastry brush until most of glaze soaks in. Decorate with artificial holly and serve.

Serves 10 to 12.

Chocolate Carrot Cake with Chocolate Cream Cheese Frosting

2½ ounces unsweetened chocolate

1⅓ cups unbleached white flour

⅔ cup unsweetened cocoa powder

1½ teaspoons baking powder

1½ teaspoons baking soda

½ teaspoon salt

1 teaspoon ground cinnamon

3 eggs, room temperature

1¼ cups honey

⅔ cups vegetable oil

2 teaspoons vanilla extract

Finely grated zest of 1 lemon

¾ cup buttermilk, room temperature

1½ cups grated carrots

Frosting:

½ cup (1 stick) butter, softened

1 (8-ounce) package Neufchantel cheese, softened

¾ cup honey or maple syrup

¾ cup unsweetened cocoa powder

2 tablespoons Cafix (a coffee substitute made from grain) or instant coffee

1 tablespoon Grand Marnier, rum or Crème de Cocoa

Heat oven to 350°. Have all ingredients at room temperature. Melt chocolate in top of double boiler. Set aside to cool. In medium bowl combine flour, cocoa, baking powder, baking soda, salt and cinnamon. In separate bowl beat eggs. Add honey to eggs and beat until light. Add oil to eggs and beat. Stir in vanilla and lemon zest. Add cooled chocolate and mix well. Stir in buttermilk. Stir in dry ingredients, just until combined. Blend in grated carrots. Butter and flour 2 (9-inch) round or square cake pans. Pour cake batter into prepared pans.

Bake 35 to 40 minutes or until cake tester inserted in the center comes out clean. Let cool before removing from pans. Let cake cool completely before frosting.

Beat butter in medium bowl. Add cream cheese and beat until very smooth and creamy. Add honey or syrup and beat again. Add cocoa, Cafix or coffee and liqueur. Beat until well combined. Makes enough to fill and frost 9-inch two-layer cake.

Serves 10 to 12.

Contributed by Brenda Langton, owner/chef of Café Brenda.

Apple Cake with Hot Caramel Sauce

¹/₂   cup pecan halves

2¹/₂   cups chopped firm cooking apples (i.e. McIntosh)

¹/₂   cup (1 stick) butter at room temperature

1   cup granulated sugar

1   egg

1   teaspoon baking soda

¹/₂   teaspoon salt

1   teaspoon ground cinnamon

1   teaspoon ground nutmeg

1   cup all-purpose flour

Hot Caramel Sauce:

¹/₂   cup (1 stick) butter

1   cup light brown sugar

¹/₂   teaspoon salt

1   teaspoon vanilla

¹/₂   cup evaporated milk

Sweetened whipped cream for garnish

Sliced unpeeled apple slices for garnish

Heat oven to 350˚. Place pecans in food processor and process until fine. Set aside. Peel, core and quarter apples. Add to processor and process until they are in medium-coarse shards, about the size of almonds. Set aside.

Place butter in large mixer bowl, add sugar and beat until fluffy. Add egg. Beat until blended. Add soda, salt, cinnamon, nutmeg and mix lightly. Add flour and blend gently. Stir in apples and nuts. Pour mixture into greased 9-inch round cake pan and bake for 30 minutes or until top springs back when touched. Cool slightly. Center may sink somewhat.

Melt butter in small saucepan over medium heat. Add brown sugar and salt. Bring to boiling stirring with whisk. Remove from heat and add vanilla and milk. Stir again with whisk.

To serve, cut cake in eight wedges. Ladle hot sauce onto 8 dessert plates. Place cake on top of sauce. Garnish with whipped cream and apple slices.

Serves 8.

Sauce may be made ahead of time and reheated over hot water. Refrigerated cake will keep for one week.

Family Favorite Rum Cake

1	cup chopped pecans or walnuts
1	(18.5-ounce) package yellow cake mix
1	(3.25-ounce) package instant vanilla pudding mix
4	eggs
½	cup vegetable oil
½	cup cold water
½	cup dark rum

Glaze:

½	cup (1 stick) butter
¼	cup water
1	cup granulated sugar
½	cup dark rum

Heat oven to 325°. Grease and flour 10-inch tube or bundt pan. Sprinkle chopped nuts on bottom of pan. Combine cake mix, pudding mix, eggs, vegetable oil and water in large mixing bowl. Stir in rum. Pour batter over chopped nuts. Bake 1 hour. Remove cake from oven and set on rack to cool before removing from pan.

Melt butter in saucepan. Add water and sugar. Beat 5 minutes, stirring constantly. Allow to cool and stir in rum. Pour glaze over cake. Slice and serve.

Serves 16 to 20.

This cake keeps well in refrigerator for up to 2 weeks and may also be frozen.

Pineapple Cake

2	cups all-purpose flour
1½	cups sugar
2	teaspoons baking soda
2	eggs
1	(16-ounce) can crushed pineapple with juice

Topping:

½	cup brown sugar
½	cup coconut
½	cup chopped pecans

Glaze:

1½	cup (1 stick) butter
1	(5-ounce) can evaporated milk
1	cup sugar

Heat oven to 350°. Combine flour, sugar and baking soda in large bowl. Add eggs and pineapple with juice. Mix thoroughly. Pour into greased and floured 13x9-inch pan.

Combine brown sugar, coconut and pecans in small bowl. Sprinkle over cake batter. Bake 45 minutes or until tester comes out clean.

In small saucepan boil butter, evaporated milk and sugar 2 minutes. Pour glaze over hot cake. Pierce cake with fork so glaze will be absorbed.

Cool cake and refrigerate. Top with whipped cream before serving if desired.

Serves 12.

Russian Tea Cakes

1   cup (2 sticks) butter, softened

¹/₂   cup powdered sugar

1   teaspoon vanilla

2¹/₄   cups flour

¹/₄   teaspoon salt

³/₄   cup finely chopped nuts

Powdered sugar for coating

Heat oven to 325°. Cream butter and sugar in large bowl. Add vanilla. Work in flour, salt and nuts until dough holds together. Shape dough into balls. Place balls on ungreased baking sheet. Bake 10 to 12 minutes until set but not brown. While warm roll in powdered sugar. Cool and roll in sugar again.

Makes about 4 dozen.

An old-fashioned favorite especially at Christmas time.

Italian Cream Cake

5   eggs, separated

2   cups sugar

¹/₂   cup (1 stick) butter, softened

¹/₂   cup shortening (i.e. Crisco)

1   teaspoon vanilla

2   cups all-purpose flour

1   teaspoon baking soda

³/₄   teaspoon salt

1   cup coconut, shredded

1   cup buttermilk

Frosting:

¹/₂   cup (1 stick) butter, softened

1   (8 ounce) package cream cheese, softened

1   teaspoon vanilla

1   pound powdered sugar

1   cup chopped pecans

Heat oven to 350°. Beat egg whites until stiff in medium bowl until stiff, but not dry. Set aside. Cream sugar, butter and shortening and vanilla in separate large bowl. Add egg yolks one at a time. Stir together dry ingredients including coconut. Add to creamed mixture alternately with buttermilk. Fold in egg whites. Pour into 3 greased and floured 8 or 9-inch round cake pans. Bake 30 minutes. Cool.

Cream butter, cream cheese and vanilla in medium bowl. Beat in powdered sugar. Add pecans. Frosting may be frozen or kept in refrigerator for at least a week.

Frost three layers of cake, cut into small wedges and serve.

Serves 12.

Triple Treat Crème de Menthe Bars

First Layer:

2   cups graham cracker crumbs

1$\frac{1}{2}$ cups chopped walnuts

1   cup coconut

$\frac{1}{2}$ cup powdered sugar

$\frac{1}{4}$ cup unsweetened cocoa powder

$\frac{3}{4}$ cup (1$\frac{1}{2}$ sticks) butter or margarine, melted

1   teaspoon vanilla

1   egg, well beaten

Second Layer:

2   cups powdered sugar

2   teaspoons dry vanilla pudding mix, not instant

$\frac{1}{2}$ cup (1 stick) butter, softened

3   tablespoons Crème de Menthe

Third Layer:

1   (12-ounce) package semi-sweet chocolate chips

$\frac{1}{2}$ cup (1 stick) butter

Combine first eight ingredients in large bowl. Mix well. Pat into ungreased 13x9-inch pan. Refrigerate 1 to 2 hours.

In medium bowl beat together powdered sugar, pudding mix, $\frac{1}{2}$ cup butter and Crème de Menthe. Pour over crust. Refrigerate 2 hours.

Heat chocolate chips and second $\frac{1}{2}$ cup butter in small saucepan over low heat stirring until smooth. Spread over Crème de Menthe layer. Refrigerate until set. Cut into small squares.

Makes 36 small bars.

Hot Fudge Sauce

5   squares unsweetened chocolate

$\frac{1}{2}$ cup (1 stick) butter

1   (14$\frac{1}{2}$-ounce) can evaporated milk

3   cups powdered sugar

1$\frac{1}{4}$ teaspoons vanilla

Melt chocolate and margarine in saucepan or top of double boiler. In small bowl combine sugar gradually with milk. Add to chocolate mixture and bring to boiling over medium heat. Cook and stir 8 minutes or until thick and creamy. Remove from heat and stir in vanilla. Serve warm. Keeps well in refrigerator.

Makes 3 cups.

Contributed by Judith Kavanaugh, CSJ who teaches at Cretin Derham Hall.

After Dinner Brownies

2	squares (2 ounces) unsweetened chocolate
2	squares (2 ounces) semi-sweet chocolate
6	tablespoons butter
$1/2$	cup sugar
1	egg
$1/4$	cup light Karo syrup
$1/2$	teaspoon vanilla
$1/2$	cup all-purpose flour
1	cup finely chopped pecans, optional

Icing:

8	ounces semi-sweet chocolate squares
$2/3$	cup whipping cream
2	tablespoons liqueur of choice

Heat oven to 350°. In microwave melt chocolate and butter in small bowl. Cool. In large bowl beat sugar and egg together until smooth. Add corn syrup and vanilla. Blend well. Stir in flour and mix thoroughly. Add nuts. Pour into well buttered $11^{3}/4$ x $7^{1}/2$-inch pan. Bake 20 to 25 minutes or until sides pull away from pan and tester comes out clean. Cool.

In small bowl melt chocolate and cream in microwave. Stir until smooth. Add liqueur and mix well. Frost brownies and chill.

Serves 16 to 20.

May be made ahead and frozen until ready to serve.

Oatmeal Carmelitas

1	cup all-purpose flour
1	cup quick rolled oats
$3/4$	cup brown sugar, firmly packed
$1/2$	teaspoon baking soda
$1/4$	teaspoon salt
$3/4$	cup ($1^{1}/2$ sticks) butter, melted

Topping:

1	cup chocolate chips
$1/2$	cup chopped walnuts or pecans

Caramel:

$3/4$	cup caramel ice cream topping
3	tablespoons all-purpose flour

Heat oven to 350°. Combine bar ingredients in large bowl until mixture forms coarse crumbs. Press half of crumbs in pan and bake 10 minutes.

In small bowl mix topping ingredients well and sprinkle over baked crust.

Combine caramel and flour in small bowl. Drizzle over chips and nuts. Sprinkle remaining crumbs over caramel topping. Bake an additional 15 to 20 minutes until golden brown. Chill bars for easy cutting.

Makes 24 bars.

Bars stay firmer if kept in refrigerator.

Chocolate Raspberry Bars

6	ounces unsweetened chocolate, chopped
12	tablespoons (1$\frac{1}{2}$ sticks) butter
$\frac{1}{2}$	cup regular or seedless raspberry jam
4	eggs
2	cups sugar
1$\frac{1}{2}$	teaspoons vanilla
1	cup all-purpose flour

Topping:

$\frac{1}{2}$	cup whipping cream
$\frac{1}{4}$	cup regular or seedless raspberry jam
1	tablespoon butter
8	ounces bittersweet or semi-sweet (not unsweetened) chocolate, chopped
3$\frac{1}{2}$	pints fresh raspberries

Powdered sugar for garnish

Heat oven to 350˚. Line 13x9-inch baking pan with foil, letting foil overhang edges. Butter foil. Combine chocolate, butter and jam in heavy saucepan. Stir over low heat until smooth. Remove from heat. Whisk eggs in large bowl until foamy. Add sugar and vanilla. Whisk until thoroughly incorporated. Stir in chocolate mixture. Add flour. Mix just until blended. Spread batter in prepared pan. Bake 30 minutes or just until springy to touch and tester comes out with a few moist crumbs attached. Cool on rack.

Combine cream, jam and butter in medium saucepan. Bring to simmer, stirring until jam and butter melt. Remove from heat. Add chocolate, stirring until smooth. Let stand until cool but still spreadable, about 30 minutes. Spread topping over brownies. Immediately top with fresh raspberries, arranged in rows. Chill until cold. Using foil as aid, remove bars from pan. Fold down foil sides. Cut into bars. Sift powdered sugar over bars.

Makes 24 bars.

Old Fashioned Cereal Cookies

1	pound white almond bark
2	cups Captain Crunch
2	cups Rice Krispies
1	cup mixed nuts

Melt almond bark in microwave. Place nuts and cereals in large bowl and pour melted bark over. Mix thoroughly. Drop by teaspoonsful on baking sheet. Let stand until firm. Store in tight container.

Makes about 36 cookies.

Mom's Sugar Cookies

1	cup (2 sticks) butter
1	cup sugar
1	egg
2	cups all-purpose flour
1	teaspoon vanilla

Heat oven to 375˚. With electric mixer beat butter with sugar in large bowl until light and fluffy. Add egg. Beat well. Fold in flour and add vanilla and mix thoroughly. Roll into small balls. Use bottom of sugared glass to flatten balls on ungreased baking sheet.

Bake until lightly brown, 5 to 6 minutes.

Makes about 36 cookies.

Sprinkle cookies with red and green sugar while still warm if baking them for the holidays.

Ranger Cookies

1	cup (2 sticks) butter
1	cup brown sugar
1	cup white sugar
2	eggs, beaten
1	teaspoon vanilla
2	cups all-purpose flour
$1/4$	teaspoon baking powder
1	teaspoon baking soda
$1/2$	teaspoon salt
2	cups corn flakes
1	cup oatmeal
1	cup coconut

Mix all ingredients in large bowl. Chill at least 30 minutes.

Heat oven to 375˚.

Roll into balls and place on ungreased cookie sheet. Flatten with fork dipped in flour. Bake 10 to15 minutes.

Makes 3 dozen.

May add chocolate chips, coarsely chopped apricots or raisins to dough. May also be frozen in a roll and cut into slices for baking.

Jingle Bells

1	cup (2 sticks) butter
1½	cups brown sugar
2	eggs
2½	cups plus 2 heaping tablespoons flour
1	teaspoon soda
½	teaspoon salt
1	teaspoon ground cinnamon
½	teaspoon vanilla
4	slices candied pineapple, chopped
½	pound candied red and green cherries, chopped
1½	pounds dates, chopped
1	cup chopped filberts
1	cup chopped pecans
1	cup chopped walnuts

Heat oven to 325°. Cream butter and brown sugar in large bowl. Add eggs and blend well. Sift flour, soda, salt and cinnamon together in separate bowl. Add dry ingredients and vanilla to butter mixture. Mix in fruits and nuts. Drop by teaspoonsful onto greased baking sheet. Bake 20 minutes.

Makes 8 dozen.

A wonderful cookie for the Christmas season.

Butter Thins

1	cup (2 sticks) butter
¾	cup plus 2 tablespoons sugar
2	egg yolks, well beaten
1¾	cups sifted cake flour
1	teaspoon vanilla

Heat oven to 350°. In large electric mixer bowl cream butter. Add sugar gradually and mix well. Add egg yolks, flour and vanilla. Drop by teaspoonsful onto ungreased cookie sheet and bake about 10 minutes or until slightly brown around edges. Watch closely while baking; cookies brown in a short time. Space carefully because these cookies spread. Let stand only 1 minute before removing from baking sheet. Place on paper towels to cool. Store in airtight container.

Makes about 30 cookies.

Ginger Cookies

1	cup sugar
³/₄	cup shortening (i.e. Crisco)
4	tablespoons dark molasses
1	large egg
1	teaspoon ground ginger
1	teaspoon ground cinnamon
¹/₂	teaspoon ground cloves
1¹/₂	teaspoons soda
1	teaspoon baking powder
2	cups all-purpose flour
¹/₂	cup additional sugar

Heat oven to 325°. Mix sugar and shortening in large bowl. Add molasses until well blended. Add egg and beat well. Mix next 6 dry ingredients in medium bowl. Blend with first 4 ingredients. Refrigerate. When chilled, roll into balls and dip in granulated sugar. Place on ungreased baking sheets. Bake cookies 15 minutes.

Makes 3 dozen.

A food editor with the New York Times, a friend of this contributor, gives these cookies 5 stars.

Almond Roca

1	cup (2 sticks) cold butter, not margarine
1	cup sugar
1	cup crushed almonds
3	ounces Hershey's milk chocolate

Boil butter and sugar in medium saucepan on medium to medium-high heat, stirring constantly, until it registers 150° on candy thermometer.

Remove from heat and add ²/₃ cup almonds. Pour into ungreased 13x9-inch pan. Immediately spread chocolate over top. Sprinkle with remaining almonds. Cool.

Break into pieces with knife. Store in airtight container.

Makes about 30 pieces.

This candy is addictive. It comes in handy as an addition to holiday cookie plates or as a hostess gift.

Delicious Drops

1	**egg white**
¹/₂	**cup powdered sugar**
1	**tablespoon cocoa**

Pinch of salt

1	**cup chopped dates**
1	**cup chopped nuts**

Heat oven to 350°. In small bowl beat egg white until stiff. Combine sugar, cocoa, and salt in separate bowl. Fold in beaten egg whites. Fold in dates and nuts. Drop by teaspoonsful on well-buttered baking sheet. Bake 10 minutes.

Makes 12 cookies.

There is no flour in this recipe.

Sister Jean's Cookies

¹/₂	**cup (1 stick) margarine, not butter**
¹/₂	**cup Crisco, do not substitute**
³/₄	**cup white sugar**
³/₄	**cup brown sugar**
2	**eggs**
1	**teaspoon vanilla**
1	**teaspoon soda**
1	**teaspoon salt**
2	**tablespoons water**
1¹/₂	**cups all-purpose flour**
1¹/₂	**cups rolled oats**
1¹/₂	**cups Rice Krispies**
¹/₂	**cup chocolate chips**
¹/₄	**cup coconut**
¹/₄	**cup nuts**

Heat oven to 350°. Cream margarine, Crisco and sugars in large bowl. Add eggs, vanilla, soda, salt and water. Mix in remaining ingredients. Drop by rounded teaspoon on ungreased cookie sheets. Bake 10 minutes or until golden.

Makes 24 to 36 cookies.

Many thanks to Jean Theurauf, CSJ, for sharing this recipe from Sister Jean's Cookie Cart, a bakery business providing inner-city youths with valuable work experience.

Catholic Grace Before Meals

Bless us, O Lord, and these, Thy gifts, which we are about to receive from Thy bounty, through Christ our Lord. Amen.

Anglican Table Grace

Bless this food to our use and us to Thy loving and faithful service, and keep us ever mindful of the needs of others. In Christ's name we pray. Amen.

Islamic Prayers Before and After a Meal

In the name of God, the Merciful One who bestows mercy. (Before a meal.)

Bless your hands. (Often said to the cook after the meal is over.)

Lutheran Table Prayer

Come, Lord Jesus, be our guest, Let this food to us be blest.

A Jewish Blessing (Birchot Hanahnin) Prior to Eating and Drinking (c. 300 B.C.E.)

On eating bread: Praised are You, Adonai our God, Sovereign of the Universe, who brings forth bread from the earth.
On drinking wine: Praised are You, Adonai our God, Sovereign of the Universe, who creates the fruit of the vine.

Buddhist Blessing

Make of yourself a light.

Complements

Bootlegs

2   **(12-ounce) cans frozen limeade**

1   **(12-ounce) can frozen lemonade**

Lots of fresh mint leaves, stems removed

Gin, vodka or light rum (optional)

Club soda or quinine water

Combine first 3 ingredients in blender. Pulse 30 seconds. Strain if desired.

For 1 serving, mix 6 ounces bootleg mix with $1^1/_2$ ounces liquor, if desired, in tall glass. Fill remainder of glass with soda or quinine water and ice cubes. Excellent and refreshing without the liquor as well.

Makes about 8 servings.

This drink closely resembles the famous Minikahda Club beverage.

Pantry Pickles

1   **quart plain dill pickles**

1   **cup sugar**

$^1/_4$ **cup tarragon vinegar**

1   **teaspoon pickling spice**

$^1/_2$ **teaspoon salt**

Drain juice from pickles into medium bowl. Add sugar, vinegar, spice and salt to juice. Cut ends off pickles and cut pickles into $^1/_4$ to $^1/_2$-inch chunks. Stir chunks into juice. Let stand at room temperature 2 to 3 days. Drain and rinse. Place pickles in covered container and refrigerate. Pickles keep for months.

Makes 1 quart.

Caramel Corn

2   **cups brown sugar**

1   **cup (2 sticks) butter**

$^1/_2$ **cup light corn syrup**

1   **teaspoon salt**

1   **teaspoon soda**

1   **teaspoon butter flavoring**

6   **quarts popcorn**

1   **cup toasted pecan pieces, optional**

Heat oven to 200°. Mix brown sugar, butter, corn syrup and salt in large kettle. Boil 5 minutes. Remove from heat. Blend in soda and butter flavoring. Toss with popcorn until well blended. Add nuts, if desired.

Spread popcorn on 15x10-inch baking sheet. Bake approximately 1 hour, stirring every 15 minutes. Store in covered tins.

Makes 24 cups.

Papaya Dream Boats

2	tablespoons mango chutney (i.e. Major Grey's)
12	ounces cream cheese, softened
$^1/_2$	cup cottage cheese
1	teaspoon curry powder
$^1/_2$	cup chopped water chestnuts
3	tablespoons white raisins
4	papayas, cut in half and seeded
$^1/_2$	cup sugar
1	teaspoon ground cinnamon
$^1/_2$	cup (1 stick) butter, melted

In blender puree chutney, cheeses and curry powder. Remove from blender. Stir in water chestnuts and raisins.

Fill fresh papaya halves with cream cheese mixture. Sprinkle with sugar and cinnamon. Drizzle with butter. Refrigerate up to 3 hours.

Heat oven to 450˚. Bake papaya uncovered 15 minutes or until heated through.

Serves 8.

An unusual accompaniment for meat or poultry entrees.

Lemon Curd

Rind and juice from 3 large lemons

1	cup sugar
$^1/_4$	cup ($^1/_2$ stick) butter
3	eggs

Finely grate lemon rind. Squeeze lemon juice into small bowl. Blend rind, juice, sugar and butter in heavy medium saucepan or top of double boiler. Heat until butter is melted. In small bowl beat eggs with electric mixer until thick and lemon-colored. Slowly add eggs to lemon mixture. Cook, stirring continuously, just to boiling point. Cool and store in covered container in refrigerator up to 2 weeks.

Makes 2 cups.

An elegant topping for fresh fruit, meringues or scones.

Punch for 50

6	**cups sugar**
4	**cups water**
1	**(12 ounce) can frozen orange juice concentrate**
12	**ounces lemon juice or lemonade concentrate**
4	**cups pineapple juice**
4	**teaspoons vanilla extract**
4	**teaspoons almond extract**
1/3	**cup citric acid, dissolved in 1 cup water**

Boil sugar and water together in large kettle until they form light syrup, about 10 minutes. Blend in remaining 6 ingredients. Chill.

Makes 50 cups.

Orange Froth

2	**cups milk, divided**
2	**cups water, divided**
1	**(12-ounce) can frozen orange juice concentrate, thawed and divided**
2	**teaspoons vanilla extract, divided**
1/2	**cup sugar, divided**
20	**ice cubes, divided**

Orange slices and mint sprigs for garnish

In blender combine half of each ingredient: milk, water, orange juice concentrate, vanilla, sugar and ice cubes. Blend at high speed about 30 seconds or until ice cubes are crushed. Repeat with remaining ingredients. Pour into goblets. Garnish with orange slice and mint sprig.

Serves 8 to 10.

This refreshing drink resembles an "Orange Julius".

Sangria

1/2	**cup fresh lemon juice**
1/2	**cup fresh orange juice**
1/2	**cup sugar**
1	**bottle (4/5 quart) dry red wine**
1	**(7-ounce) bottle club soda**

Choice of fresh fruits

Pour juices and sugar into large pitcher. Stir to dissolve sugar. Add wine and soda. Stir well. Add slices of orange, lemon, pineapple, strawberries or peaches just before serving. Serve over ice in clear glasses.

Makes 8 servings.

Sauce Buerre Blanc

3   shallots, peeled and minced

1   cup dry white wine

1/4   cup white vinegar or lemon juice

1   cup (2 sticks) butter, cut in 1/2-inch cubes

Salt and pepper to taste

Simmer shallots, wine and vinegar in medium saucepan until reduced by three-fourths. Add butter cubes one at a time, stirring continuously, until fully emulsified. Season to taste with salt and pepper.

Makes 1/2 cup.

A delicious sauce from Chef Rene at the Hyatt Regency Hill Country Resort. Perfect with fish or red meat.

Hot Buttered Rum Mix

2   cups (4 sticks) butter, melted

1   teaspoon ground cloves

1   teaspoon ground cinnamon

1   teaspoon ground all-spice

1   teaspoon ground nutmeg

2   pounds golden brown sugar

3   eggs, well beaten

Rum

Hot water

Mix melted butter with spices in large bowl. Add brown sugar and eggs. Beat 20 minutes with electric mixer set at medium speed. Pour into container. Cover and refrigerate up to 1 month.

To make each serving, mix 1 tablespoon brown sugar mixture, 1 cup hot to boiling water and 1 ounce rum.

Makes about 50 cups.

A great thing to have on hand over the holidays or on a cold Minnesota winter night--very medicinal!

After almost 40 years of operating out of rented space, the League of Catholic Women purchased its own headquarters in 1950. Located at **207 South Ninth Street** this white brick building with its signature green door is the center for LCW outreach projects and in-house activities. **Visitors are always welcome.**

Fruit and Spicy Sausage Stuffing

$3/4$ **cup fresh tangerine or orange juice**

$1/4$ **cup dried cranberries**

$1/4$ **cup dried apricots, chopped**

1   **tangerine or orange, sectioned, seeded and chopped**

Zest of 1 tangerine or orange

1   **pound andouille or other spicy sausage**

1   **medium onion, diced**

2   **stalks celery, diced**

4   **pears, peeled, cored and chopped**

1   **tablespoon chopped fresh tarragon or 1 teaspoon dried**

Salt and pepper to taste

7   **cups bread cubes, crusts removed**

$1^{1}/_{2}$ **cups vegetable broth**

Heat oven to 400˚. Pour freshly squeezed tangerine or orange juice into small bowl. Add dried cranberries, apricots, tangerines, and tangerine zest. Set bowl aside a few minutes to "plump" fruit.

Remove casing from sausage and chop meat. Sauté sausage with onions and celery. Add tangerine juice along with dried fruit and pears. Sauté briefly until pears are slightly tender. Toss meat mixture with tarragon, salt, pepper and bread cubes in large bowl. Add broth to moisten.

Transfer stuffing to buttered 13x9-inch baking dish. Cover and bake 30 minutes. Uncover and bake additional 15 to 20 minutes until browned.

Serves 6 to 8.

Add $1/2$ teaspoon fennel seed if serving with pork or poultry.

Seana's Iced Tea

2-3   **sprigs mint, stems removed**

Zest from 1 lemon, cut in thin strips

Zest from 1 orange, cut in thin strips

8   **small tea bags or 4 tablespoons loose tea**

4   **cups boiling water**

$2/3$ **cup sugar**

8   **cups cold water**

Juice of $1/2$ orange

Juice of $1/2$ lemon

Add first 4 ingredients to 4 cups boiling water. Steep 10 minutes. Strain. Add final 5 ingredients. Cool. Serve over ice in tall glasses.

Serves 12.

Candy Spice Peanuts

1	**egg white**
1	**teaspoon water**
1$1/2$	**cups salted dry roasted peanuts**
$1/2$	**cup sugar**
1	**teaspoon ground cinnamon**
$1/4$	**teaspoon ground ginger**
$1/4$	**teaspoon ground nutmeg**

Heat oven to 250°. Beat egg white until frothy in medium bowl. Add water and nuts to egg mixture. Mix until well blended. In a separate bowl, mix sugar and spices, add to nuts and mix well. Spread in oiled 13x9-inch pan.

Bake 1 hour turning with spatula every 15 minutes. Remove from oven and cool. Nuts will turn crispy as they cool.

Serves 12 to 16.

Never-Fail Hollandaise Sauce

2	**egg yolks**
$1/2$	**cup butter (1 stick) do not use margarine**
	Juice of 1 lemon (about $1/4$ cup) or less to taste
	Dash of lemon pepper

All ingredients MUST be at room temperature. Whisk all ingredients in medium saucepan over medium high heat until thick.

Makes $1/2$ cup.

Jicama Relish

1	**large or 2 small jicama, diced**
2	**red bell peppers, cut in julienne strips**
1$1/2$	**green bell peppers, cut in julienne strips**
1	**small serrano chile pepper or milder pepper, seeded and chopped**
$1/2$	**cup chopped cilantro**
$1/2$	**cup seasoned rice vinegar (i.e. Nakano)**
1	**tablespoon sugar**
$1/2$	**teaspoon salt**

Mix all ingredients in medium bowl or shake in large glass jar. Store in refrigerator at least 12 hours or up to 3 days.

Makes $3/4$ cup.

Be careful when peeling and chopping hot peppers like serrano. Wear gloves!

Black Bean Salsa

1	**poblano chile**
2	**cups cooked black beans**
2	**tablespoons fresh pomegranate juice or frozen cranberry juice cocktail mix**
1/4	**cup diced raw red pepper**
1/4	**cup diced raw yellow pepper**
2	**cloves garlic, minced**
1	**slice white onion, 3/4-inch thick**
1	**tablespoon canned diced chipatte chilies**
1	**tablespoon minced fresh cilantro**
1/4	**teaspoon cumin seed**
	Salt to taste

Roast poblano chile in dry skillet or in 400° oven until blistered. Place in paper bag, seal and cool. Remove chile. Peel, seed, devein and dice. Place in bowl and mix together with next 9 ingredients. Salt to taste. Cover bowl. Refrigerate at least 6 and up to 48 hours.

Makes 2$\frac{1}{2}$ cups.

Corn Relish

2	**(15-ounce) cans black beans, drained**
6-7	**cups fresh sweet corn, cut off cob**
5	**tablespoons olive oil**
2	**cloves garlic, minced**
2	**teaspoons orange zest**
3/4	**cup lime juice**
2	**hot banana peppers, seeds and veins removed, finely chopped**
1	**cup vinegar mixed with 1/2 cup sugar**
1/2	**cup chicken broth**
4	**tablespoons chopped cilantro**

Mix together all ingredients until well blended. Place salsa in one large or several small tightly covered containers. Refrigerate at least 12 hours and up to 1 week.

Makes 3 pints.

Mango Salsa

1   clove garlic

Vegetable spray

1   white onion, thinly sliced

1   serrano chile, minced with seeds

1   mango, peeled, seeded, diced

1   tablespoon chopped fresh cilantro

½   cup diced raw red bell pepper

In small dry skillet over medium heat, roast unpeeled garlic clove until slightly charred. Remove from pan and cool. Peel and mince.

Spray skillet with vegetable oil. Add sliced onions. Roast, stirring often, until dark brown in color. Cool.

Mix minced garlic and roasted onions with other ingredients and place in bowl or jar. Cover and refrigerate at least 6 and up to 24 hours.

Makes 1 cup.

Tropical flavors of this salsa go well with grilled pork, shrimp or chicken.

To roast garlic in oven, place in pan or on cookie sheet. Roast in 400° oven for about 10 minutes, turning once. Garlic clove will still be firm enough to mince.

Another way to roast garlic is in a skillet. Toss a few unpeeled cloves into small heavy skillet over medium heat. Cover and cook 5 minutes turning cloves once. Uncover. Cook 3 to 5 minutes more turning occasionally until skins are lightly charred and cloves can be easily pierced with knife. Cool. Peel and mash. Makes 2 tablespoons garlic puree.

Tarragon Pesto

2	cups fresh tarragon leaves, stems removed
1/2	cup parsley leaves
1/2	cup olive oil
3	tablespoons walnuts
2	cloves garlic, peeled
3/4	cup freshly grated Parmesan cheese
2	tablespoons butter, softened

Salt to taste

Place first 5 ingredients in food processor and blend. Remove to medium bowl. Add cheese and butter. Mix by hand. Salt to taste. You may substitute basil and pine nuts for tarragon and walnuts.

Makes 2 cups.

If you are freezing pesto add cheese and butter after thawing. Excellent as sauce for pasta, fish or vegetables.

Cranberry Chutney with Ginger

1 1/2	cups fresh cranberries
16	dried apricots, chopped
3/4	cup golden brown sugar, packed
1/3	cup dried currants
2	tablespoons fresh gingerroot, minced
2	tablespoons cranberry juice
3/4	teaspoon ground cinnamon
1/4	teaspoon ground cayenne pepper

Combine all ingredients in heavy saucepan and cook at medium heat to dissolve sugar. Increase heat to high, bring to boiling and keep boiling for 3 minutes.

Transfer to bowl and cool. Can be stored in refrigerator, tightly covered, 1 to 2 weeks.

Makes 3 cups.

A zingy complement to poultry or pork. Rated a "ten" by 15 tasters!

Berry Sparkler

2	tablespoons strained pureed frozen strawberries

Chilled champagne or sparkling wine to fill wine glass

1	whole strawberry
1	fresh mint spring

Mix pureed strawberries into champagne or wine. Pour into champagne flutes. Garnish with whole strawberry and fresh mint sprig.

Serves 1.

Herbed Mayonnaise

1/3	cup minced fresh Italian parsley
1/3	cup minced fresh cilantro
1/4	cup green onions, minced
2	tablespoons red wine vinegar or less to taste
1/2	teaspoon minced fresh garlic
1/4	teaspoon dried oregano
1/4	teaspoon freshly ground black pepper
1/8	teaspoon ground cayenne pepper
1	cup prepared mayonnaise

In small bowl combine 1/3 cup parsley, cilantro, green onions, vinegar, 1/2 teaspoon minced garlic, oregano, pepper and cayenne. Stir until well blended. Let stand at room temperature 30 minutes or cover with plastic wrap and chill overnight.

Just before serving, stir mayonnaise into chilled herb mixture and serve.

Makes 1 1/4 cups.

Especially good with salmon.

Pickled Mushrooms

2/3	cup tarragon vinegar
1/2	cup salad oil
1	medium clove garlic, minced
1	tablespoon sugar
2	tablespoon water
1 1/2	teaspoon salt
	Freshly ground pepper
	Tabasco sauce
1	medium onion, sliced
4	cups small fresh, whole mushrooms or 2 (6-ounce) cans whole mushrooms

Combine vinegar, salad oil, garlic, sugar, water, salt, pepper and Tabasco sauce. Add mushrooms and onions. Cover and refrigerate for 8 hours or overnight.

Remove from refrigerator. Stir and drain before serving.

Makes 1 quart.

Smoothies: Theme and Variations

Classic Smoothie

1	**cup orange juice**
1	**cup sliced fresh or frozen strawberries**
2	**fresh or frozen bananas, sliced**

Combine ingredients in blender. Pulse until smooth.

Serves 2.

Karen's Soothing Smoothie

1	**cup vanilla frozen yogurt**
1/2	**cup peach or orange juice**
1/2	**ripe medium banana, sliced**
1/8	**teaspoon ground cinnamon**
1/8	**teaspoon ground nutmeg**

Place frozen yogurt, fruit juice, banana and spices in blender container. Cover and blend until smooth.

Serves 2.

Tropical Smoothie

1	**cup coconut sorbet**
1	**cup diced frozen pineapple**
1	**cup diced frozen mango**
1	**frozen banana, sliced**

Combine ingredients in blender. Pulse until smooth.

Serves 2.

Smoothies are a perfect way to use over-ripe fruits like bananas, peaches, pineapple, etc. Simply place fruit in freezer bags and store until you are ready to whip up a treat.

Spicy Black Bean and Corn Salsa

2   **(15-ounce) cans black beans**

1   **(16-ounce) can whole kernel corn or 2 cups frozen or fresh corn, slightly cooked**

1/2   **cup chopped fresh cilantro**

3   **tablespoons olive oil**

1/4   **cup minced green onion**

6   **tablespoons fresh lime juice**

1/4   **cup minced red onion**

1/2   **tablespoon ground cumin**

Salt and pepper to taste

1   **cup chopped fresh tomatoes**

Drain beans and corn. Mix all ingredients except tomatoes in large bowl. Season to taste with salt and pepper. Cover and refrigerate until cold. May be prepared one day before serving. Just before serving, add tomatoes. Serve with chips or as an accompaniment for pork.

Makes about 3 cups.

May add chopped jalapeno peppers if you like more zip. Try filling heated flour tortillas with salsa for a tasty lunch, adding shredded chicken and/or cheese if desired.

Pat's Pineapple Dressing

1/2   **cup (1 stick) butter**

1   **cup sugar**

4   **eggs**

1   **(18-ounce) can crushed pineapple, well drained**

5   **slices white bread, cubed**

Heat oven to 350°. Cream butter and sugar in large bowl. Beat eggs. Add 1 egg at a time to butter/sugar mixture, beating well after each addition. Stir in drained pineapple. It is important to completely drain pineapple. Fold in bread cubes. Turn into lightly greased 1 1/2-quart baking dish. Bake covered 1 hour.

Serves 6.

A 40 year old favorite in this contributor's family and a big hit with Tuesday Club guests at the League. Especially good with ham.

Beginning in 1989, the League of Catholic Women began providing enrichment programs at **Northside Child Development Center**. At present the LCW provides funding and volunteers for special projects involving northside children and their parents.

The League of Catholic Women

*is an independent, non-profit, volunteer organization
committed to Christian values.
We provide creative community service
for women and families
and offer programs for spiritual, educational
and personal growth.*

Current Community Services at the League of Catholic Women:

AIDS Ministry - Women affected by HIV/AIDS have the opportunity to share their stories and gain courage and strength from each other at gatherings planned by League members in conjunction with the Archdiocesan AIDS Ministry.

By Your Side Program - League members offer friendly one-to-one support to single parent health care and nursing students at the College of St. Catherine/Minneapolis. This includes funds for emergencies and child care.

College of St. Catherine Scholarship Grant - Scholarship assistance is provided to single female parents who are students in the health care professions.

First Impression - Career clothing is provided to women entering or re-entering the work force upon completion of job training or work readiness programs.

Northside Breastfeeding Campaign - The campaign, through physician training and community education, works to increase breastfeeding rates and support for breastfeeding mothers in the Near Northside of Minneapolis.

Northside Program - Members support special projects for children and families at Catholic Charities' Northside Child Development Center.

Risen Christ Tutoring - This project supports the tutoring of children at Risen Christ by funding the volunteer director position for this inner-city Catholic school and providing volunteer tutors from the League.

Tuesday Club - League members provide lunch, games and entertainment for the elderly and socially isolated at the Downtown Center twice monthly.

Women/Becoming - Educational programs inform, challenge and encourage women to seek their full potential.

Membership is open to all women who wish to share in this mission. For more information about the work of the League of Catholic Women, current social services, enrichment programs and membership materials, please contact:

The League of Catholic Women
207 South Ninth Street
Minneapolis, MN 55402

Tele: 612-332-2649
Fax: 612-332-2668
Web: www.mplsleagcatholicwomen.org

A Taste of Spring

An Easter Feast

Asparagus Roll-ups, p. 9
Stuffed Lamb with Current Jelly Sauce, p. 156
Parsley New Potatoes, p. 106
Sweet Carrots with Green Grapes, p. 111
Lemon Pie, p. 199

Brunch on the Porch

Spinach Strawberry Salad, p. 31
Baked Eggs on Artichoke Bottoms, p. 90
Lemon Loaf, p. 89
Rhuberry Pie, p. 200

A Fisherman's Catch

Popovers, p. 88
Herb Salad, p. 46
North Shore Walleye, p. 185
Asparagus with French Aigrelette Sauce, p. 108
Strawberries Jubilee, p. 190

A Taste of Summer

A Chilled Soup Buffet

Harbor View Cucumber Soup, p. 54
Cold Strawberry Soup, p. 57
Fresh Tomato Soup with Basil Aioli, p. 65
Sweet Corn Chowder, p. 70
Cheese Puffs, p. 81
Herbed Pita Crisps, p. 12
Triple Treat Crème de Menthe Bars, p. 207

Grilling on the Patio

Crabby Quesadillas, p. 4
Grilled Pork Tenderloin, p. 169
Creamy Greens Quinoa, p. 124
Martha Stewart Asparagus, p. 115
Fresh Strawberries with Raspberry Puree and Pistachio Nuts, p. 189

A Cool Treat on a Hot Day

Sangria, p. 218
Cucumber Canapes, p. 11
Curried Chicken and Grape Salad, p. 36
Peaches and "Skyr", p. 193

A Taste of Fall

A Hunter's Dinner

Spinach Balls with Mustard Sauce, p. 15
Honey Wild Duck, p. 152
Nutted Wild Rice, p.123
Glazed Brussels Sprouts with Pine Nuts, p.108
Happy Cranberries, p.195

A Family Football Snack Spread

Beef Tortilla Pinwheels, p. 2
Sweet and Sour Meatballs, p.3
White Castle Appetizers, p. 4
Fiesta Layered Dip, p. 11
Chicken Nips, p. 2

A Simple Supper

Apple Slices with Gorgonzola, p. 9
Sloppy Josés, p. 164
Marinated Carrot Salad, p. 20
Creamy Orange Ice Cream Pie, p. 198

A Taste of Winter

A Festive New Year's Eve

Black Caviar Mousse, p. 5
Flaming Spinach Salad, p. 22
Beef Tenderloin Deluxe, p. 162
Accordion Potatoes, p. 114
Green Beans with Shallots, p. 111
Crème Brulée de Cirque, p. 192

An Informal Gathering of Friends

Sesame Chicken Wings, p. 3
Spinach Salad with Dried Cranberries, p. 40
Pork Tenderloin Stroganoff, p. 165
Food Processor French Bread, p. 79
Gateau Chocolate au Rhum, p. 202

A Hearty Supper by the Fire

Cheese Triangles, p. 10
Senator Lodge's Family Bean Soup, p. 55
Simplicity Salad, p. 41
Chocolate Mousse, p. 193

A Party Planner

An easy way to simplify entertaining and avoid duplicating menus for the same guests is to keep a record of get-togethers with friends and/or family. Please feel free to make copies of this sampler, adding your own ideas.

Date and time of party: _____

Theme, if any _____

Menu: _____

_____

_____

_____

_____

_____

Grocery List: _____ _____

_____ _____ _____

_____ _____ _____

_____ _____ _____

_____ _____ _____

Table Setting (linens, centerpieces, etc.): _____

_____

Seating: _____ _____ _____

_____ _____ _____

_____ _____ _____

Post Party Comments: _____

_____

Acknowledgements

The League of Catholic Women gratefully acknowledges the following dedicated Cookbook committee members, recipe testers and contributors, and financial patrons:

Julie Allen
Barbara Allivato
Deb Anderson
Jan McKenzie Anderson
Betty Andrews
Carole Arnold
Mary Madonna Ashton,
 CSJ
Jayne Bachman
Eileen Barbe
Mardonna Bartholet
Gary Bedsworth
Gretchen Beiswanger
James Beiswanger
Joan Bernet
Tom Blessing
Trish Blessing
Virginia Blevins
Dwayne Borg
Maxine Borg
Lynn Bowe
Laura Boyle
Carol Brahms
Jacqueline Breher
Colleen Brennan
Judy Brick
Bill Brick
Gen Brophy
Kathy Budge
Kay Bunker
Roger Bunker
Nancy Burbidge
Don Burns
Mary Burns
Antonio Burrell
Mary Byron
Emily Carlin
Julian (Bing) Carlin
Patricia Carlin
Verle Carlin
Corky Carlsen
Chuck Carlsen
Penny Carr

Darlene Carroll
Anne Casey
Billie Cashman
Jim Cashman
Rev. Robert Cassidy
Theresa Christianson
Jane Clifford
Rusty Cohen
Jan Collins
Carol Connelly
Marjorie Connelly
Ann Cronin
Mary Culhane
Donna Cunningham
Judy Dawes
Jane Deckenbach
Bonnie Dehn
Margaret Delmore
Betty Nell Dolan
Marlene Dolan
Kathy Dougherty
Michael Dougherty
Dianne Dufresne
Denny Dyrhaug
Juneal Dyrhaug
Mary Kay Egan
Judi Eggleston
John Emmer
Ramona Emmer
Anne Everette
Bill Everette
Cathy Farrell
Eleanor Farrell
Sally Friedlander
Lidia Filonowich
Arlene Finley
Judy Fischer
Shawn Glish Fischer
Dave Fitzgerald
Helen Fitzgerald
Roberto Flores
Suzanne Flotten
Most Rev. Harry Flynn

Rosemary Flynn
Bill Foley
Eileen Foley
Fran Foley
James Foley
Rev. John Forliti
Margaret Foster
Rosemary Froehlich
Beverly Frothinger
Eugene Frey
Mary Frey
Bob Fritz
Sally Fritz
Phyllis Fudali
Jan Gainor
Barbara Gallagher
Fran Galvin
Jacqui Gardner
George Gardner
Betty Garrity
Lorraine Gearty
Judy Gendron
Barbara Gillham
Joanne Gillis
Rev. Joseph Gillispie
Marie Goblirsch
Marcella Gordon
Patricia Greer
Patricia Gries
Evelyn Gudorf
Harriet Haeg
Paul Haik
Ray Haik
Sally Haik
Bob Hamel
Mary Hamel
Katie Hamel
Andrea Hammann
Richard Hanousek
Kathy Hanousek
Mary Helen Hayes
Deidre Hedrick
Bill Hedrick

Marge Hergott
Betty Higgins
Karen Hilger, CSJ
Ginny Hill-Dobbs
Betty Hidding
Paul Hinderlie
Mary Lou Hines
Tom Hines
Mary Kay Hoban
Patty Holloran
Mary Holmes
Albina Horsch
Doretta Hughes
Bettie Hunchis
Cathleen Indrehus
Jim Indrehus
Jane Jaeger
Paul Jaeger
Marty Jansen
Neal Jansen
Nancy Johnson
Roy Johnson
Ruth Johnson
Barbara Jordano
Rita Juettner
Judith Kavanaugh, CSJ
Bobbie Keegan
Joyce Kegley
Anne Dolan Kelly
Joan Kelly
Peggy Kelly
David Kennedy
Mary Helen Kennedy
Patricia Kennedy
Tom Kennedy
Marge Keppel
Bob Keppel
Patricia King
Judith King
Sharri Kinkead
Mary Kirchner
Megan Kirchner
Ed Klis

Marilyn Klis
Lucy Klos
Mary Kluener
Marcelline Kochevar
Madonna Koenig
Liz Krezowski
Margaret Kruse
Suzanne Kuhn
Mary Kunz
Carol Ladner
Jodeen LaFrenz
Phil LaGrandeur
Yvonne LaGrandeur
Mary Elizabeth Lahiff
Kathleen Laird
Mary Lou Lamberton
Kay Lang
Phyllis Langfield
Brenda Langton
Joan Lapensky
Joe Lapensky
Gail Lappen
Cliff LaRose
Peggy Lathrop
James Layer
Judith Layer
Mary Gerry Lee
Dick Lee
Tom Lee
Laverne Lewis
Gordy Lewis
Rose Linnihan
Anne Lohmann
John Lohmann
Anne Luxem
Barbara Lynch
George Maas
Patricia Maas
Rita Mach
Rev. Ambrose Mahon
Myrna Maloney
Sheila Manley
Florence McCarthy
Cynthia McGarvey
Dorothy McGlauchlin
Andrea McGough
Larry McGough
Florence McHugh
Joan McHugh
Colleen McMahon
Mary McNamara
Marta Melin
Marie Merrigan

Michael Merrigan
Carol Michalke
Ernie Micek
Sally Micek
Teresa Miller
Ceil Misencik
Susan Morrison
Michael Morse
Virginia Mulcahy
Margi Mullin
Ruth Mullin
Catherine Murphy
Jeremiah Murphy
Judy Murphy
Virginia Murphy
Gerry Murray
John Murray
Mary Murray
Marlene Muske
Patricia Myser
Marilyn Nelson
Joanna Nielson
Ken Nordling
Sally Nordling
Marna Nylander
Claire O'Connell
Gina O'Connor
Irene O'Neill, CSJ
Doirothy Ollmann
Anne Bowen Olson
Cliff Olson
Elizabeth Olson
Marguerite Olson
Joyce Ostlund
Janice Ott
Iris Osekowsky
Treva Paparella
Olga Paul
Mollie Paulson
Holmes Pedelty
Jane Pedelty
Ludy Peller
Karen Perlich
Sandra Phillips
Helen Pollock
Theresa Ann Powell
Don Prettyman
Kay Prettyman
Joan Pride
David Raab
Peggy Raab
Donna Ramsey
Marcia Reis

Susan Renwick
Alice Rice
Mary Ripper
Susan Harper Ritten
Gertrude Rocheford
Bud Rooney
Kay Rooney
Bill Rosengren
Rosemarie Rosengren
Billie Jo Scallen
Mary Hamel Scallen
Ray Scallen
Connie Schilling
Jerry Schilling
John Schiltz
Patricia Schoeppe
Marcia Schug
Rhea Schugel
John Schumacher
Kathleen Scott
Sandra Seibert
Lucia Seidel
Evelyn Selim
Susan Sell
Charlene Sheahan
Marjorie Sheehan
Sue Simons
Mary Simonds
Jackie Smith
Mary Lou Smith
Maureen Soller
Janet Spokes
Joyce Staba
Emerita Stallman
Teresa Stemmer
Anne Stocks
Bill Stocks
Mary Strother
Kay Student
Dick Student
Fay Sullivan
Laura Sullivan
Marilyn Sullivan
Karen Swanson
Helen Swanson
Jack Swift
Nancy Swift
Cynthia Tambornino
Jean Theurauf, RSM
Dave Thies
Marlys Thies
Richard Thomas
Barbara Tiede

George Tillson
Judith Tillson
Patricia Vagnoni
Carol Vasatka
Dick Vasatka
Beverly Vieno
Mimi Villaume
Don Waddick
Helen Waddick
Maggie Walters
Lucia Watson
Mary Webber
Paul Webber
Laurie Wehage
Mary Wehman
Betty Weingartner
Mary Weir
Nat Welch
Mary White
Rochelle White
Teryle Wilharm
Lucy Wilhoit
Dee Wilke
Mary Winum
Mary Wiser
Agnes Wolf
Paul Wrazielo
Josephine Zimmar

Special thanks to:
Editors:
Mary Ritten
Jane Coen

Advisors:
Gloria Allen
Barbara LaRose
Gloria Smith

Computer Specialist:
Michelle Haik

Graphic Design and Illustration:
Sara Weingartner

Front cover art and Textile Design:
Martha Murphy

Index:
Patricia Sinclaire

Index

Cooks of the Green Door Order Form

Name _____

Address_____

City/State/Zip_____

Phone_____

Please send _____ copies @ $20 each, plus $3 ea. for S & H. Enclosed is a full check or credit card payment of $_____. Please make checks payable to The League of Catholic Women. Please allow 4 weeks for delivery.

Payment type: ❑ Visa (13 or 16 digits)
　　　　　　　　　❑ MasterCard (16 digits)

Credit Card Account Number:

Expiration date: ☐☐ — ☐☐
　　　　　　　　(mo)　(yr)

Full name on card: _____

Signature:_____

Cooks of the Green Door Order Form

Name _____

Address_____

City/State/Zip_____

Phone_____

Please send _____ copies @ $20 each, plus $3 ea. for S & H. Enclosed is a full check or credit card payment of $_____. Please make checks payable to The League of Catholic Women. Please allow 4 weeks for delivery.

For Credit Card Use Only:

Payment type: ❑ Visa (13 or 16 digits)
　　　　　　　　　❑ MasterCard (16 digits)

Credit Card Account Number:

Expiration date: ☐☐ — ☐☐
　　　　　　　　(mo)　(yr)

Full name on card: _____

Signature:_____

Cooks of the Green Door Order Form

Name _____

Address_____

City/State/Zip_____

Phone_____

Please send _____ copies @ $20 each, plus $3 ea. for S & H. Enclosed is a full check or credit card payment of $_____. Please make checks payable to The League of Catholic Women. Please allow 4 weeks for delivery.

For Credit Card Use Only:

Payment type: ❑ Visa (13 or 16 digits)
　　　　　　　　　❑ MasterCard (16 digits)

Credit Card Account Number:

Expiration date: ☐☐ — ☐☐
　　　　　　　　(mo)　(yr)

Full name on card: _____

Signature:_____

Cooks of the Green Door Order Form

Name _____

Address_____

City/State/Zip_____

Phone_____

Please send _____ copies @ $20 each, plus $3 ea. for S & H. Enclosed is a full check or credit card payment of $_____. Please make checks payable to The League of Catholic Women. Please allow 4 weeks for delivery.

For Credit Card Use Only:

Payment type: ❑ Visa (13 or 16 digits)
　　　　　　　　　❑ MasterCard (16 digits)

Credit Card Account Number:

Expiration date: ☐☐ — ☐☐
　　　　　　　　(mo)　(yr)

Full name on card: _____

Signature:_____

Please send order form and payment to:

The League of Catholic Women
207 South Ninth Street
Minneapolis, MN 55402

If you have questions or for more information, please contact the LCW at 612-332-2649
or visit the web at www.mplsleagcatholicwomen.org.

Thanks for your order!

Please send order form and payment to:

The League of Catholic Women
207 South Ninth Street
Minneapolis, MN 55402

If you have questions or for more information, please contact the LCW at 612-332-2649
or visit the web at www.mplsleagcatholicwomen.org.

Thanks for your order!

Please send order form and payment to:

The League of Catholic Women
207 South Ninth Street
Minneapolis, MN 55402

If you have questions or for more information, please contact the LCW at 612-332-2649
or visit the web at www.mplsleagcatholicwomen.org.

Thanks for your order!

Please send order form and payment to:

The League of Catholic Women
207 South Ninth Street
Minneapolis, MN 55402

If you have questions or for more information, please contact the LCW at 612-332-2649
or visit the web at www.mplsleagcatholicwomen.org.

Thanks for your order!